Oil in the Economic Development of Venezuela

Jorge Salazar-Carrillo

Oil in the Economic Development of Venezuela

PRAEGER SPECIAL STUDIES IN INTERNATIONAL ECONOMICS AND DEVELOPMENT

Praeger Publishers New York Washington London

Library of Congress Cataloging in Publication Data

Salazar-Carrillo, Jorge.
    Oil in the economic development of Venezuela.

    (Praeger special studies in international economics and development)
    Includes bibliographical references.
    1. Petroleum industry and trade—Venezuela—History.
2. Venezuela—Economic conditions—1918-   I. Title.
HD9574.V42S36   338.2'7'2820987   75-19815
ISBN 0-275-55890-8

PRAEGER PUBLISHERS
111 Fourth Avenue, New York, N.Y. 10003, U.S.A.

Published in the United States of America in 1976
by Praeger Publishers, Inc.

Printed in the United States of America

To Mary Gene, my wife

The main effort for this study was carried out while the author was a Research Fellow at the Brookings Institution. I am very grateful to Dr. Joseph Grunwald, at Brookings, who helped me in different ways during that stage. I am also indebted to Professor John Letiche, of the University of California (Berkeley), for his suggestions, and the encouragement that he always gave me.

This book would not have been possible without the helpful attitude and cooperation of many individuals in the Central Bank of Venezuela, the Ministry of Mines and Hydrocarbons, and the oil firms. My special appreciation goes to Antonio Casas Gonzáles, Bernardo Ferrán, Antonio Fernández, Alberto Flores, Ruth de Krivoy, Alirio Parra, Carlos Pérez de la Cova, Hugo Romero, Carlos Rafael Silva and Romano Suprani, who gave their invaluable support on different occasions. Needless to say, none of them is responsible for any defects in workmanship that may still be present in this book.

CONTENTS

LIST OF TABLES

x

xi

Oil in the Economic Development of Venezuela

SCOPE OF THE STUDY

In explaining the patterns of international trade for different countries, economists have usually relied on the concepts of labor productivity and factor proportions. Such explanations have been challenged by a group of economists who, in turn, point out that labor productivities and factor proportions are, themselves, a function of the previous pattern of trade and production. The latter group of economists would recommend to developing countries the promotion of patterns of trade and production leading to economic development and, thus, to the desirable factor proportions and labor productivities characterizing the present advanced nations.[1] Such a trade and production mix, they believe, would deviate from the dictates of comparative advantage.

However, many of today's high per capita income countries started with patterns of trade and production that were no different from those which the peripheral countries had in the past,[2] and still have now, and which agreed with the comparative advantage rule. Diverse patterns of trade appear to have been conducive to development and to desirable labor productivities and factor proportions for these countries. Is this also applicable to the developing countries? Can a traditional pattern of trade based on primary production for export be conducive to such economic change in the periphery?

To answer these questions, the sources of growth in economies characterized by a pattern of trade based on primary production for exports have to be specified.[3] If the dynamic sector in such an economy is either total exports—with heavy concentration on primary products—or one of a few export-oriented primary producing sectors, would this help or hinder the development of the economy?

1

Many of the advanced countries of today, which had a pattern of trade based on primary type exports, also developed when the primary producing export sector, constituting their main source of growth, experienced an expansion in value terms. It could very well be presumed that these experiences should be applicable to other countries. However, according to the dissident economists mentioned above, this presumption has been proven wrong by the experiences of the peripheral countries.

These are important issues being presently debated in the field of trade and development. Hla Myint was referring to them when he stated:

> The critics start with the intention of showing that the 'nineteenth century pattern' of international trade whereby the underdeveloped countries export raw materials and import manufactured goods, has been unfavorable to the economic development of these countries. But instead of trying to show this directly, they concentrate their attacks on the 'classical theory,' which they believe to be responsible for the unfavorable pattern of trade. The orthodox economists then come to the defense of the classical theory by reiterating the principle of comparative costs which they claim to be applicable both to the developed and underdeveloped countries. After this, the controversy shifts from the primary question of whether or not the nineteenth century pattern of international trade, as a historical reality, has been unfavorable to the underdeveloped countries to the different question of whether or not the theoretical model assumed in the comparative costs analysis is applicable to these countries. [4]

As Myint implies, these issues should be illuminated by empirical verification. But the issues, as well as the different points of view taken in the debate, also need to be clarified and simplified. Only then can testing be undertaken. [5]

The only extensive survey on this problem is that undertaken by Gerald Meier in The International Economics of Development. [6] Even then, Meier does not specify the different issues involved or the facets within them, or, when covering different points of view, does he appreciate that they sometimes have been formulated with varying degrees of inclusiveness in mind. In fact, Meier, himself, is not explicit about the type of countries covered in his survey.

As suggested above, the dearth of empirical studies that could permit the testing of different points of view on these issues is appalling. There is, nevertheless, a growing awareness of this fact, and, as a consequence, there have been a few important contributions to the subject in recent years.

The present study will hopefully contribute to bridging these gaps. It will provide a brief but systematic review of these issues within the context of peripheral countries with patterns of trade and leading sectors or main sources of growth based on primary-type exports. [7]

Apart from the simplification and clarification of the theoretical issues and the elaboration of an alternative position, this study will be devoted entirely to an examination of the Venezuelan oil industry as a potentially leading sector or main source of growth and to the degree of success it may have had in leading the economic growth of the other economic sectors in the Venezuelan economy.

Venezuela was chosen for several reasons. It has a promising combination of sectoral and aggregate historical data available. The sectoral data on the petroleum sector is compiled by the Ministry of Mines and Hydrocarbons. The oil companies could provide data otherwise unobtainable in the ministry. Furthermore, the changes in the configuration of the petroleum industry, and in the petroleum policies of the Venezuelan government can be easily followed. It is possible, therefore, to derive useful conclusions as to the effects that evolving institutional arrangements have had on petroleum's impact upon the economy.

This study does not attempt to examine other export activities or their impact on Venezuelan economic development, nor does it deal with the market structure that characterizes the oil industry.

USEFULNESS OF THE FINDINGS

An examination of these issues could result in new ideas that might possibly alter the economic policy outlook in the developing countries. The underdeveloped countries have had a bias against primary production and primary exports, due, in part, to the influence of the interpretation of their economic history given by certain economists. These countries have preferred to rely instead upon import-substituting industrialization when implementing their development programs. Consequently, import-substituting industries top their investment priority lists. They are protected from foreign competition and receive, overall, favorable treatment. The reverse is true with primary production for exports. Furthermore, although inconsistent with most of the theoretical ideas that have nurtured the opposition to primary production for exports, the bias and its effects have affected in a general way other types of production for exports.

The use of different protective and promoting devices to favor import-substituting activities has gone too far in many developing countries, if long-run efficiency and economic growth considerations are kept in mind. As a result of such policies, an inefficient industrial sector has emerged. This holds down the possibility of furthering the industrialization of these countries, and the high cost economy, which it creates, also affects primary and tertiary activities. Paradoxically, import-substitution does not alleviate balance-of-payments pressures. Imports are not curtailed as expected; exports grow at a slow pace. As a result, insufficient foreign exchange receipts become the more serious bottleneck to growth. In some cases, development is forced to come to a complete standstill. Actually, the problem is much more complicated than this, as it is also related to monetary, fiscal, and exchange rate policy problems. Examples of economies to which this analysis is applicable are Argentina, Chile, and Uruguay.

In recent years, pressures have increased for a revision of the import-substitution policies. The possibilities of export stimulation are being reconsidered. Therefore, the conclusions from this study may well be opportune. Hopefully, they will aid in the revision of past and present economic policy tenets and in the formulation of more effective economic programs.

In addition, this study will focus specifically on policies that the underdeveloped countries can devise in order to augment the contribution of a primary export activity to the economy and to use this contribution in the most effective way. These policies are complementary to the broad guidelines of development programming policy. An examination of their use by the Venezuelan government will shed some light on these matters.

Research on the economic history of the peripheral countries is still in the nascent stage. Thus, this book will also constitute a contribution to the study of the Venezuelan economic history, particularly through the quantification of the development of the petroleum sector in Venezuela and its effects on the rest of the economy. This is not only important for policy making in this country, but it will probably be helpful to policy makers in other oil-producing nations.

NOTES

1. Terms such as advanced and advancement are used here as a convenient abbreviation for relatively high per capita income.

2. The definition of "peripheral countries" used here is that defined by Raul Prebisch in "Commercial Policy in the Underdeveloped Countries, " American Economic Review (May 1959).

3. It should be understood that this pattern of trade is compatible with different sources of growth. These could stem from an industrial expansion based on an import-substitution process, an expansion of primary exports, and so forth.

4. Hla Myint, "The 'Classical Theory' of International Trade and the Underdeveloped Countries, " The Economic Journal (June 1958): 137.

5. Myint himself provides an example of the confused state of the literature in this area. In the paragraph above, he fails to

distinguish between patterns of trade and sources of growth. It is really the effectiveness of primary activities as a source of growth that is central to the discussion and not the patterns of trade as Myint seems to believe.

6. Gerald Meier, The International Economics of Development (New York: Harper & Row, 1968).

7. Of course, the concept of leading sectors or main sources of growth can only be used in an a priori fashion, that is, before examining the evidence, it is only possible to determine if a sector could qualify as a leading sector. Therefore, in a strict sense, these sectors can only be "potentially leading sectors." It is only after a detailed empirical inquiry that it can be said whether or not a sector has behaved like a leading sector or a main source of growth.

2

Some controversial issues in the trade and development area were briefly referred to in the introductory chapter. They concerned prospects for economic growth under varying patterns of trade and types of potentially leading sectors. It may be worth repeating that this study is only devoted to cases in which (a) the potentially leading sector is of a primary type, (b) the pattern of trade is based on the exports of primary products, and (c) the country is a peripheral one. Its purpose is to examine the possibility of economic growth under these circumstances. In this context, what is needed are testable models that can explain the events of the past and whose implications would be useful in formulating present economic policy.

The field of trade and development stands at a juncture where the derivation of operational propositions and their subsequent empirical testing is a most urgent endeavor.[1] The literature in the field has expanded in an amazing fashion; yet, attempts of this kind are quite scarce. Because of the "statistical revolution" that has been going on in the underdeveloped countries, there is a wealth of useful material that could be used for testing. There is, thus, a felicitous concurrence of opportunity and need that should not be passed by.

Since the industrial revolution in England, a sizeable number of nations have attained relatively high levels of income per capita. International trade and related international factor movements usually have played an important role in the economic development of these countries. In fact, international contacts seem to have acted as a mechanism through which economic growth was transmitted from the more developed nations to those less developed. A great number of the presently advanced nations experienced development processes in which the export sector was predominant or, at least, contributed significantly to economic growth. In many cases, these exports were primary products.

But most of the present peripheral countries, which were more or less integrated in the international economy, were not successful in achieving such goals. These countries have still not attained comparable levels of economic advancement or per capita income, even though their exports seem to have expanded quite significantly. [2]

Many explanations of these failures have been attempted, and these could be classified in different ways. But it is particularly enlightening for our purposes to dwell upon one particular classification that divides the explanations into two types. The first attributes the lack of development to a failure in transmitting the export expansion to the rest of the economy. The second class holds that a carry-over took place and that these countries grew during these periods. However, their economic progress faltered because they could not adjust to adverse circumstances in the international markets. [3] This study attempts to inquire primarily about the validity of the first type of explanation, although its conclusions will also have a bearing on the other one.

DIFFERENT POINTS OF VIEW

The Traditional Position of Classical and Neoclassical Economists

Classical and neoclassical economists expressed some ideas on these issues. Their views, in essence, are contained in an oft-used quotation from D. H. Robertson. "The specializations of the nineteenth century were not simply a device for using to the greatest effect the labours of a given number of human beings; they were above all an engine of growth."[4]

In fact, what Hla Myint calls 'productivity' doctrine is a concrete expression of the belief these economists had that production for international markets could successfully promote growth. For them, there was no incompatibility between the gains from trade and the gains from growth. According to Myint,

The 'productivity' doctrine looks upon international trade as a dynamic force which, by widening the extent of the market and the scope of division of labor, raises the skill and dexterity of the workmen, encourages technical innovations, overcomes technical indivisibilities and generally enables the trading country to enjoy increasing returns and economic development. [5]

Furthermore, as expressed as John Stuart Mill, there are important
indirect benefits in such specialization, such as the tendency of every
market extension to improve the process of production. By producing
for an external market, Mill argued, greater use of machinery and the
introduction of innovations in the production process are fostered. [6]

The expansion of trade also aids the country's economic development through what Gerald Meier calls "the education effect." The
classical and neoclassical economists were well aware of the importance of this effect, which includes several influences. These would
range from incentives to production, resulting from the desired consumption of imported goods, to the workings of the international transmission of skills, knowledge, know-how, and technology.

Finally, the classical and neoclassical economists maintained that
a trade expansion based on comparative advantage brings about a more
efficient resource allocation. This efficiency is tied to a higher real
income in the present and a potentially greater capacity to save. The
contribution of a greater volume of real savings per capita to economic
development can be considerable.

This constitutes the essence of classical and neoclassical ideas.
A corollary which follows is that "if trade increases the capacity for
development, then the larger the volume of trade the greater should be
the potential for development."[7] The bigger the increments in trade,
the larger the growth of the economy. If expressed in terms of the
present-day terminology of leading sectors, the classical and neoclassical position would be that any country should grow as a result of
an expansion in terms of value in one or more export lines—or in the
export sector taken as a whole—no matter what the types of products
exported or the country's pattern of trade.

Development Economists: Their Reactions to
Traditional Views

After World War II, interest in the economic development of backward countries mounted. A new field of economics dealing specifically
with these matters began to take shape. Considerable attention was
devoted to a reexamination of the connections between international
trade and economic development. The conclusions gradually derived
from an examination of these issues by development economists,
such as Hans W. Singer, Gunnar Myrdal, Hla Myint, and so forth;
clashed with the classical and neoclassical beliefs.

The development economists maintained that not all types of
potentially leading sectors were successful in spreading their expansion
to the rest of the economy, at least in relation to peripheral countries
with a primary-type pattern of trade. Primary export lines were singled
out as activities that should not be relied upon as the main potential

source of growth in an economic development drive. Although other export lines were not explicitly included in the same category, the general line of reasoning implied a tighter economic policy, in which any type of export would play only a secondary role. India could be seen as an example of a country exporting manufactures without experiencing successful development.

These writers attribute the failure of the transmission mechanism in the case of primary export products to different causes. One of them is related to the behavior of the terms of trade in peripheral countries. They maintain that the actual operation of the terms of trade, by sapping the purchasing power of a unit volume of exports of the primary products traditionally exported by these economies, has been quite unfavorable for underdeveloped countries. The force of this argument is mainly lost when the export expansion is expressed in value terms, as any deterioration in export prices would automatically deflate it. Nevertheless, it still could be valid when rising import prices become unfavorable to the developing country by increasing the import bill at a fast pace.

If there is an expansion in the volume of exports accompanied by a disappointing performance in terms of value, what may be basically at fault is the mechanism of adjustment in the economy and not the particular export line, that is, the economy may be failing to heed the price signals it receives. But, if the cost of producing that particular commodity is lowered at the same time, that is, if the single factoral terms of trade do not deteriorate, then the situation cannot be considered as harmful.

According to the "factors of production" argument, the characteristics of factor mobility in the past and the consequences of factor inflows into peripheral countries have been unfavorable to these countries. Most of the factor inflows are supposed to have resulted from the needs of primary production for exports in backward economies. The importation of labor damped possible wage increases and the creation of labor skills. This minimized the adoption of modern techniques and, in general, had an adverse effect of the economy. Because production for export was organized like an enclave, with more external than domestic contact, the skills and techniques that had to be implanted in the export sector did not spread to the rest of the economy.

These enclaves, largely foreign-owned, frequently enjoyed a monopsony position in the market for labor and other domestic goods and services and a monopoly—at least inside the country—over the goods they produced or sold. These companies, which had an overruling position in the economy, discouraged its development through its buying and selling practices. No incentives were provided for the accumulation of capital or for the implementation of more advanced techniques, nor were enclaves helpful in financing other sectors of the domestic economy—with foreign investment concentrated in the development of "only the country's natural resources for export, to the neglect of production in the domestic sector."[8]

Thus, enclaves created by foreign investment in the production of primary products for exports have given rise to dual economies, characterized by a lopsided economic structure. This dual structure is not only economically inefficient, but it is allegedly inimical to the development of the backward sector, which constitutes the major part of the economy (mainly because the factor combinations typical of the modern sector do not provide an adequate demand for the plentiful labor in the backward sector).

Lastly, there are very few spillover effects emerging from the enclaves, because they strive to restrict the interactions with the rest of society. Stimulating income effects are therefore lost via disproportionate leakages.

As a result of the interactions of all these forces, primary production for export in peripheral countries cannot be relied upon to ignite the development of the rest of the economy. If export activities are in the hands of domestic capitalists, the situation improves, but only to a small extent, since many of the characteristics described above are equally applicable.

The other main causative factor generally mentioned is the harmful operation of the international demonstration effect. It supposedly puts pressure on the balance of payments and hampers the attainment of an adequate savings ratio (through high import propensities to consume and to import). This results from the indiscriminately open character of a backward country integrated in the international economy through its primary product exports and the desire to imitate the consumption habits and patterns of the more advanced economies with which they enter into contact.

These arguments are a condensed and unified expression of the main factors determining the position of the development economists mentioned above. However, not every one of them uses all these arguments or gives exactly the same slant to them. Some use other arguments, also. But these arguments, and the doctrine of enclave or dualistic development, in particular, stand on their own as an anonymous expression of the ideas of many economists from developing countries in the present day.

Some of the other ideas of the development economists who have been the main contributors to the above thoughts are important enough to merit attention. Myrdal, for example, talks in terms of a cumulative mechanism of causation. International trade is such kind of mechanism. By its operation, underdeveloped countries are led to stagnation or impoverishment and developed countries into automatic cumulative growth.

International trade and the contacts evolving from it have favorable and unfavorable effects on developing economies. The favorable ones, or spread effects, are weaker than the unfavorable ones, or backwash effects. As long as the mechanism of causation continues to be weighted in this fashion, the outcome of international contacts will be a cumulative impoverishment or stagnation of the poor countries. Furthermore, according to Myrdal, there is no force inherent in this mechanism that could break its ill-fated operation.

The spread effects mainly consist of an expanding external demand for the traditional products of the developing countries. The most important backwash effects are those arising from the adverse impact of the factor movements discussed above: (a) the perverse movements of the most efficient factors of production from the backward countries to the advanced nations, (b) the higher rates of population growth, which characterize the poorer nations after international contacts have been established, (c) the inferior capabilities of the developing nations for building an infrastructure to compensate for the lack of investment incentives resulting from their relatively unfavorable economic conditions, and (d) the weakening of the local productive structure catering to the domestic market due to the competition of cheaper imports from the advanced nations.

In turn, Singer considers that domestic industry, in contrast to primary production for export, would be effective in the promotion of economic progress in underdeveloped countries because of its intrinsic characteristics, which are not shared by primary production. "Industrial endeavors are capable of being growing points for increased technical knowledge, urban education, the dynamism and resilience that goes with urban civilization, as well as the direct Marshallian external economies."[9] He recognizes that, under different circumstances, commerce, farming, and plantation agriculture have proved capable of being such 'growing points.' Nevertheless, Singer concludes that, for the underdeveloped countries, investment in these traditional lines has been incapable of generating domestic development.[10]

Singer also contends that the effects of the cyclical changes in the terms of trade of primary producers discourage investment in sectors other than the export sector and have been unfavorable to these countries. When export prices are high, then there are no incentives to invest in other sectors, even though funds are available. When prices are low, the incentives for the diversification of investments are there, but no funds are available.

Another interesting viewpoint is that of Albert Hirschman. He believes that "agriculture certainly stands convicted on the count of its lack of direct stimulus to the setting up of new activities through linkage effects . . . . This may yet be the most important reason militating against any complete specialization of underdeveloped countries in primary production."[11]

In short, this group of development economists concludes that a primary-type export sector, or a particular line within this sector, could not fulfill the role of leading sector—even if potentially qualified—in a peripheral country with a pattern of trade based on raw material exports.

International Trade Theorists: Reaffirmation of
Traditional Thought

These pessimistic views, in turn, generated another reaction. Other economists, mainly international trade specialists, expounded and reinforced the classical and neoclassical ideas. The most notable contributors in this group have been Gottfried Haberler, Jacob Viner, Alec Cairncross, and Peter Bauer. In general, this group maintains that trade can, indeed, promote the growth of the rest of the economy. An expansion of trade in any type product generates spillover effects, which have a favorable impact on other sectors by arousing and leading their expansionary forces.

Cairncross's statements can be considered representative: "I confess to some skepticism about the supposed ineffectiveness of foreign trade in producing innovation and development. It does not strike me as entirely plausible to speak as if foreign trade could be contained within an enclave without transmitting its dynamic influences to the rest of the economy."[12] Cairncross stresses the beneficial "educative effects" of trade, which spread aspirations, skills, and ways of doing things.

Haberler argues that, apart from the static gains, trade bestows important indirect benefits, which are of a dynamic nature, to the trading countries. He concludes that "international trade has made a tremendous contribution to the development of less developed countries in the 19th and 20th centuries and can be expected to make an equally big contribution in the future, if it is allowed to proceed freely."[13]

But how does this allegedly positive influence on economic development operate? Haberler stresses the indirect benefits of trade.

First, trade provides material means (capital goods, machinery and raw and semifinished materials) indispensable for economic development. Secondly, and even more important, trade is the means and vehicle for the dissemination of know-how, skills, managerial talent and entrepreneurship. Thirdly, trade is also the vehicle for the international movement of capital especially from the developed to the underdeveloped countries. Fourthly, free international trade is the best antimonopoly policy and the best guarantee for the maintenance of a healthy degree of free competition.[14]

Bauer completes the argument of this group of economists with the following observation: "But is it not the case that now, as in the past, the most advanced of the underdeveloped regions and sectors are those in contact with developed countries?"[15] As pointed out above, these economists build upon the classical and neoclassical position in order to construct an improved version. Consequently, their conclusions are, in essence, identical with those of classical and neoclassical economists.

Staple and Export Base Theories and Extensions

Work on this issue has been conducted separately by other economists. Their ideas have not originated from an examination of the
problems faced by the developing countries of today, either now or in
the past. As an example of this, certain economists and economic historians from Canada and others that have studied its economic history
have constituted a school of thought based upon an interpretation of
Canada's economic growth. They have formulated what is known as "the
staple approach" to the economic history of Canada, which had its ori-
gins in the work of Harold A. Innis. Its applications have been mainly
restricted to Canadian economic history, although the approach has also
been used in examining the economic history of other countries, particularly other areas of recent settlement. Some economists do believe
that this model is equally applicable to peripheral countries.

The staple approach to economic history considers the staple
product line or lines as the main force or leading sector in the process
of economic development. It defines "staple" as "a product with a
large natural resource content"[16] catering mainly to the external market. The staple approach holds that these primary products, depending
upon their particular characteristics, have diverse effects on the growth
of an economy. The combination of inputs used in production and the
resultant income distribution, the sociological aspects of the productive
organization, the technological requirements, and so forth vary from
product to product. The impact of a particular line on the economy of a
country is more or less successful, depending on how effective its
characteristics are for the transmission of growth to other sectors.

Most of these characteristics stem from the technological relationship of production—in other words, the production function. From a
specified production function and the necessary ceteris paribus assump-
tions, it is possible to derive the demand for inputs, the distribution of
income, and so forth.

The staple approach, as the previous paragraphs indicate, concentrates on the direct contribution of primary production for export to the
rest of the economy. This stands in contrast with the position of the
classical and neoclassical economists and their contemporary followers,
which stresses the indirect benefits of trade.

Because of this concentration on the direct contribution, it has
been suggested lately that the staple approach is a theory of induced
capital formation. The purchase of local goods and services provides
inducements to investment in the domestic supply activities. The same
thing holds for industries using the staple product as an input via the
forward linking output of the staple industry. An estimate of its backward and forward linkages would then represent an approximate measure
of the inducement to invest provided by the staple activity. There are also
inducements to invest operating via the income originated in the staple
industry that affects the industries catering to the domestic market.

Proponents of the staple approach provide an optimistic viewpoint on the reliability of primary products as leading sectors in the economic development of peripheral countries. In this respect, their position is in agreement with the thoughts of the classical and neoclassical economists and with the ideas expressed by their followers. They have added a word of caution, however, pointing out that primary products differ in their growth-promoting characteristics. Robert E. Baldwin, who built on the staple approach to come up with a similar theoretical construct, would go a step further. He believes that the characteristics of the export products determine if the carry-over is successful or not. [17]

A concept similar to the staple export has been used for a long time by regional economists: the export or economic base of a region. This concept can be applied to countries as well, as long as they are open economies. This is the case for most of the peripheral countries, which have high foreign-trade ratios.

The concept of economic or export base can be traced to the international trade multiplier. Naturally, it has been adapted to the needs of the regional economist for short-run and long-run analysis. The economic base of a region can be defined as those industries principally engaged in exporting from the region under consideration to other regions. An empirical multiplier can then be estimated on the basis of the historical relationship between these export activities and the overall economic activity in the region. On occasions, the economic or export base is taken as the whole export sector, with the multiplier redefined accordingly.

There are several minor differences between the staple product and export base concepts. The staple approach concentrates on one or a few important export lines; the export base includes all the industries mainly producing for export or, sometimes, the export sector as a whole. In the case where there is a high degree of concentration in exports, the difference between the staple and export base concepts disappears almost completely.

Then, the staple approach is more complete. It not only goes beneath the total income and expenditure originated in the primary export activity, examining the characteristics of the productive process in the export lines, but it considers all other growth-promoting forces emanating from the staple industry. On the other hand, the export base concentrates on autonomous income effects and multiplier relationships, considering also nonprimary lines. Douglass North achieved a very fruitful blend of both approaches in his analysis of historical growth in the U.S. economy.

The economic base approach to long-run regional economic development considers export activities as the autonomous growth-promoting force in the economy. The export base can be considered as a leading sector consisting of a group of export lines. When exports are concentrated in just a few lines, then the export base reverts to the case of one, two, or a few leading sectors.

North, meshing these two models, considers that the carry-over from the export base activities to the rest of the economy has usually been successful. However, when the export base is composed of one or a few agricultural products and their characteristics do not favor the expansion of the domestic economy or the diversification of the export sector, this will not happen. On the other hand, North believes that if the export base is diversified, then its expansion succeeds in being transmitted to the other sectors of the economy.[18]

In sum, staple theory economists, such as Richard Caves, believe that expanding primary product lines could successfully lead the economic development process in peripheral countries; however, the degree of success would depend on the particular line or lines. Certain regional economists believe that an export base composed of primary products could promote growth in the rest of the economy in peripheral countries with relatively high foreign-trade ratios. North mixes these two approaches in developing the hypothesis that only if the primary export sector is diversified or if it comprises a primary product line or lines with certain growth-promoting characteristics can its expansion successfully carry over into the other sectors of the economy.

Views of Economic Historians

Economic historians assume contradictory positions in interpreting the historical facts related to this issue. They recognize the strategic role that the expansion of primary exports have had on the economic growth of today's advanced economies. In many cases, the contribution of primary product exports successfully acted as the main source of growth during the crucial preconditions and take-off stages. As Cairncross has said: "Whether one thinks of Britain at the outset of the industrial revolution or of the United States in the nineteenth century or of Japan in the twentieth, the expansion of exports gave a conspicuous momentum to the economy and helped it on its way to industrialization."[19]

Nevertheless, some economic historians point out that distinctions must be made in regard to the effects of primary export expansions in different types of economies. A primary export expansion in the economies of the Old World, with its centuries of evolution, and in some economies of the East, with developed internal markets, is one thing; quite another is the expansion of primary exports in the regions of recent settlement and in the peripheral countries. For the latter, there are greater facilities for external rather than for internal trade, with specialization between countries evolving before that between regions within a country. As a result, potential favorable repercussions are inhibited, and the effects of increasing exports do not spread with ease to the rest of the economy. In contrast, there are economic historians

who maintain that no distinction should be made as to the type of economy on this issue. They believe that an expansion in primary export
lines will lead to economic growth, irrespectively.

That the impact has been favorable for the regions of recent settlement cannot be denied. These regions did have as a common characteristic the "dependence on growth through primary commodity exports
and on the private foreign investment which, directly or indirectly, was
thereby induced."[20] But can the same thing be said for the peripheral
countries? According to the first group of economic historians, this is
not the case.

An Hypothesis by Gerald Meier

Recently, Meier took a close look at the issue that has been
explored in this chapter and came up with conclusions that differ significantly from the ideas previously examined. His observations stem
from a specific consideration of the experiences of peripheral countries
in the past as to the effects of an expansion in the export sector—or in
one or a few lines in it—on the rest of the economy. He fails to specify
the types of exports to which he refers, but seems to imply that he is
dealing with primary products.

Meier combines two main streams of thought in his explanation.
One refers to the characteristics of the particular export product as a
significant factor in the promotion of economic development in the rest
of the economy. As has been seen, these thoughts originated with the
staple product economists and, later, were expounded by Baldwin. The
other is concerned with the importance of sociocultural factors and market imperfections as general prerequisites or preconditions to sustained
growth. Both economic historians and development economists, like
Julius Herman Boeke, for example, had been exploring the latter.

Meier believes that the transmission mechanism has failed to
operate in the peripheral countries; this can be attributed to "the differential effects of different exports, and . . . the domestic market conditions of the poor country."[21]

Meier tells us that the extent of the carry-over from the expansion
in external demand varies with the characteristics of the product or
products involved. As these differ not only for primary, secondary, and
tertiary production but also among primary products, it follows that the
success or failure in the transmission of growth varies with the particular product spearheading the export drive. Therefore, the blanket con-
demnation of trade via exports of primary products is not warranted.
Neither is the indiscriminate position that considers all types of export
production capable of promoting a successful development drive.

This could partially explain the contrasting experiences that the
advanced nations and the peripheral countries have had in export-led

development. There are important differences in the characteristics of the primary export products of the latter and those that were important for the development of a number of countries in the former group. For example, the production function of plantation crops in the tropics has relatively weak growth-promoting effects, and this could determine an unsuccessful carry-over from expanding exports.

Up to this point, Meier's position appears akin to Baldwin's and similar to the ideas of North. But then comes the second portion of his thesis, which is really the crucial part of the explanation. It considers why even products with characteristics amenable to a successful carry-over into the other sectors will fail to get the peripheral countries moving.

Clearly, differences in the growth-promoting characteristics of the products is not the complete explanation, for countries exporting the same type of primary products have differed in the results obtained from the expected stimulation via exports. Some other factor has to determine such differences.

Meier gives a lucid description of domestic impediments as obstacles to the spillover of primary export expansions into the rest of the economy:

> In connection with these domestic impediments, we can recognize that the pervasiveness of market imperfections has severely limited the carry-over from exports. The economies of poor countries are characterized by factor immobility, price rigidity, restrictive tendencies in both the factor and goods markets, ignorance of technological possibilities, limited knowledge of market conditions, and few centers of entrepreneurship. . . . Many of these inhibiting factors are a function of socio-cultural customs and institutions . . . In terms of Rostow's scheme, the failure of the export sector to have been a primary growth sector, setting in motion expansionary forces elsewhere in the economy, may be attributed in large part to the absence of the pre-conditions necessary for the take-off into self sustained growth. [22]

Meier constructs his hypothesis in such a way that the presence of domestic impediments ends up overshadowing the product peculiarities and practically remains as the sole explanation. He recognizes this himself, when stating:

> When intersectoral relationships are many and the response to an expansion in exports is rapid and extensive in scope, then even a weak stimulus can still result in a significant carry-over. In contrast, when there are formidable domestic impediments to a transmission of the gains from exports to

other sectors, then even a strong stimulus will have only
slight penetrative powers. [23]

In conclusion, Meier maintains that if, as he believes happened
in the past, expansion in a primary producing export sector, or in one
or a few primary product lines within this sector, fails to bring about
economic growth in a peripheral country, it is because of the following:
(a) weak spillover effects from the external expansion, as a consequence
of the characteristics of the product or products involved; and (b) domestic impediments, which inhibit the operation of the transmission mechanism. The latter he regards as the decisive factor.

A Brief Summation

Some of the hypotheses considered were formulated to cover all
possible cases involving the relation of an external demand expansion
with the internal growth of an economy. Others were limited to an
examination of a subset of such cases. However, all these ideas are
of interest, inasmuch as they apply to the case of primary production
for export in peripheral countries with patterns of trade based on
primary exports.
It should be stressed that only the potentially successful expansions of primary product exports are being dealt with here. If the
expanding sector could not potentially lead a growth process, then
there is no point in considering the question of its success or failure
in transmitting this expansion to other sectors. As noted in Chapter 1,
for a primary product export sector or line to be considered as potentially leading, its must have a certain size as well as a significant
rate of expansion.
The different positions examined as to the success or failure of
a transmission of an export expansion by a potentially leading primary
sector or line, in peripheral countries with a pattern of trade based on
primary product exports, can be summarized as follows:

1. Classical and neoclassical economists, and their present-day
followers, take an affirmative position.
2. As a reaction to such views, development economists (Myrdal,
Singer, and so forth) took a negative position.
3. Staple approach economists, as well as most regional economists, have a positive view overall, with the former stressing that
the degree of effectiveness in the transmission mechanism depends on
the characteristics of the product.
4. North, although having a generally affirmative position, considers that lacking a diversification of the export base, the characteristics of certain products would determine the failure of the

transmission mechanism. Baldwin would agree only with the latter part of the proposition.

5. Meier agrees with North and Baldwin as to the importance of product characteristics in determining the success or failure of the expansion of a potentially leading primary sector. However, he goes further, believing that, even when those characteristics are favorable, a potentially leading primary export sector would not be able to lead the development of the rest of the economy if basic obstacles to growth, such as market imperfections and lack of adequate socioeconomic institutions, are present.

AN ALTERNATIVE HYPOTHESIS

Imagine a peripheral country that engages in trade. It exports primary products and imports mostly manufactures. Exports are concentrated, with one line constituting a significant percentage of the total. The value of exports in this main line shows an expanding trend over the long run. This expansion is not neutralized by contractions in other export lines or other autonomous sectors of the economy. Such main export activity is the principal potential source of growth in the economy. Which factors, then, are important in determining the success or failure of the main export line in transmitting its growth to the rest of the economy and, therefore, its success or failure as a leading sector?

There are four main factors determining such performance: (a) the size of the expanding primary export line relative to the economy as a whole, (b) its rate of expansion, (c) its direct and indirect contribution to the development of the other sectors of the economy, and (d) the effectiveness with which this contribution is used. As pointed out above, only the cases of the expanding export lines that can qualify as potentially leading sectors are being considered in this study, meaning those which have the rate of expansion and relative size to permit a successful carry-over. Thus, under these conditions, the success or failure of a carry-over will depend on the other two factors specified.

The direct contribution stems from the income and expenditures originated by the potentially leading primary export line. In particular, it stems from the multiplicative and accelerative effects of its increments. These run their course through the income-product flow matrix of the economy through successive spending rounds. The direct contribution also includes: (a) the backward and forward effective linkages of the industry; (b) the external economies created; (c) the impact of its investment expenditures in the native capital goods producing sector; (d) the distribution of the income originated in the export activity, and the pattern of demand related to it; (e) the level of technology and skills, and their transfer to other sectors; and (f) the opportunities for factor substitution in the industry making it flexible to the economy's resource composition.

The indirect contribution includes the favorable forces stemming from the expanding line that affect the rest of the economy in a more general and removed way. These include: (a) the participation of the industry in total public revenues and foreign exchange proceeds and their effects on growth, inflation, availability, mobility, flexibility, and economic efficiency; (b) the improvement in the process of production in the economy as a result of efficient specialization and trade; and (c) the greater savings made possible by the higher real income resulting from a more efficient use of resources.

The impact that some of these contributions eventually has on the rest of the economy depends upon their utilization. In certain cases, government policy directly determines their use, as in the contribution to public revenues. In other instances, government policy measures only determine their utilization indirectly, as in the case of the foreign exchange proceeds deriving from the potentially leading sector.

But the extent to which a sector contributes to growth and efficiency in the rest of the economy also depends on its negative effects. The final contribution is actually determined by the extent to which the positive contribution compensates for the latter. These negative elements are the following: (a) the unfavorable demonstration effects that result from external contacts, (b) the resulting short-run increase in population growth, (c) external diseconomies, and (d) the monopsony-monopoly position and other enclave characteristics that are sometimes present in primary export lines.

Many of the positive contributions of a potentially leading sector are closely related to the concepts of value added, value of production, investment, and value of exports in that line. These concepts collapse into the broader concept of total expenditures in the particular export line.

At first glance, it might appear that the total expenditures of a potentially leading sector could be an appropriate indicator of its total combined positive contribution. However, part of the total expenditures of the potentially leading sector do not affect other domestic industries or resident factors of production. All the foreign exchange earnings of the sector are not available to the rest of the economy either, since the industry uses some of them itself. What is left, after extricating the foreign component, constitutes the portion through which the impact on the rest of the economy takes place. [24] Thus, only the national component is an adequate representation of the potential leading sector's combined total positive contribution to the rest of the economy. This part represents the value actually retained by the economy of the total potential contribution of a sector or the retained value of its total expenditures.

Although the evolution of total retained value can be a simple and summarized representation of the approximate behavior of the total

combined positive contribution of a potentially leading sector, some
of the positive contributions do not have a straightforward and stable
relation with it. In order to grasp the spread effects in their entirety
and reality, a much more detailed and complicated examination of each
of the factors involved would be required. Nevertheless, variations
in the retained value concept reflect quite accurately the change in
some of the most important contributions of the industry, such as
domestic income and expenditures originated, investment, and exports.
Thus, as total retained value is a sufficiently close, convenient,
first-hand approximation of the total combined positive contribution of
a sector to the growth of the rest of the economy, the complexity of an
elaborate measurement probably is not worth the improvement in precision that would be obtained.

What consequences can be expected for the peripheral economy if
a potentially leading primary export sector experiences a long-term
expansion in its total retained value? The direct and indirect favorable
influences discussed above will constitute positive forces acting for
the development of the rest of the economy. Undoubtedly, however,
there will be unfavorable factors working in the opposite direction.
Our hypothesis is that the positive contributions generally overshadow
the drawbacks of the primary export expansion. Thus, a potentially
leading export sector of the primary type is usually successful in
inducing growth in the rest of the economy, regardless of the type of
primary product. Yet, it is believed that the characteristics of the
different products will make some more successful than others in the
role of leading sectors. Moreover, an expansion in the total retained
value of the export line should get the rest of the economy moving, no
matter what the country's stage of development. No obstacles should
be strong enough to neutralize the operation of the transmission mechanism from a potentially leading primary export line--barring counter-
acting movements in other autonomous economic variables or abnormal
conditions.

In some cases, expansion in the total retained value of a potentially
leading export sector of the primary type may not automatically spread
to the other sectors of the economy. (This is why the statement above
has been qualified somewhat.) This might take place, if the positive
contributions of a primary export line are not adequately utilized or if
the negative effects are not appropriately neutralized. In these cases,
the automatic operation of the transmission mechanism could not by
itself be expected to ensure the growth of the rest of the economy.
Thus, an effective utilization of the sector's contributions and a
minimization of its drawbacks through government policy might be
required for a successful development process to catch on. Efficient
use of the public revenues and foreign exchange earnings contributed
by the sector, coordination of public investment policies with investment expenditures in the industry, effective taxation of its income
originated—these would be some of the appropriate policies that would

have to be instituted in order to ensure a more successful transmission of the export expansion into the other sectors of the economy.

In conclusion, it is believed that expansion in a primary export line as described above can lead the rest of the economy into a process of development; in some cases, though, the transmission of growth into other sectors will not be automatic and would necessitate the implementation of appropriate government policies. This result should be obtained regardless of the type of primary product involved and the economic stage of the country in question. In fact, depending on how prolonged the export expansion in a particular line, the country might move to the preconditions stage, grow through this period, and eventually move into the take-off stage. Or the growth could occur during take-off and continue onward, while self-sustaining growth was being consolidated.

It is believed that, if the historical experience of peripheral countries is examined more carefully, it will be found that export expansions, while they lasted, usually led to growth in the rest of the economy and, thus, to economic development. When this did not happen, it probably was due to the absence or inappropriateness of policies designed to maximize the net positive contribution of the export line and to utilize it effectively. Many have expressed ideas about these matters, but few have bothered to identify and study the relevant facts.

The hypothesis that has been unfolded deals with a potentially leading primary-producing export line. Nevertheless, the same proposition would hold for the case in which two or more primary export lines were combined. These ideas would obviously hold a fortiori if the exports were industrial goods.

NOTES

1. For a short statement of a concurring point of view, which can be considered representative, see Richard E. Caves's review of Gerald Meier's International Trade and Development, in Economic Development and Cultural Change (October, 1964).

2. All of this is generally presumed to be an approximation of what actually occurred. See Gerald M. Meier, The International Economics of Development (New York: Harper & Row, 1968), and Robert E. Baldwin, Economic Development and Growth (New York: John Wiley and Sons, Inc., 1966), as two examples.

3. Particular explanations combining both these types are also found.

4. Dennis H. Robertson, "The Future of International Trade," in Howard S. Ellis and Lloyd Metzler, eds., Readings in the Theory of International Trade (Philadelphia: Irwin, 1947), p. 501.

5. Hla Myint, "The 'Classical Theory' of International Trade and the Underdeveloped Countries," Economic Journal (June 1958): 318-19.

6. John Stuart Mill, Principles of Political Economy, ed. W. J. Ashley (New York: Longmans, Green and Co., 1929), p. 581.

7. Meier, op. cit., p. 222.

8. Hans W. Singer, "The Distribution of Gains Between Investing and Borrowing Countries" (Papers and Proceedings of the Sixty-Second Annual Meeting of the American Economic Association, 1949), American Economic Review 40 (May 1950): 477.

9. Ibid., p. 47.

10. Ibid., p. 476.

11. Albert O. Hirschman, The Strategy of Economic Development, Yale Studies in Economics, 10 (New Haven: Yale University Press, 1958), pp. 109, 110.

12. Alec K. Cairncross, "International Trade and Economic Development," Economica (August 1961): 240.

13. Gottfried Haberler, International Trade and Economic Development (Cairo, Egypt: National Bank of Egypt, 1959), p. 5.

14. Ibid., p. 11.

15. Peter Bauer, "International Economic Developments," Economic Journal (March 1959): 112.

16. Richard E. Caves and Richard H. Holton, The Canadian Economy: Prospect and Retrospect, Harvard Economic Studies, vol. 112 (Cambridge, Massachusetts: Harvard University Press, 1959), p. 31.

17. Robert E. Baldwin, "Export Technology and Development from a Subsistence Level," Economic Journal (March 1963): 80-92.

18. See Douglass C. North, "Agriculture in Regional Economic Growth," and ensuing "Discussion" by V. W. Ruttan and O. V. Wells, Journal of Farm Economics (December 1959).

19. Cairncross, op. cit., p. 236.

20. Ragnar Nurkse, Patterns of Trade and Development, Wicksell Lectures (Stockholm: Almquist, 1959), p. 15.

21. Meier, op. cit., p. 240.

22. Ibid., pp. 246-47.

23. Ibid., p. 246.

24. The foreign component has only a delayed and negligible effect on the other sectors of the economy.

In the chapters that follow, the effects of the expansion of the oil industry on the other sectors of the Venezuelan economy and on the ultimate development of the country are explored. The analysis is divided into five periods: (a) 1936-42, (b) 1943-48, (c) 1949-57, (d) 1958-65, and (e) 1966-73. The purpose of this time spacing is to separate periods in which the behavior of the industry, and of government policies in general (specifically those regarding oil), have been significantly different.

In each period, attention will be focused on the main contributions of petroleum to the economy of Venezuela. Four areas will be examined: (a) foreign exchange proceeds, (b) oil tax revenues, (c) petroleum investment, and (d) income-expenditure generation. The combined total contribution of oil in each period, as indicated by the retained value of total expenditures, will then be examined. The total combined petroleum contribution will give an idea of the behavior of the positive contributions, which are not considered individually in this study. Lastly, the relationship of the contribution of oil to investment and gross domestic product (GDP) in the nonpetroleum part of the economy will be analyzed and conclusions drawn as to the overall effects of oil on the economy.

During this period, the oil industry certainly had a rate of expansion and size that would qualify it as a potentially leading sector. On the other hand, the Venezuelan economy could be classified as a peripheral country with a pattern of trade and production based on primary activities, importing most of the industrial products it consumed. Thus, this empirical section can provide a partial test for the propositions stated in Chapter 2.

In the remainder of this chapter, the methodological and procedural problems that were faced in this section of the study will be discussed. Most of the data that will be used in the study were developed directly in the course of research or existed in unpublished form in different sources. The figures have been calculated, for the most part, in terms of current bolívares and are referred to as such in the text. Whenever the figures appear in some other form, this will be specifically mentioned.

In every period, an examination is made of the foreign exchange contribution of the oil industry, relying on estimates of total exports of goods and services and petroleum exports of goods and services. These estimates actually refer to total current account credits, including transfer payments and investment income received from abroad. Whenever data limitations do not permit such level of detail, figures covering only export of goods are used. All these figures are appropriately presented in current dollars, as they refer to the availability of international means of payments to the Venezuelan economy.

Figures referring to the net foreign exchange contribution of the other major sectors of the Venezuelan economy are also used. These data are also expressed in dollars and represent the actual foreign exchange originated in each of these sectors net of its own uses. This variable measures the contribution of a particular sector to the rest of the economy only, as it excludes the foreign exchange usage of the contributing sector.

The movement of oil export prices is followed by the use of the implicit deflator of petroleum GDP with a 1957 base and by different price series compiled by the Ministerio de Minas e Hidrocarburos (Ministry of Mines and Hydrocarbons) in terms of current dollars. For the study of the application of the funds resulting from the foreign trade contribution of oil, changes in the international monetary reserves of the country, in terms of dollars, and the breakdown of the different balance-of-payments debits are examined. As to the latter, lack of appropriate data limited the investigation to the classification of imports of goods by type—consumer, intermediate, or capital goods. The other debits that could have been examined to evaluate the utilization of the foreign exchange proceeds derived from oil are of minor importance, when compared with goods imported.

For an examination of the public sector contribution, the total public revenues derived from oil in a direct way are compared with total public revenues. Petroleum-derived tax revenues are expressed in current bolívares and have been calculated on the basis of an unambiguous and homogeneous definition throughout the periods (see the section on detailed data sources at the end of the book). In contrast, public revenues in current bolívares were compiled from different sources, with varying degrees of inconclusiveness. Up to 1950, the figures have been prepared from data appearing in the Anuarios Estadísticos (Statistical Yearbook) of the Ministerio de Fomento (Development Ministry). Unfortunately, these data do not include the revenues of autonomous administrative institutes and state enterprises. From 1950 until 1960, the latter are included in the figures published by the Banco Central de Venezuela (Central Bank of Venezuela). From then on the Central Bank published data for the public sector as a whole, as previously, but without the inclusion of state enterprises.

This introduces an element of lack of comparability in the series that were constructed using these data. Total public revenues before 1950 are not comparable to those after that date. Among the latter, there are also differences between the 1950-60 figures and the more recent ones. The same is true of the ratio of petroleum to total revenues.

The latter percentage figures could be made comparable by using the same base. Instead of using total public revenues as the base from 1950 on, the revenues of the national and regional governments could be used, as has been done for previous years. Nevertheless, this would require the use of different reporting sources in some of the periods, as the publication of the Statistical Yearbook has been incomplete since 1950.

The lack of revenue data corresponding to autonomous administrative institutes and state enterprises before 1950 somewhat clouds the behavior and trends in the participation of oil in total revenues during the early periods. With some of the components missing, the conclusions derived can be extended to total public revenues only by assuming that it behaved similarly to national and regional tax revenues. The same is true to a lesser extent of the 1960-73 period, because revenues of state enterprises are missing for those years. To be more explicit, only under this assumption could it be said that the increasing share of oil-derived revenues in national plus regional tax revenues from 1936 up to 1950 is also applicable to total government revenues. According to informed sources in Venezuela, this assumption is reasonably correct, although it is impossible to document this empirically.

The appropriation of these revenues was examined in order to evaluate how effectively the public sector contribution of the oil industry was utilized. For this purpose, the determination of the surpluses or deficits in the total public budget would first be required. Again, the best that can be done here is to determine the surplus or deficit under the most inclusive definition possible of the public sector, given the lack of complete statistics. The surpluses or deficits to which references are made below refer to different degrees of inclusiveness from 1936-50, from 1950-60, and from then on. Again, it is reasonable to presume similar results under more or less inclusive definitions.

In order to appraise the effectiveness of public expenditures, the share allocated for economic development purposes should be determined. As it is impossible to estimate the latter directly, appropriate proxies are used as a replacement. Use is made of readily available estimates of social and economic expenditures in the national and regional budgets from 1936 to 1948 and of Central Bank estimates of capital expenditures for the whole public sector from then on. There

is another break in the data here, then. Furthermore, during the
first and second periods, we have been unable to determine the breakdown for the public sector as a whole. It can only be assumed, as
previously, that the share applicable to national and regional expenditures would not be altered if the calculations would have the government
sector as a whole.

The investment contribution presents even greater difficulties.
Before 1950, the data available were provided by the Central Bank.
The series is unpublished and does not have the same degree of
reliability as more recent figures. These estimates were, in turn,
adjusted by the author because of the discrepancy between the
petroleum investment figures calculated directly from company data
and those calculated by the Central Bank.

The figures corresponding to petroleum investment likewise
present problems. In order to derive estimates for the industry as
a whole from 1936 to 1942, the figures derived from our survey of
the three main oil-producing company groups in Venezuela had to be
adjusted. This was necessary because this period was characterized
by important exploratory activities in which the smaller companies
were involved, and their investment expenditures were out of proportion to their share of oil production. The adjustment was based on
company reports, exploratory and development activities, and other
indicators as presented in the Memorias (Annual Reports) of the
Development Ministry (which, at the time, included petroleum
affairs).

Petroleum investment refers to gross fixed domestic investment.
Estimates of changes in inventories required to present gross total
domestic investment figures could not be obtained, as information
on the change of raw material stocks of the industry was not reliable.
Because the impact of the industry on other sectors takes place
through its gross investment expenditures, it is more appropriate to
use the figure of petroleum investment in such terms.

Another difficulty in estimating the investment expenditures of
petroleum involves determining out of the industry's annual purchases
of goods and services, the portion that should be charged to the
capital account. Due to accounting practices, some costs of the
petroleum industry have been inappropriately included as investment
expenditures. This is expecially prevalent in concession costs and
exploratory activities, where certain expenses, such as taxes and
intangible costs, are capitalized. It has been impossible to adjust
the investment figures downward, even in an approximate manner,
in order to take account of this problem, because the data are not
sufficiently detailed. It is better, under such conditions not to
tamper with the reported figures, recognizing only that they represent
slight overestimates.

Table 3.1 shows the total investment expenditures of the industry,
and its concession and exploratory components, for a representative

TABLE 3. 1

Total Investment Expenditures of the Petroleum Industry
and Its Concession and Exploratory Components,
as Reported by the Oil Companies, 1960-65

Year	Concession Costs (millions of bolívares) (1)	Exploratory Costs (millions of bolívares) (2)	Total Investment (millions of bolívares) (3)	Percent of (1) + (2) over (3)
1960	7	41	706	5. 8
1961	12	44	521	8. 4
1962	0	25	503	5. 0
1963	7	38	518	9. 3
1964	1	42	735	7. 3
1965	4	72	825	8. 7

Note: Figures in this table do not coincide with the corresponding
total investment expenditures of the petroleum industries reported
below, because they result from the addition of quarterly inquiries
sent to the companies and differ from the adjusted yearly totals.

Source: Prepared from unpublished data from the Ministerio de
Minas e Hidrocarburos.

subperiod in order to give an idea of the orders of magnitude involved.
Most of the concession costs represent taxes, which should not be
considered a part of the industry investment. An undetermined part
of exploratory costs is also improperly included in the investment
expenditure estimates. The remainder in these categories can be
safely considered investment.

The total investment of the Venezuelan economy is also reported
in the term of gross fixed domestic investment, as the only available
long-term investment series for the economy of Venezuela is in these
terms. This contributed to the decision to present all investment
figures in gross, fixed terms. Moreover, data on changes in stocks
have been much more unreliable until very recently.

In order to analyze better the impact of the oil contributions
upon the other sectors of the economy, the concept of nonpetroleum
gross investment is used. By definition, it is total investment minus
petroleum investment, which leaves the investment expenditures
corresponding to the other sectors of the economy. This concept is
expressed in the same terms as all the other investment concepts.

In examining the contribution of the petroleum industry arising
from the increased expenditures and income originated in the industry,

two types of variables, through which the economic activity of the industry is represented, have to be considered. Variables like the value of oil produced, the current expenditures of the petroleum industry, or the gross domestic product of oil include components that have a relatively weak effect on the rest of the economy. The opposite holds for variables like the retained value of oil expenditures, whose components impinge very strongly on the other sectors of the economy.

Changes in the current expenditures of the oil industry or in its value of production have been derived from petroleum sales values, plus or minus any variation in the inventories of crude oil and products. The latter have been derived by pricing the changes in the physical quantities of oil held in inventory by the industry. GDP was estimated by adding the appropriate payment components of the petroleum industry. For the sake of clarity, the GDP originated by the industry in the creation of capital goods for its own use should be kept separate from that created in the production of current goods and services.

More specifically, petroleum GDP was estimated as the sum of wages and salaries, profits after taxes, interest payments, depreciation and amortization, and taxes that constitute the value added by the industry. Some of these components, as reported, were related to value of sales and, thus, had to be corrected to reflect value of production. This adjustment factor used was calculated on the basis of changes in the stocks of crude oil and other oil products.

Some of these individual components required other adjustments. Profits after taxes had to be adjusted in the 1936-42 period to take account of the losses that the newcoming oil companies suffered. The methodology employed of aggregating the net value added figures of the "big three" oil groups in Venezuela (Standard of New Jersey, Shell, and Gulf), which accounted for over 99 percent of total Venezuelan production from 1936 to 1942 and, adjusting for other companies in terms of their participation in total production, could not have accounted for these losses.

As for depreciation and amortization, the figures were taken as reported by the companies. No adjustments were made to try to express this capital use concept in stricter economic terms, because the information available did not allow it. Therefore, the usual obscure amortization charges of the oil sector, related to depletion, intangible costs, development, and wildcat drilling costs, were taken at face value and included in the capital use charges. A breakdown is given in Table 3.2 of the different components of depreciation and amortization, which gives an idea of the importance of each in the total capital use charges of the petroleum industry. As far as can be seen, given that it has been impossible to separate other amortization charges from depletion, the latter, as well as intangible costs, appear to be a small part of the total charges, so their inclusion does not make that much difference.

TABLE 3.2

Capital Use Charges of the Petroleum Industry,
by Components, 1947-62*
(millions of bolívares)

Year	Production Depreciation Charges	Transport Depreciation Charges	Refining Depreciation Charges	Marketing Depreciation Charges
1947	135	9	3	2
1948	188	15	3	2
1949	199	28	29	3
1950	234	32	72	3
1951	267	32	86	4
1952	310	48	83	4
1953	341	47	85	4
1954	361	50	85	5
1955	415	54	93	6
1956	461	56	95	6
1957	508	62	119	8
1958	508	68	129	8
1959	563	83	131	10
1960	545	92	128	11
1961	528	92	120	11
1962	471	76	117	12

Year	Other Depreciation Charges	Total Depreciation Charges	Depletion and Other Amortization Charges	Intangible Costs Incurred During Other Periods
1947	6	155	35	2
1948	2	211	36	1
1949	3	263	62	2
1950	5	346	74	0
1951	16	405	90	0
1952	11	456	74	2
1953	8	486	71	8
1954	15	516	97	20
1955	18	586	94	16
1956	20	638	93	13
1957	21	717	95	16
1958	24	738	98	13
1959	22	809	130	17
1960	25	800	148	24
1961	26	778	151	28
1962	20	696	215	32

*Component figures do not necessarily add to totals because of rounding.

Source: Unpublished figures from the Ministerio de Minas e Hidrocarburos.

Finally, there is no information available regarding interest payments on capital borrowed from abroad by the oil industry before 1947. This fact does not seriously affect the estimates, because this item usually has represented a small part of the total interest payments. In addition, before and during World War II, outside borrowing by the industry was much smaller than in ensuing years.

There are two principal reasons dictating the main use of GDP rather than other types of aggregate estimates for the oil industry. The only continuing figures for the Venezuelan economy starting in 1936 are GDP estimates. It is essential that petroleum activities be expressed in equivalent terms for comparative purposes. Then, from the total value added of petroleum, other indicators of its contribution to the rest of the economy can be more exactly derived.

The concept of retained value, discussed in Chapter 2, is frequently used in the study. The retained value of total expenditures is calculated by subtracting the following elements from the total expenditures of the industry: (a) payments to foreign factors (profits after taxes and interest), (b) remittances abroad by foreign industry workers, (c) imports of goods and services, and (d) depreciation and amortization charges.

In turn, retained value of current expenditures is defined as the total value of oil produced minus profits after taxes and interest payments, remittances of foreign workers abroad, imports of current goods and services, and depreciation and amortization charges. The retained value of investment expenditures can be calculated by subtracting imports of capital goods and services from the total fixed investment expenditures of the industry.

Several variants of these concepts have been calculated in different periods. These are discussed in further detail below, but as this is done whenever the variants are introduced and since this happens at different places throughout the text, it is advisable to mention them at this point.

For one thing, the retained value concept is more precise if expressed without including foreign goods purchased from domestic importers. Nevertheless, information on such purchases is only available since 1948. Correspondingly, alternative series of retained value of total expenditures figures, adjusted to exclude the value of such purchases, is presented from 1948 on.

The petroleum industry in Venezuela has paid extraordinary concession taxes on several occasions from 1936 to 1973. The concession payments in 1956 and 1957 were comparatively very large. The Ministry of Mines and Hydrocarbons does not include this payment as part of the investment or of the current expenditures of the industry in those years. However, it is clear that these payments were a substantial part of the contribution of oil in 1956 and 1957. Therefore, the retained value of total expenditures is presented both including and excluding these tax payments.

A similar situation exists with respect to the foreign exchange taxes on the petroleum industry. For reasons given in Chapter 6, the retained value estimates presented have not generally included the proceeds from these taxes. However, if they are not taken into consideration in the 1958-65 period, the resulting picture would be a distorted one, given that these taxes increased substantially at the end of the period.

In some of these variants of the retained value concept, it is quite difficult to separate the portion corresponding to current expenditures from that related to capital expenditures. Mostly, this is due to data problems, but in some cases, as in the one involving concession payments, even the attempt to make the distinction would not appear to be valid.

It should also be pointed out that calculation of the retained value concept is based on the assumption of negligible importation of services by the petroleum industry before 1946. Everything seems to indicate that this is a reasonable supposition. Certainly, imports of any kind were quite insignificant before then, and the petroleum industry was much more self-sufficient in its operations. Moreover, this assumption was supported in interviews held with various petroleum industry specialists in the Venezuelan government and in the oil companies, some of whom actually worked in the Venezuelan oil industry during these years. This conclusion is also partially confirmed by a declining trend in services imported as one goes back in years.

In order to analyze the influence of oil on the rest of the economy—or, what amounts to the same thing, the effects of petroleum in total GDP—a variable named "nonpetroleum GDP" is defined. This variable, which is computed as the residual GDP after the impact of petroleum on the GDP has been subtracted, is carefully examined below. As a measure of inflation in the Venezuelan economy, the implicit deflator of the GDP is mainly used between 1950 and 1973. Before then, different wholesale price indices are utilized.

The estimates presented from 1936 to 1947 on different aspects of petroleum activity originated in the financial statements and supporting documents of the three most important company groups in Venezuela—Standard, Shell, and Gulf. These were blown up so as to cover the entire industry. As these groups cover over 99 percent of total production during this period, the adjustment did not endanger the accuracy of the estimates. The availability of supporting documents permitted adjustments of the figures in the main financial statements. Some of these were undertaken so that the resulting data would reflect economic rather than accounting concepts.

Finally, the different statistical series used have different sources. This introduces the problem of inconsistency, which is more acute in the early years. All work in economic history is plagued by such difficulties, and in developing nations this even extends to the examination of relatively recent trends. Such problems were relatively mild in Venezuela, however, because of its price and exchange rate stability.

4

**THE CONTRIBUTION OF
PETROLEUM AND ITS
EFFECTS ON THE
ECONOMIC DEVELOPMENT
OF VENEZUELA, 1936-42**

This chapter examines the contribution of oil to the other sectors
of the Venezuelan economy during the 1936-42 period. The oil contribution via the foreign sector is considered initially, followed by
the public sector contribution, which is generated by the oil taxes.
Next, the contribution of petroleum through its investment activity
is studied. Lastly, the contribution arising from the income and
expenditures originated in the oil industry is examined. The final
section also scans the behavior of the other contributions of the
petroleum sector, through the performance of the retained value of
total expenditures, a proxy for the total combined contribution of
petroleum.

THE FOREIGN SECTOR CONTRIBUTION

The balance-of-payments situation determines, in many cases,
the rate of inflation and the rate of growth of real income in developing economies. If the external sector constrains imports, the economy
will suffer from the following:

1. unavailability of essential goods and services
2. inflexibility in the supply-demand relationships, with imported
   goods unable to alleviate bottlenecks and excess demand situa-
   tions
3. impossibility of using imports to attain efficiency in domestic
   production through import competition

Items (1) and (2), especially when they refer to the importation
of capital or intermediate goods and services, could have an important bearing on a country's rate of growth.

The balance-of-payments situation may also influence the rate of inflation. Unfavorable movements in the balance of payments may lead to an increase in the rate of inflation through shortages and inefficient import substitution. Particularly if exports are affected, an ongoing process can be initiated. In turn, continuous inflation might hamper the rate of growth of real income.

The importance of these problems varies among developing countries. Even in those countries where they are not severe, just the impossibility of using the external sector in counterinflationary policy is a handicap in the appropriate management of a developing economy.

Therefore, countries that can use their favorable balance-of-payments situation to suppress or restrain those inflationary pressures that could prove harmful to development, as well as a direct aid to economic growth and efficiency, stand a better chance of developing at a more rapid rate. [1] This has been the case in Venezuela, as a result of the strength shown by its oil industry since the mid-1930s.

The contribution of the oil industry to the balance-of-payments position of Venezuela can be approximately measured in two ways. One is the gross contribution, defined as the sum of all the credits in current account and all the capital inflows by the industry. The other is the net contribution, which is the gross contribution minus the current account debits and capital outflows of the industry. Both of these measurements are important in their own right: the net measure refers to the contribution to the other sectors of the Venezuelan economy, while the gross contribution relates to the contribution of the Venezuelan economy as a whole, including the oil sector itself. In the gross concept, the foreign exchange used by the oil industry—in buying imported goods and services, for payments to nonresident factors, in transfer payments abroad, and for capital repatriation—is assumed to be necessary for its operation.

Either one or both of these measures will be presented, depending on the availability of data. Due to lack of balance-of-payments data on services, factor and transfer payments, and capital movements, only the gross potential balance-of-payments contribution of oil is presented in this period. Furthermore, since only data on the balance of trade is available for these years, the gross contribution of oil has to be computed solely in terms of the movement of goods.

Total exports of Venezuela grew by 25 percent during the 1936-42 period, corresponding to an average annual compounded rate of 3.7 percent. This was slower than the expansion of GDP during the same period (see Table 4.1). In current terms, then, the share of exports in total GDP, which represented close to 25 percent in 1936, was reduced over these years.

The total exports in current bolívares declined continually from 1937 to 1939, after increasing in the former year. Afterwards, they

TABLE 4.1

Gross Domestic Product, Petroleum Exports,
and Total Exports, 1936-42

Year	GDP* (millions of bolívares)	Petroleum Exports (millions of bolívares)	Total Exports (millions of bolívares)	Share of Petroleum (percent)
1936	2,531	517	602	85.9
1937	2,857	533	635	83.9
1938	2,804	515	574	89.7
1939	2,843	469	527	89.0
1940	2,989	810	929	87.2
1941	3,854	1,001	1,003	90.8
1942	3,791	637	750	84.9

*GDP in current bolívares was calculated from constant GDP figures in Table 4.9 and the corresponding implicit deflator for each year.
    Source: Ministerio de Fomento, Anuario Estadístico (Caracas, 1938); and Banco Central de Venezuela, Memoria (Caracas, 1947) and La Economía Venezolana en los Ultimos Veinticinco Años (Caracas, 1966), with adjustments.

experienced an increase lasting through 1941, only to drop again in 1942. Petroleum exports followed the same pattern, but their overall increase was somewhat lower (23 percent). Their share, which already represented 85.9 percent of all exports in 1936, declined to 84.9 percent in 1942 (see Table 4.1). Clearly, the gross balance-of-payments contribution of oil to the Venezuelan economy was formidable all throughout the period. The net contribution, although smaller, would probably be quite important also.

Although exports performed reasonably well during this period, they were not sufficient to cover the needs of the economy, which was expanding faster and generated a demand for imports that was even stronger. At particular times, the shortage of foreign exchange at the official rate even became acute.

In 1936, the expatriation of capital after the death of Juan Vicente Gómez, as well as a prolonged oil strike during the year, brought about a partial exchange control. Late in 1937, the establishment of an overall, but still informal, exchange control became necessary. Prime necessity imports were allowed without limitations,

with the exchange remaining allocated according to previous import
patterns. This situation lasted to the outbreak of war in 1939, when
exports expanded. In 1940, there was again need for import controls,
as Venezuelan producers prepared for the war. Although the official
rate was 3.19 bolívares to the dollar, the selling rate rose to 3.55
bolívares in the free unofficial market. The free market was abolished
in the middle of 1940. Through the end of 1940 and the first half of
1941, the rate was stabilized at 3.19 bolívares. In July 1941, the
official selling rate was changed to 3.35 bolívares per dollar. Import
controls continued in effect during the rest of 1941 and all through
1942. [2]

Thus, during this period, the external sector constrained the
growth of the Venezuelan economy. Although essential goods were
still generally available, the economy lacked some of the other
advantages that unrestrained imports offer. While oil's contribution
to overall foreign exchange earnings was formidable, petroleum
exports simply did not expand fast enough to do away with shortages
and controls during this period, even though oil prices rose over
these years. Rising import prices were, to a great extent, responsible for the close to 40 percent price inflation occurring from 1936 to
1942 (see Appendix, Table A.2, column 1), although import controls
and deficit spending by the government also contributed to it. [3]

Therefore, the Venezuelan experience in these years constitutes
a good illustration of the adverse consequences that balance-of-
payments problems bring about for growth and inflation.

The Use of the Foreign Sector Contribution

The gross balance-of-payments contribution of the oil industry
can be utilized by the Venezuelan economy with more or less efficiency.
That is, in every single period, government policies can influence
the economy toward a use of the exchange proceeds derived from oil
that may minimize, maximize, or affect in some way the growth of the
other sectors. This depends on how the exchange proceeds for a
given period are allocated: they can either be spent in some way or
else added to the international reserves.

Adding to reserves over and above a certain level is a costly
utilization of resources. This level is determined by such factors
as the total value of international transactions in a country, the
instability of its exports and capital inflows and their seasonal
pattern, credit arrangements, currency reserve policy, and the climate
of confidence that is believed necessary. This level can be expressed
in terms of the coverage of the estimated normal imports for a certain
number of months and can be determined by the flexible application
of the technique of optimal inventory control. [4] As shall be discussed
in the sections to follow, an accumulation of international reserves

over this level in a particular country, can only be justified by a
very low social marginal rate of return to investment.

On the other hand, if foreign exchange is devoted to the purchases
of goods and services abroad, to cover capital outflows, and so forth,
the effectiveness of its utilization can be determined by its allocation
among different types of uses. Therefore, the general pattern of
utilization of exchange proceeds is an indication of the adequacy
with which the balance-of-payments contribution of the oil sector is
employed.

The proceeds of development usually brings about a change in
the composition of imports. This is a result of several forces. Consumer goods imports are substituted as development proceeds, which
results in an increase in the demand for intermediate products. Concurrently, higher levels of investment also increase the demand for
capital goods. As developing countries are usually much less efficient
in the production of intermediate and capital goods, these are imported.
Although the demand for consumer goods also rises, this type of
import does not increase as much as the other types, as it is more
easily substituted by domestic production. Therefore, unless a
country has unusual advantages in the import substitution of intermediate or capital goods, an increase in the share of capital and
intermediate goods imports would indicate that the allocation of
foreign exchange earnings among competing types of goods imports
is proceeding efficiently.

During the period covered by this study, the Venezuelan economy
can be classified under the general case. Therefore, an increase in
the share of capital and intermediate goods imports in total Venezuelan
imports would indicate that the foreign exchange contribution of oil
is being effectively allocated among different types of goods imports.[5]

During this period, the international reserves of Venezuela remained at approximately the same level, except for the year 1942
(see Table 4.2). The latter was the result of the upheaval created
by the war economy. An excessive accumulation of international
reserves did not occur over these years, especially if one considers
that the determinants of increasing reserves expanded during the
period. Thus, it can be said that the foreign exchange contribution
of oil was effectively utilized, at least in relation to the level of
international reserves.

The pattern of utilization of foreign earnings in the purchase of
imported goods reveals that the share of capital goods imports rose
from 18 percent in 1936 to 28.9 percent at the end of the period
(see Table 4.2). This also suggests that the foreign sector contribution of oil was adequately utilized by the economy during these years.
No other tests of the change in the effective use of foreign earnings
over time can be performed, as no information is available on other
types of goods.

TABLE 4.2

International Reserves and Imports of Capital Goods, 1936-42[*]

Year	International Reserves (millions of dollars)	Share of Capital Goods Imports (percent)
1936	47	18.0
1937	51	15.7
1938	60	37.6
1939	55	35.9
1940	65	33.7
1941	66	31.0
1942	89	28.0

*Calculated on the basis of imports in constant bolívares.

Source: Ministerio de Fomento, Anuario Estadístico (Caracas, 1951) with adjustments; Banco Central de Venezuela, La Economía Venezolana en los Ultimos Veinticinco Años (Caracas, 1966); and Bernardo Ferrán, lectures on economic history, given at the Universidad Central de Venezuela, Caracas, 1962.

On the whole, the effects of the foreign trade contribution of the oil sector during this period had a mixed character. An overwhelming proportion of the total exports of goods came from the oil industry, making the gross balance-of-payments contribution quite high. On the other hand, the increase in oil exports, albeit respectable, was not quite sufficient to cover the needs of the economy, which were expanding even faster. Such a constraint undoubtedly represented an obstacle to the achievement of a higher rate of growth of real income in Venezuela. On the other hand, the economy seems to have effectively used the contribution of oil during this period, since international reserves were not unduly incremented, and the composition of imports appears to have changed in agreement with the efficient norm.

THE FISCAL CONTRIBUTION OF OIL

Part of the value stream originating in any producing sector can be affected and appropriated by the state. In the case of a potentially leading sector, this portion can be substantial relative

to the total value added by the economy. Depending on how the
particular government uses these funds, the development of the
country could be stimulated, stifled, or remain unaffected.

If taxes on the potentially leading sector are large, they could
constitute its most important contribution to the growth of the economy.
If the potential gains that this contribution can impart are to be realized,
the public expenditures financed from such funds must be allocated
according to sound criteria. The greater the departure from these
criteria, the smaller the realized gains derived from the potentially
leading sector.

The fiscal contribution of a potentially leading sector to the rest
of the economy is not only exercised through the expenditures that
can be financed from the taxes it pays. The revenues derived from
this sector might alleviate harmful tax pressures in other parts of
the economy. They also could facilitate the avoidance of budgetary
deficits, when these could be harmful, thereby preventing the rise
of inflationary pressures. However, excessive tax pressure on the
sector might, in turn, have an adverse effect on its exports or investment.

The importance of the petroleum contribution to the Venezuelan
public revenues in the 1936-42 period is now considered. An examination of Table 4.3, showing the behavior of petroleum-derived tax
revenues, provides an indication of the importance of the petroleum
contribution to Venezuelan public revenues in the 1936-42 period.
During this period, the petroleum-derived tax revenues ranged from
64 million to 168 million bolívares. With respect to the participation
of oil in government revenues in 1941, it reached 41.7 percent, nine
percentage points over the 1936-42 average. As can be seen from
Table 4.3, the relative share of oil taxes fluctuated widely during
the period, but overall, it increased from 25.2 percent in 1936 to
31.8 percent in 1942.

If oil revenues are expressed as a percentage of GDP to give an
idea of their importance in relation to the entire economy, the average
percent for the whole period is 3.9 percent. Such magnitudes, if
properly utilized, could have had a major impact on the growth of the
other sectors of the Venezuelan economy.

The increase in the tax contribution of oil during these years
was mostly due to increases in the tax rates applicable to petroleum
operations. Almost immediately after Juan Vicente Gómez died in
December 1935, his successors made clear that a revision of the
government's relationship to the petroleum industry would take place.
The new Hydrocarbons Law of 1936 only provided increases in the
minimum royalties that could be obtained from a barrel of oil. But
the concessions granted in 1936 and 1937 stipulated quite formidable
increases in most petroleum taxes, and extraordinary payments were
received as lump sums from the companies obtaining concessions. [6]
Moreover, tighter enforcement of the tax laws was instituted, and

TABLE 4.3

Share of Oil Revenues in Total Revenues, 1936-42

Year	Total Revenues (millions of bolívares)	Oil Taxes (millions of bolívares)	Share of Oil Tax in Total Revenues* (percent)	Oil Foreign Exchange Tax (millions of bolívares)
1936	254	64	25.2	0
1937	329	99	30.0	3
1938	368	153	41.6	6
1939	389	118	30.3	7
1940	371	107	28.8	19
1941	402	168	41.7	14
1942	340	108	31.8	19

*Excluding the oil foreign exchange tax.

Source: Ministerio de Fomento, Memoria (Caracas, several years); Banco Central de Venezuela, Memoria (Caracas, several years), La Economía Venezolana en los Ultimos Veinticinco Años (Caracas, 1966), and unpublished data on the historical exchange rates in Venezuela; Ministerio de Minas e Hidrocarburos, Petroleo y Otros Datos Estadísticos (Caracas, 1965); Dirección General de Estadística, Anuario Estadístico (Caracas, 1938 and 1951); Manuel R. Egaña, Tres Décadas de Producción Petrolera (Caracas, 1947); and Table 4.4.

court claims made to the companies for back taxes were settled favorably to the government. Finally, the method of valuing petroleum for royalty payment purposes was modified.

In February 1937, the government created the Oficina de Centralización de Cambios (Exchange Centralization Office), which was to purchase and sell foreign exchange in order to stabilize the bolívar at a predetermined official rate. The Oficina proceeded to establish a system of multiple buying rates for foreign exchange. Oil companies were required to sell to the Oficina all the foreign currency that they wanted to convert in bolívares. The Oficina bought them at a rate (3.09) that was lower than the general official buying rate. The Oficina was dissolved when the Central Bank, created in 1940, took over its activities.

As a result of these operations, the petroleum companies were penalized when exchanging foreign currency into bolívares, by a penalty equal to the difference between the general official and special petroleum buying rates, multiplied by all the foreign exchange converted into bolívares. This penalty was essentially a new tax imposed on the industry. [7] On the other hand, the foreign currency coming from traditional export activities, such as coffee, cocoa, and cattle, was bought at rates higher than the general official rates and, thus, represented a subsidy to these activities. These subsidies partly offset the profits that the government reaped from the sale of petroleum foreign exchange to commercial banks. [8]

The figure reported as a government revenue under the heading of profits from exchange operations is actually the net result of all profits and losses obtained in all the dealings. This, coupled with the fact that the foreign currency sold to the Central Bank was not necessarily resold by the latter to commercial banks in the same year, explains the divergence between the official figures on profits from exchange operations and the calculations of the foreign exchange tax contribution of oil, which are presented in Table 4. 3. As a very high percentage of the foreign exchange profits derive from oil, the figures presented in this study are larger than the balance from the various exchange operations reported by government sources.

As can be seen from Table 4. 3, during this period, the tax on the foreign exchange operations of the petroleum industry did not amount to much. Nevertheless, if these taxes are added to all the other government revenues derived from the oil industry, the percentage share of petroleum revenues in total revenues increases slightly. [9]

From 1936 on, expenditure and revenue statistics of federal entities or states, as well as county or municipal governments, are available. [10] Thus, the revenue and expenditure data presented in this study embrace the national, state, and county governments. During this period, the revenues and expenditures of state and local governments were not important when compared with the total government revenues and expenditures. Table 4. 4 shows that they were in the neighborhood of 10 percent of the totals for the government sector, as an average. Nonetheless, the shares of county and state revenues and expenditures expanded more rapidly than their federal counterparts. At the end of the period, they represented about 15 percent of the total government budget.

Despite fluctuations, total government revenues increased considerably during this period. If 1936 is taken as the base year (100), the index of government revenues rises to 134 by 1942, even though there was a sharp drop in that year. This represents an annual average compounded rate of growth of 5 percent a year, most of which resulted from an expansion in the revenues of state and local governments. If only the national budget is considered, the index rises only to 123 in 1942, which is equivalent to a 3. 5 percent compounded average rate of growth per year.

The course of oil revenues shows a greater variation, but a more dramatic increase. At the end of the period, the 1936-based index

TABLE 4.4

Revenues and Expenditures of Local Governments, as a Percentage of
Total Government Revenues and Expenditures, 1936-42

	Year						
	1936	1937	1938	1939	1940	1941	1942
Local revenues[a]	20	27	28	38	42	43	53
Local expenditures[a]	24	30	29	37	41	44	49
Total government revenues[a]	254	329	368	389	371	402	340
Total government expenditures[a]	281	329	370	415	410	378	352
Percent of local revenues[a]	—	—	—	10.2[b]	—	—	15.5
Percent of local expenditures	—	—	—	15.5[b]	—	—	13.9

[a]Millions of bolívares.
[b]Average percent of local revenues over total revenues for the period as a whole (1936-42).

Note: Local revenues and expenditures do not include transfers from the national or central government budget. Total government revenues and expenditures do not include those of state enterprises and autonomous government administratives institutes.

Source: Ministerio de Fomento, Anuario Estadístico (Caracas, several years).

stood at 169. In terms of compounded annual growth, this corresponds
to a 9.1 percent rate of increase. This means that the tax contribution
of petroleum expanded in relation to the Venezuelan GDP, which only
expanded at a compounded annual average rate of 6.2 percent in
current terms.

The Utilization of Tax Revenues from Oil

All this shows that petroleum taxes, if properly used, could have
had a significant impact on the growth of the rest of the Venezuelan
economy. How effectively were they utilized? The most satisfactory
procedure to measure such effectiveness in a simple, straightforward
manner is to estimate the portion of government expenditures devoted
to the fostering of the economic development of the country. The
percentage of capital expenditures in total government expenditures
would also appear to be an adequate indication of effectiveness in
the use of government funds; but this is not so, since it does not
include current expenditures promoting economic growth.

Since there are no estimates of the economic development expenditures of the public sector during the period examined, it is necessary
to rely on estimates of expenditures of a social or economic nature.[11]
These estimates are only available with respect to the expenditures
of the national government. It will, therefore, be assumed that the
pattern of expenditures at the state and county level is close enough
to that of the federal or national government. This is not an unreason-
able assumption, and, in any case, it cannot introduce significant
inaccuracies, since county and state expenditures are a small part
of total government expenditures.

Government expenditures of a social and economic type represent
an outer bound for public expenditures of an economic development
nature. But if it happens that these variables move roughly together,
it is still possible to use the former as a proxy for the latter. This
is the contention made here, based on the evidence given by Charles
Rollins in his study of public expenditures in Venezuela.[12]

From Table 4.5, it can be seen that the share of social and
economic expenditures increased from 53.4 percent in 1936 to 57.0
percent in 1942. In fact, during the in-between years, the share was
always higher than in 1942, the peak year being 1937, with 62.1
percent. As an average over the whole period, the percentage share
was 59.6 percent.

Since 1936, one of the most important principles of government
policy in Venezuela has been the use of oil funds for the long-run
development of the economy. This objective has been summarily
expressed in the "sow the oil" motto. This concept implies that oil
revenues are earmarked for long-run development projects. Thus,
instead of merely considering how overall expenditures have been

TABLE 4.5

Social and Economic Expenditures and Their Share in
Total Government Expenditures, 1936-42

Year	Social and Economic Expenditures (millions of bolívares)	Share in Total Government Expenditures (percent)	Overall Change in Social and Economic Expenditures (millions of bolívares)
1936	150	53.4	
1937	204	62.1	
1938	227	61.3	} 51
1939	251	60.4	
1940	253	61.6	
1941	224	59.3	
1942	201	57.0	

Source: Charles E. Rollins, Raw Materials Development and Economic Growth: A Study of the Bolivian and Venezuelan Experience (Ph.D. diss., Stanford University, 1956); and Tables 4.3 and 4.4.

allocated, it might be better to work under the supposition that the entire oil revenues are devoted to economic development expenditures. Thus, instead of examining the composition of total expenditures, and attributing the same breakdown to expenditures financed from oil revenues, we can inquire if the economic and social expenditures have been at least as large as oil revenues. Furthermore, the increments in both can be compared to see how marginal oil revenues have been utilized.

This test shows that social and economic expenditures were larger than oil revenues during this period and that increments in oil revenues were more than fully utilized for social and economic expenditures (see Tables 4.3 and 4.5). The tendency to run a surplus on the national government account, which was prevalent previously, was reversed. In fact, during most of these years, public expenditures were in excess of public revenues (see Table 4.4). These deficits were financed in two ways. First, by a dwindling of treasury reserves, to the accumulation of which oil revenues had contributed in the past. And second, through debt financing, to which the oil companies contributed directly by purchase or indirectly through the strength of their deposits and other assets supplied to the financial institutions operating in Venezuela.

In summary, during the 1936-42 period, the contribution of the oil sector to the rest of the economy taking place through the fiscal system was substantial, in terms of its share of the total tax burden and its increasing tax contribution. The government's utilization of these revenues also improved considerably during the period. The surplus budgets of the past were abandoned, and expenditures that could potentially contribute to the economic development of Venezuela increased in relation to total government expenses. Finally, this type of expenditures seemed to have been related to oil revenues throughout the period. All this indicates an increasing positive influence of oil on the other sectors of the economy, through its fiscal contribution. This strong showing by petroleum also helped to alleviate tax pressures on the rest of the economy and helped to expand government services, without incurring large deficits.

Finally, the petroleum companies have provided health, education, communication, transportation, and other facilities in the communities where they were located, easing the pressures on government to do so. On the other hand, the hydrocarbon department of the government has participated only slightly in the total public budget. Although it is impossible to obtain exact data on the period examined, as hydrocarbon activities were then included in the Development Ministry, it is clear that it must have been quite small, since the ministry was allotted only 2.4 percent of the total expenditures of the national government in 1940. [13]

TOTAL INVESTMENT AND THE CONTRIBUTION OF PETROLEUM INVESTMENT

After examining both cross-sectional and historical data, Simon Kuznets concludes:

In the study of economic growth, wide interest attaches to the proportion that capital formation constitutes of national product. The larger it is (i.e., the larger the part of current product retained for use in further production), other conditions being equal, the higher the rate of growth of national product that can be generated. [14]

In developing economies, the processes of capital widening, capital deepening, and technical modernization are in their initial stages. In some economies, and Venezuela is certainly one of them, inflows of factors and resources can remedy the unavailabilities and deficiencies that limit absorptive capacity. In these countries, the social marginal rates of return on investment are probably substantially higher than the opportunity cost of capital. Assuming this is correct, and barring other complications, these economies should be

expected to allocate a substantial portion of their resources to investment in order to maximize the rate of growth of output over the long
run.

The investment rate in the Venezuelan economy seems to have
been quite respectable during the period examined. The percentage
share of gross fixed domestic investment over GDP in constant 1957
prices (see Table 4. 6) was 10. 7 percent in 1937. By the end of the
period, the accumulation of capital in the Venezuelan economy was
at a much higher level (15. 4 percent in 1941 and 13. 9 percent in 1942).
In the interim, the rate had soared in 1938, 1939, and 1940, probably
as a result of the recovery from the Depression and the preparation
for World War II.

In absolute terms, the allocation of income to real gross fixed
capital formation increased up to 1939. From then on, it declined.
For the whole period, investment increased to a figure of 130, on an
index scale based on 1936 equal to 100. This corresponds to a 4. 5
percent yearly rate of compounded increase. It was much greater in
current prices, as the latter rose approximately 40 percent during the
period (see Appendix, Table A. 2, column 2).

Gross fixed domestic investment in petroleum represented an
important part of total gross fixed domestic investment during this
period. It rose from 32. 4 percent in 1936 (see Table 4. 6) to a peak
42. 8 percent in 1938. From then on, it declined. If the public
investment derived from petroleum taxes is added, the oil sector
accounts for a much larger portion of total investment.

Petroleum investment, which started recuperating from the
Depression in 1934, was spurred during the 1936-38 period by concessions taking place in 1936 and 1937 and by the prospects of
increasing demand for oil in Europe, as a result of the conflagration.
By 1939, the first factor was wearing off, and the European war was
resulting in diminishing sales in Europe. From then on, investment
contracted, the spreading war proving to be an obstacle to the expansion of the oil industry, because of transportation difficulties and
shortages of skilled personnel and capital goods. In constant 1957
prices, petroleum investment was lower in 1942 than in 1936. In
current prices, it was only 18 percent greater than in 1936 (see
Appendix, Table A. 2, column 3).

If petroleum investment is substracted from total investment, the
residual obtained indicates the accumulation of capital taking place
in the other sectors of the economy. It is important to examine the
investment activity there for further evaluation of the impact of the
autonomous forces of petroleum on the economy. Nonpetroleum
investment expressed in 1957 bolívares, is shown in Table 4. 6.
This variable increased continually and considerably up to 1940,
and decreased from 1940 to 1942. During the whole period, it moved
consistently with petroleum investment, with a one-year lag. By
1942, nonpetroleum gross investment in constant 1957 bolívares had

TABLE 4.6

Gross Fixed Domestic Investment for the Main Sectors and the Investment Rate, 1936–42

Year	Investment (millions of bolívares)	Investment Rate (percent)	Petroleum Investment (millions of bolívares)*	Share of Petroleum in Total Investment (percent)	Nonpetroleum Investment (millions of bolívares)
1936	555	10.7	180	32.4	375
1937	746	14.1	252	33.8	494
1938	1,056	19.6	452	42.8	604
1939	1,313	24.0	410	31.2	903
1940	1,290	22.4	260	20.2	1,030
1941	866	15.4	198	22.3	688
1942	721	13.9	155	21.5	566

*Constant 1957 bolívares.

Source: Banco Central de Venezuela, unpublished statistics; Appendix, Table A.2, column 2, as well as column 3; and calculations derived from the financial statements and supporting documents of the big three oil company groups in Venezuela, adjusted to obtain industry-wide estimates.

increased by 51 percent throughout the period, equivalent to a compounded annual average rate of growth of 7.1 percent, which was
much greater than that of overall gross investment.

Nonpetroleum Investment and Retained Value

The most important contributions of the oil sector are undoubtedly
exercised through the current expenditures it generates in yearly production. These expenditures consist of payments to productive factors
and to the government and other producers and are financed from exports
and other sales of current production. However, not all of these
expenditures affect the economy of Venezuela directly. Only those
going to native factors or firms or to the Venezuelan government can
be considered as a direct contribution to other economic sectors.[15]
These expenditures constitute the portion retained by Venezuela of
the current expenditures of the industry.

Looking at petroleum investment expenditures in terms of their
contribution to the strength of the domestic capital goods-producing
sector, a corresponding parallel is found. It is only the local purchase
of capital goods and their construction by native factors that represents
a direct contribution to other sectors in the economy. This portion of
the total investment of the industry constitutes the retained value of
its investment expenditures.

In fact, it has been argued above that the total combined contribution which a sector can make to an economy is somewhat related
to the retained parts of total industry expenditures (current plus
investment expenditures). As retained value of total expenditures
changes, similar variations take place in the total combined contribution of the industry to other sectors of the economy. For example,
as retained value increases, the overall contributions of the industry
to the economy also rise. However, it should be understood that each
particular contribution may not have the same relationship to total
retained value as the overall contribution.

As pointed out above, nonpetroleum gross investment expenditures
have moved with a one-year lag with respect to gross petroleum investment. Nevertheless, it was found that petroleum investment was much
more affected by the war than the other components of investment.
Would nonpetroleum gross investment be more closely related to retained value of total petroleum expenditures during this period?

Retained value of total expenditures in current prices experienced
only two setbacks in its increase during the period examined. These
were in 1940 and 1942, as can be seen in Table 4.7. For the period
as a whole, it increased 21 percent, which corresponds to a 3.2
percent compounded annual average. This increase resulted from
rising prices of crude and products, as, in real terms, retained value
was, in 1942, at the same level it had been in 1936 (see Appendix,
Table A.2, column 17).

TABLE 4. 7

Value of Production, Gross Domestic Product, and Retained Value
of Total Expenditures in the Petroleum Industry, 1936-42
(millions of bolívares)

Year	Value of Production	GDP	Retained Value of Total Expenditures
1936	401	351	204
1937	476	425	244
1938	426	415	313
1939	455	428	318
1940	445	419	271
1941	619	580	289
1942	403	393	246

Source: From calculations based on the financial statements and
supporting statements and documents of the big three oil company
groups in Venezuela, adjusted to cover the whole industry; and from
Appendix, Table A. 2, columns 4, 5, 6, 7, 8, 9, 10, 11, and 12, and
from Table 4. 6.

As noted above, petroleum was among the sectors to first recu-
perate from the Depression, not having been affected by it as much
as the other sectors. Although oil prices increased up to 1936, from
then until 1940, a decreasing trend set in once more (see Appendix,
Table A. 2, column 13). On the other hand, production increased
up to 1939. In terms of current value, the industry expanded in 1937,
decreased in 1938, and rose again in 1939. Nevertheless, if the
period is taken as a whole, the value of petroleum production was
13 percent higher in 1939 than in 1936 (see Table 4. 7). As a result
of government policy, the share of the value of oil production remaining in Venezuela increased slightly faster, with the retained value
of current expenditures, in current bolívares, rising 15 percent above
the 1936 level. [16]
However, as shown earlier, petroleum investment increased
considerably from 1936 to 1938, diminishing only slightly in 1939.
This was partly the result of a recovery from the Depression; more
significantly, however, it resulted from the 1936-37 concessions
and the positive expectations deriving from the early stages of what
was to become World War II. As a result, even during this period,
there was an increase in the retained value of total expenditures.
In response, investment expenditures in the rest of the Venezuelan
economy expanded. Part of the increased investment in the non-

petroleum sectors resulted from a rising share of government expenditures devoted to investment, a favorable outlook for future years, and the expectation of spreading war.

Nonpetroleum investment in real terms increased in 1940, but from then on, it moved downward. Petroleum indicators moved in the same direction, as the war affected the petroleum industry, except that the highest point was reached in 1939. The fact that nonpetroleum investment was still growing, even though petroleum activity had begun its downturn, is explained by three factors: (a) lags in the adjustment process, (b) the three-year development plan started by President López Contreras in 1938, and (c) the anticipation of expanding hostilities.

Investment Effectiveness

It is interesting to know that nonpetroleum investment expenditures in some years exceeded the portion of the total expenditures of the petroleum industry that were retained in Venezuela during this period (see Table 4.6 and Appendix, Table A.2, column 17). For the period as a whole, the rest of the economy invested an amount about as great as the payments received from the oil industry by native factors of production, local firms, and the Venezuelan government. This would suggest that the nonpetroleum part of the economy devoted a quite satisfactory amount of these resources to investment during these years.

Although capital formation proportions are a crucial factor for economic growth, the productivity of the resources devoted to capital accumulation is almost as important. Thus, it would be appropriate to inquire about the social productivity and efficiency of investment resources in the Venezuelan economy. But appraisals of the efficiency in the use of investment funds are scanty, as well as being limited to the public sector. The only seemingly objective evaluation found during this period concludes that significant resources were wasted by devoting them to unproductive uses. Misallocation also ruled in the shares of government investment going to the different productive sectors, as well as in the division between capital expenditures for directly productive activities and for social overhead. This is driven home with force by the fact that agricultural production declined during this period, despite increased government attention. [17]

In sum, gross fixed domestic investment in real terms increased respectably during this period, although negatively affected by war conditions in 1941 and 1942. Nonpetroleum gross fixed domestic investment in real terms did even better. While gross investment in the petroleum industry in equivalent terms failed to rise during the period, it increased considerably up to 1939. The increase in petroleum investment, coupled with an expansion in the retained value

of total expenditures in the oil industry, a promising outlook, and
war expectations seem to have been the forces promoting the investment performance of the nonpetroleum sector up to 1940. It has been
impossible to separate nonpetroleum investment in its public and
private component in this analysis.

Overall, the nonpetroleum part of the economy succeeded in
devoting to investment an amount comparable to the retained value of
the total expenditures originating in the petroleum industry. This is
consistent with an extension to the whole economy of the "sow the
oil" concept. Nevertheless, there are reasons to believe that the
social profitability of investment left much to be desired.

Finally, petroleum investment constituted a prominent portion of
total investment in this period: over one-third as an average from
1936 to 1939. Although the contribution of oil constituted a growth-
promoting force up to 1939, from then on, its impact became disappointingly small.

TOTAL DOMESTIC PRODUCT AND THE
EXPENDITURES OF THE OIL INDUSTRY

As a potentially leading sector expands, its income-expenditure
effects spread throughout the economy. Additional factor employment
in the industry usually results, and average factor earnings rise.
Government revenues deriving from the industry increase, and purchases from other business firms are raised. Finally, the expansion
probably would enlarge the industry's investment spending. The
effects of this expansion are woven through the oft-described multiplier
accelerator mechanism and reverberate throughout the economy.

Paying strict attention to the impact on other domestic economic
sectors, and barring repercussions from imports or factor payments
abroad, only a portion of these expenditures can be said to have a
direct and immediate leverage. These portions have been called
the retained values of current and capital expenditures. Retained
value of total expenditures is the sum of the current and investment
retained value components.

As pointed out in previous chapters, it is unnecessary to go
through the lengthy and still unprecise process of evaluating and
weighing each of the contributions of a potentially leading sector,
and its impact, in order to appraise with sufficient accuracy how
successful the sector has been in transmitting its growth to the rest
of the economy. Suffice it to examine some of its main contributions
and their influence on the other sectors of the economy. However,
this must be accompanied by a similar analysis of the sector's total
combined contribution, as represented by the behavior of the retained
value of its total expenditures.

The income-expenditure contribution originating in the petroleum industry throughout this period should be examined at this point. In 1936, petroleum activity in Venezuela, while recuperating from the Depression, was still quite off its previous highs. The value of oil output and the gross value added of petroleum spurted in 1937 and then moved erratically under the contradictory influences of World War II. Nevertheless, their trend was upward, and in 1941, spurred by war demand, they attained the highest level of the period. In 1942, the industry slumped, as a result of war scarcities and transportation difficulties in the Caribbean. In that year, the value of petroleum production and its GDP stood barely above 1936 levels in current terms (see Table 4. 7).

In 1936, the contribution of the oil sector to the GDP of Venezuela—in constant 1957 bolívares—was already a shade above 20 percent (see Table 4. 7). It hovered above that percentage during the next ten years, reaching a high of 28. 2 in 1941. In 1942, the participation of oil in total production declined to 20. 4 percent, lower than in 1936. These figures clearly show the importance of petroleum in the economy of Venezuela. In this period, from one-fifth to over one-quarter of all economic activity in the country was derived from petroleum. [18]

The effects of gross fixed petroleum investment on the Venezuelan economy were examined in a previous section. Reference has been made above to the behavior of the current expenditures of the petroleum industry, which generate gross multiplier-accelerator effects throughout the economy. Both the value of production and GDP of petroleum experienced an upward trend up to 1941, with a big increase in that year (see Table 4. 7). Because the oil industry exports an overwhelming fraction of its total production, these income-expenditure injections were basically exogenous in character.

From 1936 to 1940, the value of petroleum production in current terms increased 11 percent, a compounded annual average rate of 2. 7 percent. GDP, in current bolívares, rose 19 percent, for a 4. 4 percent annual average. Although a tremendous increment took place in both these variables in 1941, its consequences were short-lived, because a severe contraction occurred in 1942. But only the retained portion of the expenditures of the industry actually directly influenced the economy of Venezuela.

The behavior over time of retained value of current expenditures appears in Table 4. 8. In current bolívares, the retained value of current expenditures increased in 1937 but returned to the 1936 level the next year. From then on, it advanced continually up to the 1942 decline. At the end of the period, it had increased 24 percent, for a 3. 8 compounded annual average rate of growth. Such an increase was greater than that experienced by either the value of production or GDP of the industry. This means that the fraction of current expenditures retained in Venezuela expanded more rapidly than total

TABLE 4.8

Percentage of Retained Value of Current and Total Expenditures in the Petroleum Industry and per Barrel of Oil Produced, 1936-42*

Year	Retained Value of Current Expenditures (millions of bolívares)	Retained Value as a Percentage of Current Expenditures	Retained Value of Current Expenditures per Barrel of Oil Produced (bolívares)	Retained Value as a Percentage of Total Expenditures	Retained Value of Total Expenditures per Barrel of Oil Produced (bolívares)
1936	142	35.4	0.92	41.7	1.32
1937	162	34.0	0.87	39.8	1.31
1938	144	33.8	0.77	47.3	1.66
1939	163	35.4	0.79	47.6	1.54
1940	181	40.4	0.98	46.7	1.47
1941	215	34.6	0.94	39.4	1.27
1942	177	43.9	1.20	48.5	1.66

*Does not include foreign exchange taxes on oil

Source: Table 4.7; Appendix, Table A.2, columns 4, 5, 7, 8, and 9, 10, and 20; and Ministerio de Minas e Hidrocarburos, Petróleo y Otros Datos Estadísticos (Caracas, 1965).

current expenditures. Both government policies and more enthusiastic
industry compliance with them brought this about.

Expressed as a percentage of total current expenditures (value
of production), retained value increased throughout the period from
35.4 percent to 43.9 percent. Although this increase was not smooth,
it undoubtedly indicates that a greater portion of the current expenditures of the industry affected the Venezuelan economy directly.
Similarly, Table 4.8 shows that retained value of current expenditures
per barrel was much higher at the end of the period. This is partially
attributable to the increase in oil prices that took place during the
war. But the remainder results from an increase in the portion of
current expenditures retained in Venezuela.

The figures for retained value of investment expenditures (presented in Appendix Table A.2, column 15) do not have the same degree
of precision as the estimates of retained value of current expenditures.
If these two estimates are combined, retained value of total expenditures results. This variable had an upward course during these years,
except for 1940 and 1942, with an overall growth of 21 percent throughout the period, good for a 3.2 percent average annual compounded
growth (see Table 4.7).

The percentage share of total retained value in the total expenditures of the industry grew considerably, too (from 41.7 percent
to 48.5 percent), although in an uneven fashion. Again, this can be
attributed to government policy and industry collaboration. If this
variable is expressed in a per barrel basis, an increase is also
evident. At the beginning of the period, the retained value of total
expenditures per barrel stood at 1.27 bolívares. By the end of the
period, it had climbed to 1.66 bolívares per barrel, again in an
uneven way, for the same reasons given above.

In terms of output, the oil industry had recovered from the
Depression by 1934. But as a result of lower prices, the value of
production was even smaller than in the pre-Depression era. The
industry expected to be favorably affected by the rumbles of war in
Europe. Events fell quite short of expectations, as the spurt of
prices from the 1933 low ended in 1936. From then until 1940, prices
declined, increasing from that year to 1942 (see Appendix, Table
A.2, column 13).

As an outcome of favorable expectations, production increased
in 1937. But shattered dreams, resulting from disappointing European
demand, affected it on and off in succeeding years. The year 1941
saw an expansion in production again due to the geographical extension of the war, its greater intensity, and its effects upon other
supply sources. However, a severe setback occurred next year, as
the conflagration reached the waters of the Caribbean and war scarcities imposed heavy pressures upon the industry.

On the other hand, the oil sector was confronted from the beginning of the period by a more aggressive Venezuelan government.

Since the death of Gómez, airs of reform had filled the Venezuelan
atmosphere. These reforms were advocated by old Gómez followers
and turned out to be moderate in nature. The government received
special payments from the companies for the privilege of obtaining
concessions, even though higher taxes accompanied them. [19] Even
more, the companies were urged in other ways to increase their
expenditures in Venezuela.

The rule of duty-free importation of those goods needed by the
industry to conduct their operations, which had been included as a
matter of course clause in past concessions contracts, was questioned.
The dispute between the executive branch of the government and the
oil companies was taken before Venezuelan courts. The government
maintained that the clause was meant to apply only when such goods
were not available from Venezuelan producers. The matter was not
settled during this period. But in the meantime, the companies were
forced to submit lists of their planned imports to the Development
Ministry for approval. This resulted in the companies turning to
local firms for procurement in order to avoid the haggling involved,
even though their rightful obligation was still undetermined.

Other government actions also affected the industry. The 1936
labor law increased the required minimum representation of Venezuelans in the labor employed by the industry. Then, the minimum wage
was raised from about 7 bolívares a day to 9.77 bolívares a day, and
fringe benefits for petroleum workers were considerably increased.
Also, the law stipulated that companies would have to use more
Venezuelans in skilled, technical, administrative, managerial, and
executive capacities and begin training them for such purposes.

Finally, the government made an about-face in the refining
question. Gómez had not encouraged refining in Venezuela, and the
companies, wary about what would happen if he disappeared, had
set up big refineries in Aruba and Curaçao. The only clause in the
Venezuelan petroleum legislation promoting oil refinement in Venezuela permitted the locally refined products to pay only 50 percent of
the taxes that the imported refined products had to pay. As the
Venezuelan market was quite small, this did not prove to be a good
incentive. Government incentives to local refining became more
attractive when preference in the granting of concessions was given
to those companies that agreed to establish or expand their refineries
in Venezuela. This brought along a considerable increase in the
production of refined oil products in the country.

These measures, coupled with some labor unrest, political agitation against the companies, and litigation with the government in
other fronts had helped, by 1938, to bridle the industry's enthusiasm.
Yet, the situation had improved somewhat by 1941, and from then on,
the situation was ripe for large gains, whenever world demand would
act as the spark plug.

Effects on Population Shifts

Although this period was not one of significant expansion for the industry, the higher level of its retained value did have some beneficial effects on the Venezuelan economy. In the geographic areas where oil was produced, a moderate expansion took place. Yet, the sharp contraction of 1942 resulted in so much unemployment that an organized back-to-farm movement had to be instituted with the collaboration of the petroleum industry and the government.

Between 1926 and 1936, the population in the petroleum states increased 23.9 percent, while the increase in total population was 15.3 percent. During the same period, the population in the federal district (part of the Caracas Metropolitan Area) increased by 45.0 percent.[20] Comparable figures for the 1936-42 period show a 25.0 percent increase in the population of the petroleum states at the same time that total population increased 14.5 percent. The population in the federal district grew 34.3 percent during the latter period.

Thus, petroleum was pulling population to the areas where its activity took place, at a similar pace, over these two periods. The oil industry also contributed significantly to the movement of population to the federal district: directly, by establishing administrative offices and making purchases in the area and, indirectly, through government expenditures, which were very heavily concentrated in Caracas.

The concentration of population in the federal district apparently slackened during the 1936-42 period. However, the population increase in the federal district did not abate as much as it might appear, and perhaps not at all. This is because a comparison of the population in the federal district for the years 1926 and 1936 would tend to exaggerate its expansion. In 1936, conditions in the rural areas were influenced by the Depression, and agricultural workers had flocked to urban areas, while 1926 had been a good year for Venezuelan agriculture, which would have tended to keep the labor force in the rural areas.

Impact on Nonpetroleum Gross Domestic Product

Venezuela's GDP in constant 1957 prices, grew 11 percent from 1936 to 1941. This is equivalent to a 2.2 percent compounded annual average rate of growth. Although this might seem small, it was sufficient to maintain previous levels of income per capita, as the rate of growth of population in Venezuela by that time was approximately 2.2 percent also. The oil crisis and mounting war difficulties crippled the economy of Venezuela in 1942. GDP, in 1957 prices, fell almost as much as it had grown in the previous five years (see Table 4. 9).

GDP, in figures that exclude the petroleum component, shows just how the nonpetroleum sector of the Venezuelan economy behaves. The influence of the oil sector was eliminated in the calculation of nonpetroleum GDP in constant 1957 bolívares, which appear in Table 4. 9. Both the value of oil production and gross fixed investment in the industry were subtracted, because they are taken into account in the calculation of total GDP and because they influence the gross value added in other sectors.

Nonpetroleum GDP, in 1957 prices, seems to have grown very little from 1936 to 1942. Its expansion only amounted to 3 percent during this period. Still, this is larger than the growth of the total GDP (less than 1 percent) and of petroleum GDP (which declined somewhat). Interestingly, it was only toward the end of the period that the influence of petroleum's expansion up to 1939 was felt by the other sectors. Thus, the effect was delayed and unusually protracted. This can probably be explained by the political and economic uncertainty prevalent during the initial years of the López Contreras regime and the normal gestation period of investments. The lag does seem to have worked on a more reasonable one-year basis in the latter part of the period.

Although the retained value of total expenditures expanded up to 1939, the nonpetroleum GDP, in 1957 bolívares, declined during this period and jumped upward in 1940. As petroleum's retained value sagged in 1940, its effects on the rest of the economy were felt the following year. The same thing occurred, in the opposite direction, with the 1941 expansion in the retained value.

The total retained value of the petroleum industry expanded throughout the period at a 3. 2 percent average compounded rate of growth per year, while nonpetroleum GDP in 1957 prices rose only 3 percent in the six years. Even though the nonpetroleum part of the Venezuelan economy did better in its expansion up to 1940, it only rose at a 1. 7 percent compounded annual average, which is much lower than the average increase in petroleum's retained value for the whole period. Moreover, from 1936 to 1940, retained value expanded at a 7. 4 percent compounded yearly average.

It is easier to understand all this if the 1936-42 period is divided into two parts and each is examined in detail. From 1936 to 1939, the petroleum sector augmented its contribution to the other sectors and spread exogenous injections to the rest of the economy. The nonpetroleum part of the economy did not seem to be affected by such autonomous forces, with production only beginning to react in 1940, although investment had been affected much sooner.

The main explanation of what took place during those years must lie in the uncertain political atmosphere following the passing away of Gómez. It took some time before López Contreras emerged,

TABLE 4.9

Nonpetroleum and Petroleum Domestic Product and the
Share of Petroleum in the Total, 1936-42

Year	Nonpetroleum GDP*	Petroleum GDP*	Total GDP*	Percentage Share of Petroleum in the Total
1936	3,668	1,106	5,166	21.4
1937	3,458	1,328	5,291	25.1
1938	3,342	1,344	5,392	24.9
1939	3,316	1,462	5,468	26.7
1940	3,924	1,314	5,748	22.9
1941	3,624	1,621	5,752	28.2
1942	3,780	1,059	5,193	20.4

*Millions of constant 1957 bolívares.

Source: Appendix, Table A.2, columns 4, 5, 6, 10, 17, and
21; Bernardo Ferrán, unpublished estimates presented in lectures on
the economic development of Venezuela, delivered at the Universidad
Central de Venezuela, Caracas, 1963; and Table 4.6.

apparently in full control of the situation. It was even longer before
Venezuelans felt confident that his regime was stable.

Being one of the old dictator's strong generals, López Contreras
nevertheless admitted most of the groups that had opposed Gómez
into the political arena. Some of these were quite liberal; others had
radical ideas that they could now express rather freely. Other groups
were more moderate, but either sided with the liberals in the condem-
nation of the oil industry and in other economic matters or had
"unorthodox" ideas of their own. Many of these sat in Congress,
and even some, like Néstor Pérez, the development minister, were
in López Contreras' cabinet. Moreover, much agitation occurred
during the government of López Contreras, especially in the early
years, when unrest among petroleum workers was at its peak and
spreading to other sectors.

All this frightened the business community. It took some years
for the confidence of the economic classes to return. The economic
development program of López Contreras, which started rolling in
1938, and which included measures for the promotion of domestic
production, helped considerably in changing business attitudes.

The unfavorable performance of Venezuelan exports was another
factor that contributed to the stagnation of the nonpetroleum part of
the economy. Nonpetroleum exports declined from 1937 to 1942, and

this coincided with a considerable expansion in imports in anticipation of the spread of war, as well as rising import prices.

Just at the time the business community was reacting favorably to the expansion in oil, the latter began losing momentum and became a depressing force in the economy. Thus, during the second part of the period, the performance of the economy as a whole was quite disappointing, and nonpetroleum GDP declined from its high in 1940.

The Impact of Oil on Other Sectors: A Disaggregated Analysis

How the various Venezuelan industries have fared over time will now be examined. This will be accomplished by using output indices, as no discriminated time series in terms of values exist for this period. The petroleum industry has been examined above and will not be included in the tables presented below.

Most of the national income originated in the Venezuelan economy in 1936, if petroleum and government are excluded, corresponded to tertiary activities (45.6 percent). As Table 4.10 shows, commerce constituted the larger part of the tertiary sector. The industrial sector,

TABLE 4.10

Income Originated by Type of Activity, 1936[a]

Sectors	Income Originated (millions of bolívares)	Share (percent)[b]
Industry:	322	26.2
Manufacturing	303	24.7
Extractive	9	0.7
Construction	10	0.8
Agriculture:	343	28.1
Agriculture	255	20.9
Livestock	88	7.2
Commerce	222	18.3
Real Estate	173	14.2
Services:	161	13.2
Transport	66	5.4
Domestic service	52	4.3
Public and personal services	43	3.5
Total	1,221	100.0

[a]Does not include oil or government.
[b]Percentages do not add to 100 because of rounding.
Source: Banco Central de Venezuela, El Ingreso Nacional de Venezuela (Caracas, 1949), p. 93.

TABLE 4.11

Income Originated in Industry, by Type of Activity, 1936

Industry	Income Originated (millions of bolívares)	Share (percent)*
Textiles and clothing	162	50.3
Food	59	18.3
Hides and by-products	21	6.5
Wood	20	6.2
Construction	10	3.1
Extractive	9	2.8
Power	8	2.5
Printing	6	1.9
Chemical	6	1.9
Cement, tile, ceramics, and so forth	6	1.9
Tobacco	6	1.9
Metals	4	1.2
Other	5	1.6
Total	322	100.0

*Percentages do not add to 100 because of rounding.
Source: Banco Central de Venezuela, El Ingreso Nacional de Venezuela (Caracas, 1949), p. 100.

including extractive activities, represented 26.2 percent of the economy, after petroleum and government have been taken out. Manufacture accounted for most of this (24.7 percent). Lastly, agriculture constituted 28.1 percent, with livestock representing a sizeable part of it (7.2 percent).

Discriminating a bit further within each of these sectors, it is found that textiles and clothing were estimated to be about one-half of the income originated in industry (see Table 4.11). The food industry also seems to have accounted for an important part of industrial value added (18.3 percent). Most of the industries listed can be classified as consumer goods industries.

If a similar level of detail is presented for the agricultural sector, it is found that coffee, sugar, and corn were the major crops in 1936, representing altogether 45 percent of the total value of agricultural production. Meat, dairy products, cocoa, cassava, and bananas were also important. Many other products were grown, as can be seen in Table 4.12.

TABLE 4.12

Value of Agricultural Production, by Type, 1936

Products	Value of Production (millions of bolívares)	Share (percent)
Coffee	62	16.7
Sugarcane	58	15.6
Corn	47	12.7
Steers	29	7.8
Cheese	23	6.2
Milk	21	5.7
Cocoa	16	4.3
Cassava	15	4.0
Plantain	13	3.5
Bananas	11	3.0
Beans	13	3.5
Pigeon peas	8	2.2
Tobacco	4	1.1
Coconuts	4	1.1
Yautia	3	0.8
Goats	3	0.8
Rice	3	0.8
Potatoes	3	0.8
Fruits	3	0.8
Cotton	3	0.8
Feed	3	0.8
Vegetables	3	0.8
Wheat	2	0.5
Butter	2	0.5
Yams	2	0.5
Horses	2	0.5
Cream	1	0.3
Onions	1	0.3
Mares	1	0.3
Asses	1	0.3
Other roots	1	0.3
Celery	1	0.3
Lard	1	0.3
Garlic	1	0.3
Other products	5	2.1
Total	368	100.0

Source: Banco Central de Venezuela, El Ingreso Nacional de Venezuela (Caracas, 1949), p. 102.

A breakdown of commercial activities in 1936 shows that food predominates, with clothing and cosmetics accounting also for a large share (see Table 4.13). A similar breakdown for other services demonstrates the importance of transportation and domestic services (see Table 4.14). The latter accounted for over 70 percent of income originated in the other services category.

TABLE 4.13

Income Originated in Commercial Activities, by Type, 1936

Type of Commerce	Income Originated (millions of bolívares)	Share (percent)*
Food	62	27.8
Clothing, cosmetics, and so forth	23	10.3
Advertising, radio, and so forth	14	6.3
Banks, and insurance	11	4.9
Motor vehicles and gasoline	8	3.6
Pharmaceuticals and similar products	7	3.1
Various	98	43.9
Total	223	100.0

*Percentages do not add to 100 because of rounding.
Source: Banco Central de Venezuela, El Ingreso Nacional de Venezuela (Caracas, 1949).

Actual volume figures are only available in agriculture. In Table 4.15, the breakdown of agricultural production is shown for 1936; corresponding figures for 1945 are presented whenever possible, in order to give an indication of how the different agricultural activities have fared over time. In Table 4.15, the years 1936 and 1945 are compared by means of an index. It is found that most categories and certain important products declined.

In particular, farm food crops appear to have declined. This is true for each of its subcategories, except fruits and vegetables, on which no figures are available. The latter could not have increased much, as they rose just over 10 percent between 1936 and 1948 (see Tables 4.15 and 4.12). The production of industrial crops, as well as coffee and cocoa, also diminished. The animal products category expanded, mainly due to fish production, because most other products contracted. Lastly, timber production expanded considerably, but from a slim base.

TABLE 4. 14

Income Originated in Services, by Type, 1936

Type of Service	Income Originated (millions of bolívares)	Share (percent)*
Domestic services	52	32. 5
Land transport	33	20. 6
Water transport	19	11. 9
Other transport	11	6. 9
Repair shops	10	6. 2
Diverse services (including private hospitals)	10	6. 2
Realtors and employment agencies	7	4. 4
Restaurants and hotels	7	4. 4
Barber shops and community swimming	6	3. 8
Entertainment	2	1. 2
Air transport	1	0. 6
Photographic services	1	0. 6
Laundry and cleaners	1	0. 6
Total	160	100. 0

*Percentages do not add to 100 because of rounding.
Source: Banco Central de Venezuela, El Ingreso Nacional de Venezuela (Caracas, 1949), p. 106.

Hence, it appears that there was a contraction in agriculture during the period. Although the government demonstrated its worry about agriculture (in the "sow the oil" motto), it was not successful in this sector. Overall, government policy was mainly directed toward self-sufficiency and diversification and, together with aid to local industry, tried to stimulate agricultural production. But

> while a considerable share of public investments of a directly productive type have been devoted to agricultural development, in general, urban development has been emphasized at the expense of providing basic facilities in the rural areas. Some of the investments specifically designed for agricultural development have not been well conceived, so that the capital created has not been fully utilized. [21]

A general index for manufacturing and extractive activities is presented in Table 4. 16, together with indices for particular industrial

TABLE 4.15

Volume of Agricultural Production, by Product, 1936 and 1945
(thousands of metric tons)

Product	1936	1945
Farm food crops:	1,129.7	—
Cereals:	380.5	290.3
Corn	361.3	253.8
Shelled rice	12.7	29.6
Wheat	6.5	6.9
Legumes:	56.8	43.1
Beans	30.8	22.1
Pigeon peas	4.3	5.0
Kidney beans	14.3	8.0
Peas	7.4	8.0
Roots and tubers:	181.7	164.0
Cassava	115.4	—[a]
Yautia	35.1	—
Yams	14.7	150.0
Sweet potatoes	n.a.[b]	—
Celery	5.9	—
Mapuey	n.a.[b]	—
Potatoes	10.6	14.0
Fruits and vegetables:	510.7	—
Bananas	281.9	'n.a.[b]
Plantain	159.2	n.a.[b]
Other fruits	56.8	n.a.[b]
Vegetables	12.8	n.a.[b]
Industrial crops:	179.1	—
Fibers and oils:	16.6	12.6
Sesame	0.7	2.0
Peanuts	0.3	0.3
Copra	7.0	n.a.[b]
Raw cotton	8.5	10.3
Sisal fiber	0.1	n.a.[b]
Others:	162.5	—
Sugar	21.0	27.2
Unrefined sugar	136.6	50.0
Tobacco	4.9	n.a.[b]
Coffee:	74.6	58.1
Cacao	24.1	15.1
Animal products:	252.2	277.8
Meat	72.5	70.1
Poultry	2.0	2.0
Fish	16.0	54.7
Eggs	1.0	1.5
Dairy products:	160.7	149.5
Milk	74.2	62.0
Cheese	86.5	87.5
Forestry[c]	24.7	98.8

[a]Estimated production of all roots and tubers, except potatoes.
[b]Not available.
[c]Timber in cubic meters.

Source: Derived from Juan P. Pérez Castillo, Some Aspects of Venezuela's
Economic Development: 1945-1960 (Ph. D. diss., Tulane University, 1963).

TABLE 4.16

Indices of Industrial Production, by Line and Sector, 1936-48

Sector and Line	1936	1937	1938	1939	1940	1941	1942	1943	1944	1945	1946	1947	1948
Lines:													
Rayon	—	—	100	n.a.[b]	600	2,233	3,600	3,766	4,100	5,566	—	—	—
Cotton	—	—	100	140	170	227	680	797	733	713	—	—	—
Sugar	—	—	—	—	—	—	100	116	108	90	—	—	—
Butter	—	—	—	—	—	—	100	126	116	133	—	—	—
Meat	—	—	—	—	—	—	100	95	103	111	—	—	—
Beer	—	—	—	—	—	—	100	112	146	185	—	—	—
Pasteurized milk	—	—	—	—	—	—	100	109	111	102	—	—	—
Crackers	—	—	—	—	—	—	100	118	124	219	—	—	—
Textiles[a]	—	—	100	119	142	181	131	151	141	176	—	—	—
Electricity	—	—	100	107	129	155	162	167	181	207	242	284	344
Tires	—	—	—	—	—	100	85	172	265	246	298	283	285
Energy[a]	—	—	100	112	98	142	142	150	195	211	261	400	484
Cement[a]	86	71	100	98	200	287	303	283	289	289	325	353	502
Sectors:													
Extractive	100	104	102	96	150	166	149	128	135	127	182	175	248
Manufacturing	—	—	100	—	—	—	—	—	—	245	255	234	350

[a]Consumption.
[b]Not available.
Source: Evelyn M. Baran, The Economic Development of Venezuela (Ph.D. diss., Radcliffe College, 1959).

and manufacturing lines. They show expansion, especially for manufacturing in general, and for textiles, energy, cement, beer, and
crackers, in particular.

The figures exaggerate the growth that actually took place. First,
some of the indices refer to consumption rather than output, and, when
referring to particular lines, they represent growth from quite slim
bases. Second, the growth in manufacturing is to 1945, which undoubtedly was much more than the expansion to 1942, as other indices and
all evidence indicates.

Different policies were instrumental in bringing this industrial
growth about: tariffs were raised, quotas were established, and
exchange controls were enforced at different times during the period.
Toward the end, the breaking of hostilities became a central factor
in the expansion of industry. The scarcities it brought about facilitated the substitution of imports by Venezuelan producers.

This analysis shows that the small growth in the nonpetroleum
activities during this period concentrated on the industrial sector
(extractive activities included). Tertiary activities may have grown
somewhat, as was shown above for government.

It is difficult to pinpoint which lines have felt a stronger impact
from petroleum, as the breakdown available is not sufficiently detailed.
Still, the expansion in the consumption of cement and energy are clearly an outcome of petroleum activity and its indirect effects. The per
capita consumption of energy in Venezuela expanded substantially from
1937 to 1952. In the terminal year, it was the highest in South America.[22] Cement and timber consumption were tied to construction in
the petroleum industry and to the expansion in government expenditures
and increased urbanization it fostered. The trend in other consumer
product lines is tied in a more roundabout fashion to the expansion of
oil.

SUMMARY

In conclusion, during the first part of this period, all the contributions examined—with the exception of petroleum exports—and the
total combined contribution of petroleum to the rest of the economy
expanded considerably. Because of an unfavorable political and
economic climate, the other sectors of the Venezuelan economy failed
to expand pari passu in real terms. While some of the contributions
examined continued to expand in the second part of the period, the
total combined contribution of oil declined from 1939 on. The rest
of the economy followed suit. In real per capita terms, the Venezuelan
economy, as a whole, did not grow from 1936 to 1941. Surprisingly,
all this took place while the investment rate—gross fixed investment
over GDP—constituted a respectably high figure. This was particularly
true at the beginning of the period, during which investment expanded.

     This seeming contradiction can be explained by an increasingly higher investment component in the public sector, by capital spending in anticipation of the war, and by the lag existing between the particular investment expenditure and the time when it actually became productive. Moreover, public investment was heavily weighted in favor of social overhead projects. This assumes no excess capacity in the economy, which is a realistic supposition for this period, as the economy had recuperated from the depression by 1936.

     By the end of 1942, the structure of the Venezuelan economy had only changed slightly from what it had been in 1936. Industrial production was in its infancy, and the economy was completely dependent upon oil.

NOTES

     1. This is especially true, if such beneficial conditions in their external sectors have not resulted from large devaluations or entailed adverse movement in the terms of trade. This would ensure that the national currencies involved would maintain their purchasing power in terms of other currencies and that no decline in the standard of living has occurred.

     2. On all this, see United States Tariff Commission, Economic Controls and Commercial Policy in Venezuela (Washington, D.C.: U.S. Government Printing Office, 1945).

     3. In economies with a high average propensity to import, the overall price level tends to be greatly influenced by the behavior of the prices of imported goods. On this see, Henry Wallich, Monetary Problems of an Export Economy, Harvard EC Studies, vol. 88 (Cambridge, Mass.: Harvard University Press, 1950).

     4. For a survey of different views on reserve levels, see Herbert Grubel, "The Demand for International Reserves: A Critical Review of the Literature," Journal of Economic Literature (December 1971).

     5. For some evidence on all these points, see Nassau A. Adams, "Import Structure and Economic Growth: A Comparison of Cross-Section and Time-Series Data," Economic Development and Cultural Change (January 1967).

     6. The Hydrocarbons Law of 1938 raised all petroleum taxes considerably. But it was applicable only to new concessions. As the companies, in opposition to the law, did not apply for them, and since they decided against converting or adapting the old concession to this law, the rate increases embodied in the law had little practical effect.

     7. The Venezuelan Ministry of Finance includes it among its tax revenues as profits from exchange operations. The latter is slightly different from the concept discussed above, as shall be shown below, being also extended to other industries covered under the same regulations.

8. These proceeds were also partly used for covering the expenses incurred in the administration of the foreign exchange program.

9. If foreign exchange tax revenues from the oil sector are included in oil revenues and compared to total government revenues, the participation of oil in the latter becomes exaggerated. But as has been seen above, if they are not included, the share of oil in total tax revenue is underestimated. As the exact percentage share cannot be determined, these two different measures are used and determine a range that includes the exact share.

10. The same cannot be said for state enterprises and autonomous government administrative institutes.

11. See Charles Rollins, Raw Materials Development and Economic Growth: A Study of the Bolivian and Venezuelan Experience (Ph. D. diss., Stanford University, 1956).

12. Rollins, op. cit., ch. 2.

13. On this point, see Banco Central de Venezuela, La Economía Venezolana en los Ultimos Veinticinco Años (Caracas, 1966), Sección Finanzas Públicas.

14. Simon Kuznets, Six Lectures on Economic Growth (Glencoe: Free Press, 1959), p. 70.

15. Even in this case some of the local purchases are actually imported goods not produced in Venezuela. Strictly speaking, these purchases should not be classified together with those directly affecting the domestic economy. These purchases could only be considered different from direct imports by the companies on the basis that they might help to strengthen the native commercial sector.

16. This increase would have been somewhat greater if the foreign exchange tax had been included in retained value.

17. See Evelyn M. Baran, The Economic Development of Venezuela (Ph. D. diss., Radcliffe College, 1959). The author also finds some indication that the same characteristics were present in the investment activities of the private sector.

18. The estimates of petroleum GDP referred to above only comprise the value added by the petroleum sector in the production of oil. But the petroleum sector also engages in the production of capital goods for its own use. The factor payments and taxes related to such activity are capitalized by the companies and do not appear as part of the value of petroleum's current output. If the income originated in the capital goods section of the petroleum industry is added to the estimates presented above, the petroleum share of GDP would be even larger. Estimates of the national income originating in capital goods production in the petroleum industry are presented in Appendix, Table A. 2, column 14.

19. The procedure was that different companies bid for the concessions, with the highest bidders usually receiving them.

20. Economic Commission for Latin America, United Nations, Recent Facts and Trends in The Venezuelan Economy (México, D. F., 1951), p. 54.

21. Evelyn M. Baran, op. cit.

22. See United Nations, <u>Statistical Yearbook</u> (New York, 1954),
p. 277.

5

THE CONTRIBUTION OF PETROLEUM AND ITS EFFECTS ON THE ECONOMIC DEVELOPMENT OF VENEZUELA, 1943-57

This chapter examines the impact over the decade and a half in which oil's potential contribution to the Venezuelan economy appeared to attain its peak. As shall be seen, this appeared to coincide with a period of unparalleled growth in the other economic sectors of Venezuela.

In order to best examine the impact of petroleum's contribution, and how effectively it was utilized, as well as to evaluate the extent to which oil acted as a leading sector, it is important to separate these 15 years into two quite distinct subperiods. The first begins with the abatement of World War II and the conversion and granting of oil concessions that took place in 1943, and continues through the end of the war and the early postwar years. The second starts with the downfall of the Acción Democrática regime, which ruled in Venezuela from 1945 to 1948 and which introduced many reforms, especially with respect to the government relations with the oil industry. It ends with the oil concessions of the late 1950s and the overthrow of the Perez Jiménez military dictatorship.

Thus, this chapter will be divided into two chronological sections, with the approach introduced in Chapter 4 being followed in each of the subperiods.

THE 1943-48 SUBPERIOD

The Foreign Sector Contribution

Total exports of goods increased considerably from 1942 to 1948. Almost a fivefold increase was registered (see Table 5.1). This expansion was continuous, with the exception of 1945. The growth was much faster than that of the GDP. The share of exports in the latter was enlarged from 20 percent to 30 percent, reversing the pattern of the preceding period.

TABLE 5.1

Share of Petroleum Exports in Total Exports, 1942-48

Year	Petroleum (millions of dollars)	Total (millions of dollars)	Share of Petroleum (percent)
1942	206	226	91.2
1943	254	275	92.4
1944	342	356	96.1
1945	332	351	94.6
1946	485	512	94.7
1947	664	691	96.1
1948	1,069	1,102	97.0

Source: Banco Central de Venezuela, La Economía Venezolana en los Ultimos Veinticinco Años (Caracas, 1966).

Petroleum exports expanded even faster. The share of oil in total goods exported rose from 91.2 percent in 1942 to 97.0 percent in 1948 (see Table 5.1). Thus, the gross balance-of-payments contribution of oil was very considerable, as well as expanding. Undoubtedly, oil was the basic force, ensuring the strong foreign payments position attained by Venezuela toward the end of the period, in spite of the high import levels sustained during these years. As in the previous period, no data are available for calculating the net balance-of-payments contribution of oil.

The strong showing of oil exports ended the need for import controls in 1944. The Import Control Commission was then replaced by the National Supply Commission, a body to control the demand and supply of certain goods that were scarce because of the war. After the war, normal trading conditions were slowly reestablished, and totally unrestrained imports became the rule once more for the first time since the late 1920s.

Although the rate of inflation was somewhat high during this period—over a 7 percent compounded annual average—it resulted from abnormal conditions prevailing in the second half of World War II and in the initial postwar years. It was not at all connected to Venezuelan balance of payments problems. Price hikes in Venezuela followed those in its trading partners, whose prices rose as a result of post-war conditions such as rationing and scarcity of nonmilitary goods. The inflation, moreover, had no adverse effect on the economy's development.

The import capacity of Venezuela broadened during this period. However, the net barter terms of trade evolved unfavorably from 1942 to 1945 and started to move in favor of Venezuela in 1946, although never regaining the 1942 or 1943 levels (see Table 5.2).

The effectiveness with which the foreign exchange proceeds contributed by oil were actually used during this period can be evaluated by looking at the composition of the total Venezuelan goods imports. Although this constitutes a partial measurement, as it does not refer to other kinds of foreign exchange uses, such as imports of services and capital outflows, again, it is the only one possible in this period.

TABLE 5.2

International Reserves and Import Capacity and
Net Barter Terms of Trade, 1942-48

Year	International Reserves (millions of dollars)	Import Capacity (index)*	Net Barter (index)*
1942	89	25.4	172.9
1943	115	28.8	160.2
1944	142	33.6	131.2
1945	208	31.0	95.8
1946	232	43.2	111.9
1947	234	53.2	123.4
1948	362	68.2	141.8

*1959 = 100.

Source: Banco Central de Venezuela, La Economía Venezolana en los Ultimos Veinticinco Años (Caracas, 1966).

Table 5.3 reveals that the percentage of imported goods devoted to capital formation during this period rose from 28.0 percent in 1942 to 46.1 percent in 1948. This is a general indication that the allocation of foreign exchange proceeds among different types of import goods was efficient. Such a shift must be interpreted with caution, because, in 1942, there were import controls, and capital goods were in scant supply. On the other hand, in 1948 there were no import restrictions, and the scarcity of capital goods was more benign. Thus, most of this shift can best be explained in terms of changing circumstances.

Venezuela accumulated international reserves throughout this period (see Table 5.2). However, this accumulation was small in almost all of these years, as world commerce and international availability of goods were still affected by war conditions.

TABLE 5.3

Share of Capital Goods in Total Imports, 1942-49

Year	Percentage Share of Capital Goods
1942	28.0
1943	10.8
1944	19.8
1945	37.9
1946	22.8
1947	36.0
1948	46.1
1949	40.4

Note: Imports expressed in terms of constant 1957 bolívares.

Source: Bernardo Ferrán, lectures on Venezuela's economic history, given at the Universidad Central de Venezuela, Caracas, Venezuela.

In summary, over these years, an overwhelming and growing portion of the foreign exchange earnings of Venezuela were derived from the oil industry. Petroleum exports expanded quite rapidly, assuring the Venezuelan economy of a strong balance-of-payments position. This meant that the external sector served as an aid to growth. On the other hand, the terms at which Venezuela traded in foreign markets deteriorated somewhat throughout the period. Finally, the economy utilized this increasing oil contribution more effectively, as an apparently larger share of the total imports of goods were used for capital formation, while no excessive accumulation of international reserves took place. Therefore, the foreign sector contribution of oil was an important force working for development during this period, and the economy took advantage of it. This represented a great improvement over the previous period.

The Fiscal Contribution of Oil

Petroleum's impact upon the government sector—and, through the latter, upon the rest of the economy—was examined for the years 1936-42 in the preceding chapter. In the subsequent period, the contribution of oil to government revenues increased considerably;

concurrently, the usage of these funds by the government improved significantly. An examination of Table 5.4 shows how petroleum-derived tax revenues behaved during 1942-48.

The same forces that caused the increase in the percentage share of oil revenues in the previous period were again instrumental in eliciting a higher level of oil participation. Petroleum GDP became a larger proportion of total GDP, and petroleum taxes were raised, this time radically.

Most petroleum taxes were raised by the Hydrocarbons Law of 1943, to which practically all petroleum companies converted their concessions, and which, therefore, became applicable to the industry as a whole. Moreover, petroleum operations were further affected by the establishment of an income tax, applicable almost exclusively to the petroleum companies. [1]

Then, during 1944 and 1945, the government granted new concessions, which resulted in special concession payments and increased exploration tax revenues. In addition, when the Acción Democrática Party came to power in 1945, it instituted the famous "fifty-fifty" provision, ensuring that total oil profits would be divided equally between the companies and the government.

In 1943, the participation of oil in government revenues jumped to 42.9 percent, ten percentage points over the 1936-42 average. Table 5.4 shows that the percentage share increased from 1943, with the exception of 1947, until it reached 60 percent in 1948. The average for the whole period is 52.9 percent—19.6 percentage points higher than the average for the preceding period.

If the taxes of oil companies are compared to GDP during this period, they would amount to 7.5 percent as an average for the whole period. Thus, it is clear that the potential contribution of oil to the economy via the government sector was quite sizeable during these years, even in terms of the total economic activity of Venezuela.

If the exchange tax is taken into consideration, then oil's contribution looms still larger. In July 1941, the bolívar was devalued. The buying rate for foreign exchange of commercial banks was raised to 3.32 bolívares to a dollar; the devaluation did not affect the special buying rate for the petroleum sector. As a result, the contribution of the foreign exchange tax on oil to government funds was computed on the basis of a higher tax rate all throughout the 1943-48 period. Oil revenues from this source also rose due to an increase in the amount of foreign currency exchanged into bolívares by the oil companies (see Table 5.5).

Both total revenues and oil revenues increased continually during this period. The former expanded to almost six times its 1942 level. Oil revenues expanded faster. They registered a tenfold increase from 1942. The index of government revenues increased from 100 in 1943 to 517 in 1948, a compounded average growth of 31.5 percent per year. Oil revenues increased to 722 from the base value of 100 in 1943, for a compounded yearly average rate of 39 percent.

TABLE 5.4

Share of Petroleum Tax Revenues in Total Government Revenues, 1942-48

Year	Petroleum (millions of bolívares)	Total (millions of bolívares)	Share of Petroleum in Total Revenues (percent)	Yearly Change in Petroleum Revenues (millions of bolívares)	Overall Change (millions of bolívares)
1942	108	340	31.8	53	
1943	161	375	42.9	129	
1944	290	599	48.4	79	
1945	369	734	50.3	128	1,055
1946	497	943	52.7	198	
1947	695	1,417	49.0	468	
1948	1,163	1,939	60.0	—	

Note: Petroleum revenues do not include foreign exchange taxes on oil. Government revenues encompass all the public sector, with the exception of state enterprises and autonomous administrative institutes; they include profits from foreign exchange operations.

Source: Ministerio de Fomento, Anuario Estadístico (Caracas, 1949); Ministerio de Minas e Hidrocarburos, Petróleo y Otros Datos Estadísticos (Caracas, 1965); and J. J. Bracho Sierra, Cincuenta Años de Ingresos Fiscales (Caracas, 1963).

TABLE 5.5

Share of Oil Revenues in Total Revenues, Including the
Foreign Exchange Tax on Oil, 1942-48

Year	Oil Foreign Exchange Tax (millions of bolívares)	Share of Oil Taxes in Total Taxes (percent)
1942	19	40.3
1943	21	48.5
1944	28	53.1
1945	48	56.8
1946	69	60.0
1947	102	56.2
1948	155	68.0

Source: Banco Central de Venezuela, Memoria (Caracas, several years); La Economía Venezolana en los Últimos Veinticinco Años (Caracas, 1966); and Table 5.4.

Oil-derived revenues contributed substantially to the financing
of the government sector. As a result, the other sectors had to bear
a much lighter burden in government financing, which undoubtedly
helped to strengthen them.

Effectiveness in the Use of the Fiscal Contribution

In order to judge the Venezuelan government's effectiveness in
the use of these funds, it is necessary to estimate the portion of
total government expenditures devoted to the furthering of economic
development. Total social and economic expenditures were utilized for
this purpose in the previous period. Lacking a better alternative, the
same variable will be used once more.

In the 1943-48 period, a slightly higher proportion of the government budget was devoted to social and economic expenditures when
compared to the previous period: 60.8 percent, as compared to 59.6
percent. This resulted from the more soundly based appropriations
of the Acción Democrática party, which came to power in 1945.

In 1943, the share of expenditures for social and economic objectives continued the downward trend begun in 1941, reaching its lowest
level since 1936 (see Table 5.6). But it rebounded in 1944, and at
the end of the period, it stood at 64.3 percent. In absolute terms,
social and economic expenditures increased all throughout the period.
In another test of the effectiveness in the utilization of oil revenues,
it was found that during this period the social and economic expenditures of the government were larger than the revenues derived from
oil in absolute terms (see Tables 5.4 and 5.6). [2]

Furthermore, the growing oil revenues appear to have been devoted
to expenditures of a social and economic character during this period,
as their increase was more than matched by an increase in this type
of expenditures (compare Tables 5.4 and 5.6). The "sow the oil"
policy was evidently taken seriously over these years.

Budgets showed alternating deficits and surpluses in this period,
as Table 5.7 shows. No treasury reserve accumulation policies were
followed. Therefore, taking the period as a whole, those impulses
originating in petroleum and directed to the government sector were
not neutralized, being used for increased expending. At the same
time, the plentiful tax revenues derived from oil allowed the Venezuelan government to expand needed public services, while relatively
little tax pressures were imposed on other economic sectors—and
without any resort to chronic deficit spending. The latter has been
isolated as perhaps the major proximate cause of inflation in Latin
American countries. If deficit spending had been utilized to a
greater extent, it probably would have aggravated the inflationary
process that, mostly as a result of war and postwar scarcities, Venezuela was experiencing.

TABLE 5.6

Social and Economic Expenditures, as a Share of Total Government Expenditures, 1942-48

Year	Social and Economic Expenditures (millions of bolívares)	Percentage Total Government Expenditures	Yearly Change in Social and Economic Expenditures (millions of bolívares)	Overall Change (millions of bolívares)
1942	201	57.0	15	
1943	216	54.7	69	
1944	285	59.4	126	
1945	411	63.0	172	986
1946	583	55.3	304	
1947	887	68.4	300	
1948	1,187	64.3	—	

Note: Table does not include expenditures of state enterprises and autonomous administrative institutes.

Source: Charles Rollins, Raw Materials Development and Economic Growth: A Study of the Bolivian and Venezuelan Experience (Ph. D. diss., Stanford University, 1958); and Table 5.7.

TABLE 5.7

Revenues and Expenditures of Local Governments, as a Percentage of Total Revenues and Expenditures, 1942-48

Year	Local Revenues (millions of bolívares)	Local Expenditures (millions of bolívares)	Total Revenues (millions of bolívares)	Total Expenditures (millions of bolívares)	Percentage of Local Revenues	Percentage of Local Expenditures
1942	53	49	349	352	—	—
1943	56	58	375	394	—	—
1944	65	70	599	480	—	—
1945	74	71	734	652	11.2*	11.3
1946	94	102	943	1,054	—	—
1947	136	123	1,417	1,434	—/	—
1948	163	137	1,939	1,846	8.4	7.4

*Average.

Note: Local revenues and expenditures do not include those arising out of transfers from the central government.

Source: Ministerio de Fomento, Anuario Estadístico (Caracas, several years).

In sum, petroleum's contribution to government revenues increased tremendously during this period. The share of oil in total revenues rose. Oil-derived revenues expanded very fast, facilitating a high level of public expenditures, with no undue pressure on the rest of the economy and without recourse to public indebtedness. Effective use of the oil contribution to public revenues even improved during this period.

The Contribution of Petroleum Investment

As a proportion of GDP, gross fixed investment dropped to 12. 3 percent in 1943, the lowest it had been since 1936. [3] From then on, investment surged, until this percentage stood at 38. 3 percent in 1948 (see Table 5. 8). The increase was even more phenomenal in absolute terms. Gross investment in real terms rose continually from 1942, except for a mild decline in 1943. From 1943 to 1948, gross investment in real terms increased over sixfold (see Table 5. 8), representing a 45 percent average annual compounded increase. In current prices, the increase was even greater (see Appendix, Table A. 2, column 2).

The investment rate—gross fixed domestic investment over GDP—was much higher in this period than in the preceding one. As shall be seen below, this reflected itself in comparatively higher growth rates, which is in agreement with Simon Kuznet's findings. [4]

During this period, gross petroleum investment in current terms also increased continually. In 1943, the industry invested 161 million bolívares, an increase from 1942. By 1948, the amount devoted to investment expenditures climbed to 1, 630 million bolívares (see Appendix, Table A. 2, column 3), which meant a little over a tenfold increase since 1943. Petroleum investment expressed in real terms also increased considerably throughout the years. In constant bolívares of 1957 (see Table 5. 8), gross investment increased over sixfold from the 1943 base, after making a healthy advance in 1943. This increment was equivalent to approximately a 36 percent average compounded rate of growth per year.

The share of gross petroleum investment in total gross investment shifted upward in 1943, going from 21. 5 percent to 32. 6 percent (see Table 5. 8). It was even higher at the end of the period (37. 1 percent in 1948), so that the contribution of petroleum to total Venezuelan investment rose impressively, and the capital goods sector was considerably strengthened under its impact. (The contributions of oil would loom much larger if account were taken of the oil-derived revenues used for public investment.) From 1939 to 1949, net investment by government represented over 34 percent of total net investment as an average, according to the Central Bank. [5]

TABLE 5.8

Gross Fixed Domestic Investment, the Petroleum Share, and the Investment Rate, 1942-48

Year	Total Gross Fixed Domestic Investment (millions of bolívares)*	Petroleum Gross Fixed Domestic Investment (millions of bolívares)*	Nonpetroleum Investment (millions of bolívares)*	Share of Petroleum in Total Gross Fixed Domestic Investment (percent)	Investment Rate (percent)
1942	721	155	566	21.5	13.9
1943	675	220	455	32.6	12.3
1944	1,061	350	711	33.0	16.3
1945	1,717	563	1,154	32.8	22.6
1946	2,228	843	1,385	37.8	25.6
1947	3,478	1,238	2,240	35.6	35.1
1948	4,304	1,598	2,760	37.1	38.3

*Constant 1957 bolívares.

Source: Appendix, Table A.2, columns 2 and 3; Table 5.7; Banco Central de Venezuela, unpublished statistics; and Bernardo Ferrán, lectures on the economic history of Venezuela, presented at the Universidad Central de Venezuela, Caracas, 1963.

In 1948, investments in petroleum refineries represented 21 percent of total petroleum investment, while investments in production amounted to 56 percent, an important part of the latter being devoted to roads, camps, houses, schools, and hospitals. [6]

As to nonpetroleum investment, after suffering a setback in 1943, it rose continually until 1948. In real terms, the growth was nearly 500 percent from the 1943 base, for approximately a 43 percent average annual compounded rate of advance (see Table 5.8).

Nonpetroleum investment seems to have reacted to petroleum investment, and to retained value of total petroleum expenditures, with a one-year lag during this period. As mentioned previously, there should be stronger connections between the levels of nonpetroleum investment and retained value of total expenditures. A very high correlation was found between these two variables. The relationship, as depicted by a linear regression equation, is:

$$NPI = 252.575 + 1.284 \ RV \qquad R^2 = .953$$
$$(.126)$$

where

NPI = nonpetroleum investment with a one-year lag

and

RV = retained value of total petroleum expenditures.

This suggests that nonpetroleum investment responded to changes in the total retained value of petroleum. As the contribution of oil rose, investment activity in the rest of the economy moved in a parallel fashion, but with a one-year lag. No other variables in the Venezuelan economy were strong enough in this period to have induced these changes in investment.

Throughout the period, nonpetroleum gross fixed domestic investment did not exceed the retained value of petroleum expenditures, that is, the payments made to local factors of production and producing firms, as well as the government (compare Table 5.8 and Appendix, Table A.2, column 17). This means that at least the rest of the economy did not invest an amount greater than the immediate domestic expenditures originated in the oil sector during this period. As to the social productivity of the investment resources, at least with respect to public investment, the allocation of investment funds seems to have improved relative to the previous period, especially under the Acción Democrática Administration, during the years 1945 to 1948.

The impressive expansion in external sales, tax proceeds, and investment expenditures in the oil sector occurred when the transportation difficulties, the capital and technical shortages, and the war scarcities began clearing up in 1943 and, especially, in 1944. Venezuelan oil began to flow unrestrictedly once again to meet increasing demand. The worldwide conflagration proved that access to oil was essential for military power. After the war, the pent-up demand and the reconstruction effort assured increased needs for "black gold." Demand increased, and prices moved upward. This proved to be a boom for oil producers, particularly for Venezuela, which still produced very large quantities of oil at a very low relative cost.

On the national front, as a result of several reforms—the most important being the new tax legislation—the retained portion of the petroleum expenditures increased even more than the other petroleum variables. This, combined with a better use of the contribution of petroleum in the foreign trade and public sectors, spearheaded the expansion in investment activity in the rest of the Venezuelan economy.

To recapitulate, petroleum investment expanded sharply during this period, contributing significantly to the high level of capital accumulation sustained by the economy and promoting some local production in its wake. However, the investment rate of the country was not high enough to ensure that the amount of nonpetroleum income invested was greater than the retained value in the oil industry.

Both petroleum investment and the overall contribution of the oil industry to the economy, expressed in terms of the retained value of its total expenditures, were the exogenous elements inducing an expansion in investment in the nonpetroleum part of the economy. It was found that the retained value explained 95.3 percent of the lagged variation in nonpetroleum investment. Certainly, another important factor in the investment surge was a more effective utilization of oil's public sector and foreign sector contributions by the economy, resulting to a great extent from more enlightened government policies.

Total Domestic Product and the Expenditures of the Oil Industry

In examining some of the important variables determining the contribution of oil to the other sectors of the Venezuelan economy, it has been seen that during this period, they were characterized by a sharp upward trend. Understandably, the same can be said about oil's output and its value of production. As a consequence of an increase in the price of oil, the latter rose eightfold from 1942 to 1948. This represented a corresponding annual average compounded rate of approximately 44 percent from 1942 (38 percent from 1943). A similar increase took place in the GDP of petroleum in current prices. In constant 1957 prices, the trend is identical, but with smaller increases (see Table 5.9).

Petroleum became even more important to the Venezuelan economy in terms of its share in GDP in real terms (1957 prices) during this period. Petroleum accounted for a participation of 20.4 percent in

TABLE 5.9

Value of Oil Production, Petroleum Gross Domestic Product and Its Share in
Total Gross Domestic Product, and Nonpetroleum Gross Domestic Product,
1942-48

Year	Value of Oil Production (millions of current bolívares)	Petroleum GDP (millions of current bolívares)	Petroleum GDP (millions of constant 1957 bolívares)	Nonpetroleum GDP (millions of constant 1957 bolívares)	Total (millions of constant 1957 bolívares)	Share of Petroleum in Total (percent)
1942	403	393	1,059	3,780	5,193	20.4
1943	600	474	1,283	3,736	5,478	23.4
1944	832	738	1,838	3,981	6,515	28.2
1945	1,059	912	2,312	4,283	7,592	30.5
1946	1,473	1,292	2,778	4,566	8,707	31.9
1947	2,389	2,028	3,109	4,976	9,911	31.4
1948	3,564	2,920	3,503	5,462	11,225	31.2

Note: Nonpetroleum GDP is not simply calculated as the difference between the total GDP and petroleum GDP. Thus the petroleum and nonpetroleum GDP do not add to total GDP. See text for further information on the different sources used and adjustments made in the calculation of these concepts.

Source: From calculations based on the financial statements and documents of the big three oil company groups in Venezuela, adjusted to cover the whole industry; Ministerio de Minas e Hidrocarburos, Petróleo y Otros Datos Estadísticos (Caracas, several years); Appendix, Table A.2, columns 4, 5, 6, 10, 25, and 27; Bernardo Ferrán, lectures on the economic history of Venezuela, presented at the Universidad Central de Venezuela, Caracas, 1963; and Table 5.8.

1942 and of 31.2 percent in 1948. The enhanced participation of
petroleum is not so great, however, if compared with the year 1941,
when petroleum represented 28.2 percent of total GDP. Yet, these
two years (1941 and 1942) cannot be considered representative of
petroleum's contribution to the total production of the Venezuelan
economy. In 1941, petroleum was at a peak, while the rest of the
economy was still in a lull; in 1942, just the opposite took place. It
would be more reasonable to compare the 1948 percentage share of
petroleum in total GDP, with the average for the previous period.
Such a comparison indicates that the participation of oil in the economy
increased significantly over a short spell, as the previous period
average was 24.3 percent, while the 1943-48 average was 30.0 percent. [7]

Thus, the petroleum industry generated exogenous injections
into the Venezuelan economy during this period. As the multiplicand
enlarged, the multiplier-accelerator mechanism acted in a continuous
and reinforcing fashion. The value of production and the formation
of capital in the oil industry constitute what can be called the "gross
income-expenditure generating base" of the industry, which expanded
considerably. But only the retained part of the gross expenditures of
the industry has direct and immediate impact on the Venezuelan
economy. The retained value of current expenditures expanded continually throughout the period, increasing over elevenfold from 1942
to 1948, for an average increase of over 50 percent a year compounded
(43 percent from 1943), which is higher than that of any other petroleum
indicator examined (see Table 5.10).

The share of retained value of current expenditures in the total
current expenditures of the petroleum industry reached 43.9 percent
in 1942. By 1943, it had jumped to 50.5 percent. Except for 1946,
it continued to increase until 1948, when it reached 59.0 percent.
This increase was due, to an important degree, to increasing tax rates
for the petroleum industry. Other contributing factors included the
following: (a) a change in the procedures for determining the oil
prices to be used in calculating the income and royalty taxes to be
paid by the industry, (b) a more efficacious administration of the tax
laws, (c) a substantial expansion in refining capacity, (d) increased
wages and more liberal fringe benefits for petroleum workers, (e) the
limitation of tariff exemption to goods not produced in Venezuela,
and (f) the special payments made to the Venezuelan government for
the new concessions granted in 1944 and 1945. [8] Retained value of
current expenditures per barrel of oil produced jumped from 1.20
bolívares per barrel in 1942 to 4.21 bolívares in 1948, an almost
fourfold increase, resulting from the expanding share of retained
value of current expenditures in the value of output and from increasing
oil prices.

In the preceding chapter, it was explained that the estimates of
retained value of investment expenditures were not considered as

TABLE 5.10

Retained Value of Current Expenditures in the Petroleum Industry,
as a Percentage of Total Current Expenditures in the Industry
and per Barrel of Oil Produced, 1942-48

Year	Retained Value of Current Expenditures (millions of bolívares)	Percentage of Total Current Expenditures	Per Barrel of Oil Produced (bolívares)
1942	177	43.9	1.20
1943	303	50.5	1.69
1944	437	52.5	1.70
1945	616	58.2	1.91
1946	821	55.7	2.42
1947	1,399	58.6	3.22
1948	2,103	59.0	4.21

Note: The foreign exchange taxes on oil are not included in retained value.

Source: Appendix, Table A.2, columns 4, 5, 6, 7, 8, 9, 19, 20; and Ministerio de Minas e Hidrocarburos, Petróleo y Otros Datos Estadísticos (Caracas, 1965).

reliable as the other retained value estimates. These have been presented in Appendix, Table A.2, column 17, and suggest a meteoric ascension in the retained value of investment expenditures, in keeping with the growth of petroleum investment during the period.

Retained value of total expenditures also had an astounding increase. At the end of the period, it had risen more than twelvefold, which is even greater than the increase experienced by the retained value of current expenditures (see Table 5.11). If retained value of total expenditures is taken as a share of value of production plus investment expenditures in the petroleum industry, it would represent an estimate of the degree of participation by domestic factors, producers, and government in the total activity of the sector. This percentage stood at 48.5 percent in 1942, rose to 57.6 percent in 1943, and stood at 60.9 percent in 1948. As can be seen in Table 5.11, it did not increase smoothly throughout the period, having mild setbacks in 1944 and 1947.

The same forces causing the increase in retained value of current expenditures determined the expansion of the retained value of investment expenditures. With raising demand and increasing sales of Venezuelan oil, favorable prospects for the future, and new concessions to work on, investment in the Venezuelan petroleum industry expanded considerably from 1943 on. With the spurt of investment and an increasing proportion of capital expenditures being directed to local producers and native factors, the retained value of investment expenditures was the petroleum indicator rising the fastest during this period. As retained value of investment expenditures is a component of total retained value, its increase greatly contributed to the expansion of the latter and explains why it was greater than the expansion in retained value of current expenditures.

The expansion of all these concepts was much less in terms of constant 1957 prices, but nonetheless impressive, as Appendix, Table A.2, columns 16, 17, and 18 demonstrate. Again, the growth rate for the period is smaller if an average for the previous period is used, instead of taking the 1942 low as the base year, but results are not appreciably changed.

The Impact of Oil on the Rest of the Economy

What overall effects did the oil sector's contributions from 1943 to 1948 have upon the overall behavior of the other sectors of the

TABLE 5.11

Retained Value of Total Expenditures, as a Percentage of
Total Expenditures in the Oil Industry, and
per Barrel of Oil Produced, 1942-48

Year	Retained Value of Total Expenditures (millions of bolívares)	Retained Expenditures as a Percentage of Total Expenditures	Per Barrel of Oil Produced (bolívares)
1942	246	48.5	1.66
1943	439	57.6	2.45
1944	607	55.2	2.36
1945	862	57.5	2.67
1946	1,280	59.3	3.30
1947	2,077	59.0	4.77
1948	3,167	60.9	6.46

Note: Retained value estimates do not include foreign exchange taxes on the oil industry.

Source: Table 5.9 and 5.10; Appendix, Table A.2, columns 3, 11, 12, and 20 and Ministerio de Minas e Hidrocarburos, Petróleo y Otros Datos Estadísticos (Caracas, 1965).

Venezuelan economy? Were the positive effects of sufficient strength to offset the negative influences of the oil sector? Were the net effects important enough to draw the conclusion that oil acted as a leading sector during this period?

The impact was quite substantial in those geographic areas where petroleum activity took place. But most of retained value consisted of tax payments, and government expenditures arising from the latter were not concentrated in the petroleum areas. Moreover, a substantial part of the industry procurement within Venezuela involved nonpetroleum regions. Therefore, the influence of petroleum, and the economic growth it caused, was spread among various other regions. [9]

Population statistics give an idea of the economic expansion that occurred in those places where oil activities were concentrated. Statistics show that population in the petroleum states increased 46.8 percent between 1936 and 1947. The federal district experienced a 42.5 percent increase in population during the same period, while all of Venezuela had a population growth of only 20.2 percent from 1936 to 1947. [10]

From 1936 to 1941, the population in petroleum states grew 25.0 percent—that in the federal district expanded 34.3 percent and the overall population, 14.5 percent. If these rates are compared with those cited just above, it is immediately apparent that the growth of population in the petroleum states during the second half of the 1936-47 period was quite impressive, surpassing the population expansion in the federal district. This was to be expected, as the rise in oil activity from 1941 to 1947 was much greater than the expansion from 1936 to 1941. Such population data give an approximate indication of the remarkable economic expansion—in terms of income and product—which took place in the petroleum districts during this period. The rates of growth of regional GDP in these areas must have been much higher than those for the country as a whole. It appears then that a major part of the economic expansion in Venezuela from 1936 to 1947 was centered in the petroleum states and in the federal district.

The GDP of Venezuela in real terms more than doubled from 1942 to 1948 (see Table 5.9). To be exact, this aggregate grew about 114 percent in that time span, equivalent to a compound annual average growth rate of 13.5 percent (15.4 percent per year from 1943). As a rise in prices occurred during the period, the increase in GDP in current prices was still greater.

However, what is of greater interest is the effect of the oil expansion on the other sectors of the economy, as indicated by the nonpetroleum GDP. With the exception of 1943, this indicator grew continually during the period. In real terms, it expanded at a 6.3 percent compounded average rate per year, with the overall growth between 1942 and 1948 being 44.5 percent (see Table 5.9). From 1943 to 1948, the yearly average rate of growth was 7.9 percent. The increase in current prices was much greater.

A more disaggregated examination of how these different sectors have fared over time would be fruitful at this point. The agricultural sector appears to have rebounded from the low production levels of 1942. As has been said in the previous chapter, there is a statistical gap between 1936 and 1945 in the agricultural output series, but there are indications that production was lower in 1942 than in 1945. The actual extent of the increase in production between these two years remains a conjecture, but the data on agricultural output presented in Table 5.12 and 5.13 evidence a substantial increase from 1945 to 1948.

TABLE 5.12

Agricultural Output, 1945-48
(index, 1938 = 100)

Year	Agricultural Output
1945	95
1946	92
1947	91
1948	103

Source: Evelyn M. Baran, The Economic Development of Venezuela (Ph. D. diss. , Radcliffe College, 1959).

An index of agricultural output is presented in Table 5.12. From 1945 on, agricultural production decreased up to 1947, probably as a result of greater competition from imports just after the war. Then, it surged in 1948, when postwar readjustments were complete and more sound economic policies, attaining a better balance between the promotion of directly productive activities and social overhead investment in rural areas, began having effects. Forestry production increased considerably from 1945 on. If forestry is included with agriculture, production in the year 1946, and maybe 1947, would have been larger than in 1945. Lack of detailed information does not allow a more definite statement.

Agriculture and forestry production are shown as disaggregated as possible in Table 5.13. The table is partly incomplete before 1948, and that explains the absence of subtotals for those years. From 1945 to 1948, the greatest increases were in cereals (82.7 percent), unrefined sugar (77 percent), and eggs (106.7 percent, but from a low base). Corn was mostly responsible for the rise in cereal production in 1948. Much of this increase can be attributed

TABLE 5.13

Agricultural Production, by Product, 1945-48
(thousands of metric tons)

Product	1945	1946	1947	1948	Index[a]
Farm food crops:	—	—	—	1,332.2	
Cereals:	290.3	235.0	288.6	530.4	(182.7)
Corn	253.8	190.0	231.0	483.3	(190.4)
Shelled rice	29.6	39.0	52.1	41.7	(140.9)
Wheat	6.9	6.0	5.5	5.4	(78.3)
Legumes:	43.1	41.0	49.4	53.7	(124.6)
Beans	22.1	20.0	25.4	30.0	(135.7)
Pigeon peas	5.0	5.0	7.0	7.7	(154.0)
Kidney beans	8.0	8.0	8.3	8.0	—
Peas	8.0	8.0	8.7	8.0	—
Roots and tubers:	164.0	164.0	164.0	166.2	(101.3)
Cassava	—	—	—	95.9	—
Yautia	—	—	—	19.4	—
Yams	150.0[b]	150.0[b]	150.0[b]	17.6	—
Sweet potatoes	—	—	—	8.0	—
Celery	—	—	—	3.6	—
Mapuey	—	—	—	5.7	—
Potatoes	14.0	14.0	14.0	16.0	(114.3)
Fruits and vegetables:	—	—	—	581.9	—
Bananas	n.a.[c]	n.a.[c]	n.a.[c]	310.0	—
Plantains	n.a.[c]	n.a.[c]	n.a.[c]	155.9	—
Other fruits	n.a.[c]	n.a.[c]	n.a.[c]	60.3	—
Vegetables	n.a.[c]	n.a.[c]	n.a.[c]	55.7	—
Industrial crops:	—	—	—	142.1	—
Fibers and oils:	12.6	10.6	15.9	20.3	(161.1)
Sesame	2.0	2.8	4.9	6.2	(310.0)
Peanuts	0.3	0.3	0.4	0.3	—
Copra	n.a.[c]	n.a.[c]	4.3	5.2	—
Raw cotton	10.3	7.5	6.3	7.1	(68.9)
Sisal fiber	n.a.[c]	n.a.[c]	n.a.[c]	1.5	—
Others:	—	—	—	121.8	—
Sugar	27.2	27.4	28.5	26.6	(97.8)
Unrefined sugar	50.0	71.6	77.0	88.5	(177.0)
Tobacco	n.a.[c]	n.a.[c]	n.a.[c]	6.7	—
Coffee:	58.1	45.1	44.0	53.4	(91.9)
Cacao	15.1	20.0	17.0	23.8	(157.6)
Animal products:	227.8	294.6	306.0	324.2	(142.3)
Meat	70.1	76.9	73.3	73.4	(104.7)
Poultry	2.0	2.0	2.0	2.0	(100.0)
Fish	54.7	63.5	69.5	79.8	(145.9)
Eggs	1.5	2.0	2.5	3.1	(206.7)
Dairy products:	149.5	150.2	153.7	168.9	(113.0)
Milk	62.0	61.7	64.7	78.9	(127.3)
Cheese	87.5	88.5	89.0	90.0	(102.9)
Forestry[d]	98.8	144.7	151.3	152.4	(154.3)

[a]1945 = 100.

[b]Estimated production for the whole group of roots and tubers, minus potatoes.

[c]Not available.

[d]Timber in cubic meters.

Source: Derived from Juan P. Pérez Castillo, Some Aspects of Venezuela's Economic Development 1945-1960 (Ph.D. diss., Tulane University, 1963).

to climatological conditions. Venezuela waited for 14 years before
having a large crop of cereals.

Fibers and oils, although not as important as cereals or sugar,
expanded consistently. They increased 61.1 percent between 1945
and 1948, but from low levels. As to the traditional export products,
although cocoa output increased 57.9 percent, coffee declined.
Animal products expanded modestly from 1945 to 1948. Fish, eggs,
and milk led the expansion, which amounted to 42.3 percent overall.
Forestry products increased 54.3 percent during this time span.

Total agricultural output, excluding forestry, expanded at a
2.7 percent compounded annual average from 1945 to 1948 (see
Table 5.12). Forestry expanded at a 15.6 percent average yearly
percentage increase. From 1942 to 1945, the increases were smaller.
Hence, during these years, the growth in population outstripped the
growth of agricultural production. Imports were needed to close the
gap, especially since, in contrast with the previous period, per capita
income rose. There are data on agricultural imports showing that their
value and volume stood at 78,000 metric tons and 31 million bolívares
in 1936 and at 340,200 metric tons and 349 million bolívares in 1948.[11]

Industrial and extractive production expanded at a very fast pace
from 1942 on. In Table 4.16, an output index for extractive activities-
petroleum not included-shows an increase of 8.9 percent per year
from 1942 to 1948. Yet, the expansion took place in the second half
of the period and represented increases from a thin base.

No information on the trend of manufacturing production from 1942
to 1945 is available. Still, indices for particular manufactured products presented in Table 4.16, depict a sizeable expansion. As has
been pointed out in Chapter 4, the industrialization process picked
up momentum in these years, so a similar expansion probably held
for manufacturing as a whole.

Acute shortages resulting from World War II were the main forces
in back of the expansion in manufacturing production. Over and
above the general policies of manufacturing promotion, these sorts
of natural obstacles greatly facilitated the import-substitution process.
Increases in demand were mostly translated into expanding domestic
production.

From 1945 on, the information is more complete. The index of
manufacturing output presented in Table 4.16, rises 42.9 percent
up to 1948, representing a 12.6 percent average yearly compounded
increase. The increase in the second part of the period was probably
not as great as in the initial years. The expansion was almost
totally concentrated in 1948, with the preceding two years being a
period of readjustment to increasingly normal trade relations, with
imported manufactures regaining lost markets.

At a more disaggregated level (see Table 5.14), it can be seen
that most industries expanded between 1945 and 1948. Expanding at

TABLE 5.14

Manufacturing Production, by Industry and Commodity,
1945 and 1948

Industry	1945		1948	
	Volume	Index	Volume	Index
Food processing industries:	—[m]	100	—	132
Pasteurized milk[a]	n.a.[m]	—	15.7	100
Milk for butter[b]	n.a.[m]	—	34.4	100
Powdered milk[b]	1.5	100	1.7	113
Vegetable oils[b]	3.6	100	10.1	281
Peanut oil[b]	0.7	100	0.5	71
Sesame oil[b]	0.7	100	1.3	186
Coconut oil[b]	0.9	100	1.3	144
Cotton oil[b]	0.5	100	0.2	40
Canned fish[b]	6.0	100	9.3	155
Ground coffee[b]	n.a.[m]	—	n.a.[m]	—
Chocolate[b]	n.a.[m]	—	1.2	100
Cookies[b]	2.5	100	6.3	252
Pastries[b]	3.1	100	6.7	216
Sugar[b]	27.2	100	26.6	98
Rice[b]	12.4	100	5.0	41
Salt[b]	57.5	100	35.5	62
Fruit juices[a]	n.a.[m]	—	n.a.[m]	—
Beverage industries:	69.2	100	161.9	234
Beer[c]	40.1	100	57.8	144
Liquor[c]	3.9	100	5.6	144
Rum[c]	3.1	100	4.6	148
Gaseous drinks[c]	22.1	100	93.9	425
Textile industries:	—	100	—	100
Cotton suits[a]	7.6	100	7.2	95
Linen and canvas[a]	4.3	100	3.7	86
Cotton cloth[a]	9.4	100	9.8	104
Rayon and cotton cloth[a]	n.a.[m]	—	n.a.[m]	—
Cotton knits[d]	0.2	100	0.3	150
Cotton bedspreads[e]	0.03	100	0.07	253
Cotton blankets[e]	0.4	100	0.6	150
Cotton towels[e]	0.4	100	0.2	50
Cotton underwear[e]	1.1	100	1.3	118
Cotton footwear[e]	0.9	100	1.6	178
Rayon cloth[b]	1.7	100	3.3	194
Rayon knits[d]	0.04	100	0.30	750
Rayon footwear[f]	0.3	100	0.2	67
Rayon and cotton footwear[f]	0.7	100	0.6	86
Nylon footwear[e]	n.a.[m]	—	0.06	100
Wool suits[b]	0.10	100	0.09	90
Wool knits[b]	n.a.[m]	—	0.1	100
Linen cloth[b]	0.10	100	0.03	30
Rope[b]	0.7	100	0.9	129
Sisal bags[e]	n.a.[m]	—	n.a.[m]	—

Industry	1945		1948	
	Volume	Index	Volume	Index
Leather industries:	—	—	—	—
Leather soles[g]	—	100	—	164
Leather linings[h]	18.0	100	30.3	168
Other products[i]	0.3	100	0.5	167
Paper and cardboard industries[g]	6.1	100	8.7	143
Rubber industries:	59.0	100	72.0	122
Tires[j]	34.0	100	39.0	115
Inner tubes[j]	25.0	100	33.0	132
Tobacco industry[e]	2.1	100	1.9	90
Timber industry[i]	21.0	100	58.0	276
Chemical industries:	—	100	—	157
Paint[b]	1.0	100	1.4	140
Distilled alcohol[c]	2.4	100	3.0	125
Soap[b]	15.3	100	20.0	131
Candles[b]	n.a.[m]	—	2.6	100
Matches[e]	n.a.[m]	—	n.a.[m]	—
Industrial gas[k]	n.a.[m]	—	0.7	100
Animal feed[d]	5.7	100	10.3	181
Metal industries:	n.a.[m]	—	n.a.[m]	—
Nails[l]	n.a.[m]	—	n.a.[m]	—
Tin cans[l]	n.a.[m]	—	n.a.[m]	—
Vehicle assembly industries:	—	—	—	—
Passenger[j]	—	—	—	—
Commercial[j]	—	—	—	—
Construction materials industries:	115.0	100	215.0	187
Portland cement[l]	115.0	100	215.0	187
Lime[l]	n.a.[m]	—	n.a.[m]	—
Cement blocks[j]	n.a.[m]	—	n.a.[m]	—
Cement tubes[j]	n.a.[m]	—	n.a.[m]	—
Mosaics and so forth[l]	n.a.[m]	—	n.a.[m]	—
Bricks and tiles[j]	—	—	—	—
Total		100		164

[a]Thousands of liters.
[b]Thousands of metric tons
[c]Millions of liters.
[d]Millions of kilograms.
[e]Millions of units.
[f]Millions of pairs.
[g]Meters.
[h]Thousands of square feet.
[i]Thousands of cubic meters.
[j]Thousands of units.
[k]Millions of cubic meters.
[l]Millions of metric tons.
[m]Not available.

Source: Juan P. Pérez Castillo, Some Aspects of Venezuela's Economic Development: 1945-1960 (Ph.D. diss., Tulane University, 1963), corrected for certain inaccuracies in the 1948 index.

the swiftest pace were the beverage and timber industries, which more than doubled their production, and the cement industry, which almost doubled it. The leather and chemical industries grew by more than 50 percent. The rubber industry increased 22 percent and the food-processing industry somewhat over 30 percent, their growth being in turn slower than the overall growth of manufacturing.

The increase in the output of the utilities component of the industrial sector is suggested by the trends in the production of electricity and in energy consumption presented in Table 4.16. In this sector, consumption is a precise indicator of domestic production due to the nontradable and nonstorable nature of these products. Energy consumption more than tripled between 1942 and 1948. In terms of average compounded yearly increases, the expansion came to approximately 23 percent per year. Hence, the utilities sector appeared to expand more rapidly than manufacturing over these years.

The construction industry also expanded very rapidly. The rapid expansion of the timber and cement industries is an indication of this. (As in the utilities field, construction activities virtually are of a domestic nature. The consumption of cement can suggest the trend in consumption activities.) From 1942 to 1948, cement consumption expanded about 66 percent, for a yearly average compounded rate of growth of 8.8 percent. In contrast with the utilities sector, which grew in a continuous and regular fashion, the construction industry was adversely affected by the war and actually contracted from 1942 to 1945, because of unavailability of imported materials.

There is very little information available on the growth of tertiary activities during this period. Government expenditures, for one, showed the highest sectoral rates of growth. If expressed in real terms, to make them as comparable as possible with the output indices presented above, it is found that they quadrupled from 1942 to 1948.

If the growth of the Venezuelan economy in this period is expressed in per capita terms, a substantial rise is still found. In per capita terms, real GDP amounted to 1,472 bolívares in 1941, when a population census was taken. In 1950, when another census was conducted, the same aggregate expressed per head of population had increased to 2,518 bolívares. This amounts to an expansion of 70.7 percent over the whole period, which is equivalent to a 6.1 percent average compounded increase per year. The Venezuelan economy put on quite a performance during this period, contrasting favorably with what had taken place in any previous period.

Petroleum was the strongest force in the promotion of growth throughout these years. To a certain extent, this can be attributed to rising petroleum prices, an externally determined variable that boosted the value of production and income from petroleum in Venezuela. Most of it, however, resulted from increasing output.

The retained value of total oil expenditures experienced a very substantial increase, and the particular contributions from oil, which

have been examined, were substantially enlarged. This coincided with
a more effective use of petroleum's contributions by the Venezuelan
economy. All this was the main force in the quite satisfactory expansion of the other sectors of the Venezuelan economy. The basic
conditions for economic progress in Venezuela had been slowly laid
down since the initial oil spurt in the 1920s. The Venezuelan economy
demonstrated it was ready for the establishment of the preconditions
for take-off, and 1943 can be accepted as its start. Therefore, the
greater part of the increase in nonpetroleum GDP resulted from the
leadership role exercised by the petroleum sector in the Venezuelan
economy.

In fact, when the retained value of total petroleum expenditures
is regressed against nonpetroleum GDP, it is seen that changes in
the former explain 96.2 percent of the variation in the latter. A
linear regression equation for the set of observations on both variables
can be expressed as follows:

$$NPP = 3598.822 + .964 \quad RV \qquad R^2 = .962$$
$$(.083)$$

where

NPP = nonpetroleum GDP

and

RV = retained value of total expenditures.

Nevertheless, a quite substantial increase in the contribution
of oil to the economy was apparently needed to obtain a large, but
much smaller, expansion in the other sectors of the Venezuelan
economy. This is deceiving, however, because the large increase
in total retained value is based on much lower levels. This is clearly
shown if the absolute increase in total retained value during the
period is expressed as a proportion of the value for nonpetroleum
GDP in 1942 (77.3 percent) and this, in turn, is compared to the
overall increase in nonpetroleum GDP during the period (44.5 percent). The discrepancy is not that great in these terms and illustrates
why relative size must be taken into consideration in evaluating the
effects of potentially leading sectors on the rest of the economy.

Which activities were particularly affected by the expansion
of the petroleum industry? It appears that, as in the previous period,
construction and utilities were most directly and importantly influenced
by the expansion in petroleum.[12] Petroleum investment had a high
construction component in this period. Refineries and transportation
facilities were built; houses, schools, hospitals, and roads were
constructed; and storage and distributive facilities were provided.
This required increasing production and importation of cement, timber,
and other construction materials and services. Government expenditures in public works, education, and health increased six or seven

times in current bolívares from 1942 to 1948, mainly as a result of
the oil industry's tax contribution. [13] This also required a strong
expansion of construction activities.

The operations of the oil industry have high energy requirements
in almost all its stages. This explains the high and increasing per
capita consumption of energy in Venezuela. Heavy investment in
social overhead facilities by the government was also instrumental
in the expansion of the utilities sector.

The production of refined oil more than doubled from 1942 to
1948, but still represented only about 10 percent of the total output
of oil. [14] The utilization of petroleum by-products in other uses had
not begun in this period.

THE 1949-57 SUBPERIOD

The Foreign Sector Contribution

Oil exports continued their strong performance during the 1949-57
period. Expressed in terms of current dollars, they came to almost
two and one-half times the 1948 level by the end of this period, enough
for a 10.2 percent compounded average annual increase. While this
was not so strong a showing as in the foregoing period, it was quite
impressive (see Table 5.15).

As verified by Table 5.15, total exports expanded just a shade
faster. The participation of oil in total exports, thus, declined from
97 percent in 1948 to 93.4 percent in 1957. But this diminution still
does not detract from the gross balance-of-payments contribution of
the oil sector during this period. [15]

Since 1953, it is possible to obtain balance-of-payments data
in a more disaggregated fashion. The gross balance-of-payments
contribution of oil can then also be computed in terms of the current
account credits generated by the industry. In Table 5.16, the current
account credits of the oil industry and of the Venezuelan economy are
shown for the latter part of the period. Their trend is similar to that
in exports of goods, with the share of oil being slightly smaller in
terms of current account credits.

Table 5.15 also shows all foreign exchange proceeds of the
Venezuelan economy from 1950 to 1957, with the petroleum share
shown separately. These are the exchange proceeds contributed
by the different sectors net of their own needs. Although the foreign
exchange proceeds contributed by oil rose substantially from 1950 to
1957, its share in the total proceeds was reduced from 84.6 percent
in 1950 to 66.4 percent in 1957. Altogether, it is clear that the
net balance-of-payments contribution of oil, while smaller than the
gross contribution, was nevertheless quite significant.

TABLE 5.15

Share of Petroleum in Total Exports of Goods and in Total Foreign Exchange Earnings, 1948-57

Year	Petroleum (millions of dollars)	Total (millions of dollars)	Share of Petroleum (percent)	Petroleum (millions of dollars)	Total Exchange (millions of dollars)	Petroleum Share in Total (percent)
1948	1,069	1,102	97.0	—	—	—
1949	966	990	97.6	—	—	—
1950	1,124	1,155	97.3	557	658	84.6
1951	1,297	1,370	94.7	657	775	84.8
1952	1,384	1,446	95.7	758	917	82.7
1953	1,428	1,498	95.3	809	1,013	79.9
1954	1,564	1,648	94.9	828	1,094	75.7
1955	1,791	1,891	94.7	916	1,291	71.0
1956	2,086	2,211	94.3	1,363	1,849	68.3
1957	2,570	2,751	93.4	1,761	2,464	66.4

Source: Banco Central de Venezuela, La Economía Venezolana en los Ultimos Veinticinco Años (Caracas, 1966), Memoria (Caracas, several years), and Informe Económico (Caracas, several years).

During this period, data on net capital inflows by the oil industry also became available. Although prima facie this might appear as an important source of foreign means of payment, this was not so during these years. The inflow of foreign capital into the Venezuelan petroleum industry was concentrated in the years 1947-49 and 1956-57 (see Table 5.16). All other years were characterized by a mild decapitalization, with no foreign funds being brought into the country by the oil companies.

Exports advanced every year except 1949, the same being true for petroleum exports. Such expansion took place at improved external prices. Yet, import prices rose throughout the period, and the net barter terms of trade moved slightly against Venezuela (see Table 5.17). As a result of the increase in exports and foreign exchange proceeds, coming to a substantial degree from the oil industry, the foreign trade sector was able to play its role as growth promoter and inflation suppressant during this period. No controls were placed on imports, and a free flow of productive factors and technical knowledge took place.

Foreign exchange proceeds derived from Venezuelan exports, capital inflows, and so forth are resources that can be used to import required goods and services, or alternatively, they can be added to the international reserves of the country, to be utilized at some future date, or not at all. During this period, the total reserve holdings of Venezuela increased considerably, doubling between 1947 and 1953, and almost tripling from then until 1957, as can be seen in Table 5.17. This occurred in the face of increased unemployment toward the end of the period. With a fair degree of unemployed and underemployed resources and the possibility of bringing about an inflow of those in scarce supply, as well as improvements in techniques and capital usage, still very much possible, more expansive economic policies, which could have utilized foreign exchange more fully, could have brought about increasing growth and employment.

This is even more strongly so because of the traditionally heavy gold content of the Venezuelan international reserves, from which practically no earnings were derived (see Table 5.18). Furthermore, only part of the nongold reserves provides some yields. Throughout the years, about one-half of the nongold assets was kept in the form of deposits that could be withdrawn at sight. This was especially true during the period being examined.[16]

However, even if the reserves had been kept in income-earning assets, it is doubtful that their return would have been higher than the social marginal return to investment in Venezuela. Although there are no careful studies on the rate of return to investment in Venezuela, it is difficult to imagine that the government could not have lent (or invested) its capital in a more profitable fashion. Recent empirical evidence has found that the rate of return on investment on developing economies is at least as high as in the United States.

TABLE 5.16

Share of Petroleum in Current Account Credits, 1953-57, and
Gross Capital Inflows of the Oil Industry, 1947-57*

Year	Petroleum (millions of dollars)	Total (millions of dollars)	Share of Petroleum (percent)	Gross Capital Inflows of the Oil Industry (millions of bolívares)
1947	—	—	—	203
1948	—	—	—	278
1949	—	—	—	507
1950	—	—	—	—
1951	—	—	—	—
1952	—	—	—	—
1953	1,441	1,557	92.5	—
1954	1,572	1,705	92.2	—
1955	1,805	1,906	92.1	—
1956	2,115	2,303	91.8	371
1957	2,595	2,871	90.4	712

*Current account credits include exports of goods and services, transfer payments, and investment income.

Source: Banco Central de Venezuela, unpublished statistics; and Ministerio de Minas e Hidrocarburos, Petróleo y Otros Datos Estadísticos (Caracas, 1965).

TABLE 5.17

Import Capacity, Net Barter Terms of Trade,
and International Reserves, 1947-57

Year	Import Capacity (index)	Net Barter (index)	International Reserves (millions of dollars)
1947	—	—	234
1948	68.2	141.8	362
1949	61.6	132.5	424
1950	78.0	148.9	342
1951	80.9	136.5	379
1952	87.4	136.8	448
1953	91.8	146.4	494
1954	96.8	142.4	492
1955	111.7	144.5	539
1956	120.9	136.0	927
1957	137.5	137.9	1,396

*1959 = 100.

Source: Banco Central de Venezuela, La Economía Venezolana en los Ultimos Veinticinco Años (Caracas, 1966).

TABLE 5.18

Share of Gold in the International Reserves, 1938-63
(percentages)

Year	Share of Gold	Year	Share of Gold
1938	86.3	1951	100.0
1939	92.7	1952	86.1
1940	81.5	1953	77.9
1941	79.8	1954	84.3
1942	89.4	1955	76.9
1943	87.1	1956	62.7
1944	86.5	1957	47.4
1945	90.2	1958	65.6
1946	85.7	1959	94.1
1947	84.8	1960	73.4
1948	94.6	1961	75.6
1949	84.2	1962	76.2
1950	100.0	1963	60.5

Source: Ministerio de Fomento, Anuario Estadístico, 1957-1963
(Caracas, 1964).

Furthermore, in recent fittings of Cobb-Douglas functions to Venezuelan data, the product-factor partial elasticities of capital were above 0.30.[17] Finally, the impression obtained in conversations with Venezuelan economists, businessmen, and bankers was that the marginal rates of return to capital were without doubt above 20 percent, with an abundance of projects in which such returns could be realized.

Idle resources in the form of excessive international reserves indicate that the contribution of oil during this period was not that effectively utilized. A part was neutralized by the accumulation of reserves beyond the level dictated by the nature of international flows of Venezuela. In fact, in this respect, it appears that the use of foreign exchange funds in the previous period was comparatively superior.

A portion of the foreign exchange proceeds earned by the Venezuelan economy was utilized in the purchase of goods and services or left the country as transfer payments, capital outflows, or other payments abroad. An examination of the composition of the goods imported into the country suggests how well these funds were used. The composition shown in Table 5.19 indicates that these funds were not used inefficiently. Imports of capital goods expanded greatly, and intermediate goods also increased their share somewhat, except for the year 1957.

In summary, oil contributed most of the foreign exchange proceeds of the Venezuelan economy over these years, albeit a contracting portion. At the same time, the value of oil exports expanded considerably, providing the economy with the resources required for adequate growth and stability. Yet, the economy did not utilize this contribution as effectively as in the previous period. Even though the allocation of foreign exchange proceeds, as indicated by the breakdown in goods imports, was not inefficient, excessive international reserves were maintained.

The Fiscal Contribution of Oil

More complete public finance statistics are available for this period, so that it is possible to use figures of revenues and expenditures of the public sector as a whole from 1950 on, including autonomous administrative institutes and state enterprises. So defined, public revenues expanded greatly from 1950 to 1957. By 1957, public revenues had doubled (214), based on an index scale with 1950 equal to 100. This is equivalent to an annual average compounded increase of 11.5 percent (see Table 5.20). Between 1948 and 1949, public revenues, not including enterprises and autonomous administrative institutes, increased by 5.9 percent. From 1949 to 1950, they

TABLE 5.19

Total Imports of Goods, by Type, 1950-57
(percentages)

Year	Investment Goods	Intermediate Goods	Consumer Goods
1950	25.6	41.8	32.6
1951	28.9	43.6	27.5
1952	32.4	42.9	24.6
1953	30.7	42.9	26.4
1954	33.5	41.8	24.7
1955	33.6	44.1	22.3
1956	32.7	43.1	24.3
1957	42.5	39.9	17.6

Note: In constant 1957 prices.

Source: Computed from Banco Central de Venezuela, Memoria (Caracas, 1959), and Informe Económico (Caracas, 1963).

TABLE 5.20

Share of Petroleum Tax Revenues in Total Public Revenues, 1948-57
(in millions of bolívares)

Year	Petroleum	Total	Percent of Share of Petroleum in Total Public Revenues	Increase in Petroleum Taxes
1948	1,163	1,939	60.0	—
1949	1,277	2,169	64.5	114
1950	901	2,796	32.2	-376
1951	1,332	3,235	41.2	431
1952	1,508	3,385	44.5	176
1953	1,606	3,616	44.4	98
1954	1,515	4,022	37.7	-91
1955	1,734	4,469	38.8	219
1956	3,058	6,087	50.2	1,324
1957	3,846	7,283	52.8	788
Period change in petroleum taxes	—	—	—	2,683

Note: For the years 1948 and 1949, autonomous administrative institutes and state enterprises are not included in the total revenues of the public sector. From 1950 on, total revenues are defined as current revenues (ingresos ordinarios), including those corresponding to autonomous institutes in their own right. Petroleum taxes do not include foreign exchange taxes on oil.

Source: Ministerio de Fomento, Anuario Estadístico (Caracas, 1951); Banco Central de Venezuela, Memoria (Caracas, several years), and Informe Económico (Caracas, several years); Ministerio de Minas e Hidrocarburos, Petróleo y Otros Datos Estadísticos (Caracas, 1965); and J. J. Bracho Sierra, Cincuenta Años de Ingresos Fiscales (Caracas, 1963).

declined a little. Although such rate of expansion fell short of that
corresponding to the previous period, it was nonetheless outstanding.

Oil revenues expanded at a faster rate due to the increase in the
value of petroleum output and the payments for the 1956 and 1957
concessions. The 1949 base index rose to 331 in 1957, representing
an annual average compounded rate of growth of 16.1 percent. Between 1948 and 1949, oil revenues experienced an increase of 9.8
percent (see Table 5.20).

If compared to total GDP, oil-derived revenues represent an
average of 11.6 percent of GDP for the period—an increase from the
previous average of 7.5 percent. The participation of oil revenues
in total government revenues increased from 1950 to 1953, diminished
in 1954 and 1955, and rose again in 1956 and 1957. [18] At the end of
the period, they had increased 20 percentage points from 1950.
However, that year was sort of a low base, as petroleum revenues
had diminished sharply between 1949 and 1950. As an average, from
1950 to 1957 petroleum revenues represented 46.0 percent of total
public revenues.

As shown above, oil's contribution to the public sector was
significant in terms of the total activity of the Venezuelan economy
over these years. Moreover, a substantial portion of government
revenues were derived from the petroleum industry. Petroleum-
derived tax receipts expanded considerably, permitting the government
to use funds that otherwise probably would have been sent abroad.
Oil revenues also permitted the government to spend a substantial
amount of funds, without having recourse to deficit financing and with
very little tax pressure on other sectors. If the proceeds from the
foreign exchange levy are added, then the percentage share of oil
in total revenue would be even larger, since substantial revenues
were derived from this source (see Table 5.21).

Have petroleum taxes been appropriated according to adequate
criteria? Since this study aims at determining if and how effectively
the oil sector has been leading economic development in the other
sectors, the appropriate indicator should be the proportion of public
expenditures devoted to the furthering of economic development.
However, it has been impossible to classify expenditures according
to this criterion. Instead, the portion of public expenditures devoted
to capital formation will be used. Although not as inclusive as the
concept of economic development expenditures, which includes public
investment as well as other types of expenditures, it is the best
replacement available.

It is our belief that public capital expenditures are at least as
close as social and economic expenditures (which are too comprehensive) to the concept of economic development expenditures.
Anyhow, it is impossible to continue using the latter concept, as
no estimates are available for most of the recent years. On the
other hand, statistics on public investment are only available since

TABLE 5. 21

Share of Petroleum in Total Public Revenues,
Including Foreign Exchange Taxes on Oil, 1948-57

Year	Oil Foreign Exchange Tax (millions of bolívares)	Share of Oil Taxes (percent)
1948	155	68. 0
1949	153	65. 9
1950	120	36. 5
1951	140	45. 5
1952	171	49. 6
1953	173	49. 2
1954	176	42. 0
1955	196	43. 2
1956	301	55. 2
1957	403	58. 3

Source: Banco Central de Venezuela, Memoria (Caracas, several years), and La Economía Venezolana en los Ultimos Veinticinco Años (Caracas, 1966); and Table 5. 18.

1950. As a result of this conceptual change, and, also, because a different public expenditures definition was used previously, it is also impossible to compare the utilization of oil revenues in this period with preceding ones.

From 1950 on, public expenditures charged to capital account increased in a continuous way, with a single setback occurring in 1952. By 1957, these expenditures had increased by 233 percent, for an average annual compounded rate of growth of 18. 8 percent (see Table 5. 22). As a share of total public expenditures–including state enterprises and autonomous institutions–capital expenditures rose from 37. 1 percent in 1950 to 57. 8 percent in 1957. This increase took place mostly at the end of the period, since the share was quite stable up to 1953.

Another test of the effectiveness in the use of the funds contributed by petroleum is the ratio of public capital expenditures over oil revenues. If the "sow-the-oil" policy was taken seriously, public capital formation should have exceeded the revenues derived from oil. In this period, the ratio was both above and below unity, mostly below. As an average, it was 96. 8 percent, a respectable figure (compare Tables 5. 20 and 5. 22), suggesting again that, in terms of basic apportionment, the potential contribution of oil had been put to good use.

TABLE 5.22

Share of Public Capital Expenditures in Total Public Expenditures, 1950-57
(in millions of bolívares)

Year	Total Public Expenditures	Capital Expenditures	Share of Capital in Total Expenditures	Increases in Capital Expenditures
1950	2,984	1,108	37.1	—
1951	3,205	1,225	38.2	117
1952	3,290	1,194	36.3	-31
1953	3,479	1,281	36.8	87
1954	4,131	1,761	42.6	480
1955	4,503	2,073	46.0	312
1956	5,094	2,675	52.5	602
1957	6,390	3,692	57.8	1,017
Period change in capital expenditures	—	—	—	2,584

Source: Banco Central de Venezuela, Memoria (Caracas, several years).

Finally, although at the beginning of the period the marginal increments in oil revenues were not accompanied by marginal increases in public investment, the situation did change at the end of the period. In fact, by then, the marginal increments in the latter were greater than those in the former. Full use of petroleum tax revenues was partly circumvented by a recurrent preoccupation with balancing the budget that was reminiscent of the Gómez era. In some years, huge amounts were added to Treasury reserves, neutralizing somewhat the potential effects of oil on other sectors of the Venezuelan economy.

In conclusion, the petroleum sector was an even stronger mainstay of government finances during this period. Its revenue expansion permitted the government to greatly expand its own activities without recourse to debt financing, while only light tax pressures were put on the other sectors of the economy. This helps explain how the GDP deflator, despite more than doubling of government expenditures, rose less than 10 percent from 1950 to 1957 (see Appendix, Table A.2, column 1).

Still the contribution of petroleum was not utilized as effectively as in previous periods. Budgetary surpluses became more frequent and larger, thereby neutralizing the potential expansionary effects of oil revenues. This was especially damaging at the end of the period, when unemployment mounted. Stability was not a problem during these years, so that appropriate policies could have exploited the favorable balance-of-payments situation and the budgetary surpluses in order to foster further the country's economic growth and to solve the unemployment problem.

It is apparent that an increasing share of public expenditures was devoted to capital formation throughout the period, with much of the rise in oil revenues apparently being allotted to this purpose. On the other hand, the evidence seems to indicate that all this was accompanied by increasing waste and lower productivity in the use of capital funds by the government.

The Contribution of Petroleum Investment

Capital formation in the Venezuelan economy increased at a fast pace during this period. By 1957, gross domestic investment in constant prices was 49.4 percent above the 1948 level, equivalent to a compounded annual average rate of growth of 4.6 percent. Growth was not continuous, however, and slumps occurred in 1950 and 1955 (see Table 5.23).

However, GDP outpaced capital formation during these years. In 1957, gross fixed domestic investment represented 26.5 percent of GDP, as compared to 38.3 percent in 1948 (see Table 5.23). But the gross investment rate was at its peak during 1948. As an average, the economy devoted more resources to capital formation from 1949

TABLE 5.23

Share of Petroleum Gross Fixed Domestic Investment in Total Gross Fixed Domestic Investment, and Investment Rate, 1948-57

Year	Gross Fixed Domestic Investment			Share of Petroleum (percent)	Investment Rate (percent)
	Total (millions of bolívares)*	Nonpetroleum (millions of bolívares)*	Petroleum (millions of bolívares)*		
1948	4,304	2,706	1,598	37.1	38.3
1949	4,458	3,272	1,186	26.6	38.0
1950	3,234	2,570	664	20.5	25.7
1951	3,573	2,775	798	22.3	25.0
1952	4,379	3,328	1,051	24.0	28.8
1953	4,797	3,790	1,007	21.0	29.5
1954	5,822	4,587	1,135	19.5	32.0
1955	5,363	4,277	1,086	20.3	27.3
1956	5,584	4,232	1,352	24.2	26.2
1957	6,429	4,607	1,822	28.3	26.5

*Constant 1957 bolívares.

Source: Banco Central de Venezuela, unpublished statistics, and Memoria (Caracas, several years); Ministerio de Minas e Hidrocarburos, Petróleo y Otros Datos Estadísticos (Caracas, 1965); Appendix, Table A.2, columns 2 and 3; and Table 5.25. (The total investment figures of the Banco Central were adjusted to take account of the difference between the Banco Central estimates of petroleum gross fixed investment and the estimates of the Ministerio de Minas e Hidrocarburos.)

to 1957 than in the previous period, in which investment was very low at the beginning. In all, the investment rate must be considered highly satisfactory during the period, since it was never under 25 percent.

Investment in the petroleum industry was a substantial share of total investment (see Table 5.23). Nevertheless, as an average, its participation was the lowest ever during any period, partly as a result of a relatively slow (11.8 percent) increase in petroleum investment from 1948 to 1957 in real terms (equivalent to a 1.2 percent average compounded rate per year). Still, it represented well over 20 percent of total investment. The strengthening of the other sectors of the economy during this period also contributed to the lessening of petroleum's participation in total investment. Despite this, the average of petroleum investment in absolute terms was much greater during this period than in previous ones.

The share of investment related strictly to the production of oil grew during these years, as is shown in Table 5.24. This took place, even though it suddenly shrunk in 1956 and 1957. Actually, the participation of investment in purely productive activities changed abruptly as a result of bursts of capital expenditures in refining and transport (see Table 5.24). In Venezuela, spells in refining investment have been usually determined by government influence and generally follow concession periods. This results from the selective concession policy utilized by the Venezuelan government since 1936, in which an expansion in domestic refining is one of the requisites for obtaining (sometimes favorable) concessions. Investment in transport facilities is tied to the exploration, development, and exploitation of new concessions.

The share of transport investment increased during this period from 10 percent to 15 percent, while that of refining investment decreased somewhat, although picking up substantially in 1956 and 1957. Investment in marketing was more or less stable throughout, and all other types of investment expenditures declined considerably.

As could be surmised, nonpetroleum investment expanded much faster than total investment during this period. It grew 70.3 percent from 1948 to 1957 in real terms, equivalent to a 6.1 percent average compounded yearly rate of growth. Nonpetroleum investment grew every year with the exceptions of 1950 and 1955 (see Table 5.23).

Although petroleum investment still was an important determinant of nonpetroleum investment, with a one-year lag, the relationship was not as close during this period. This is understandable in the face of greater independence by the rest of the economy. However, the retained value of total petroleum expenditures should exert a stronger influence on the behavior of nonpetroleum investment.[19] In fact, these variables were closely related during this period, if investment is lagged one year behind retained value. A test of correlation performed on the two variables resulted in an R^2 of .834. The linear regression equation determined by least squares is:

TABLE 5.24

Petroleum Gross Fixed Domestic Investment, by Type, 1948-57

Year	Petroleum Gross Fixed Domestic Investment (millions of bolívares)	Investment in Production (millions of bolívares)	Share of Production (percent)	Investment in Transport (millions of bolívares)	Share of Transport (percent)	Investment in Refining (millions of bolívares)	Share of Refining (percent)	Investment in Marketing (millions of bolívares)	Share of Marketing (percent)	Investment in Other Activities (millions of bolívares)	Share of Other Activities (percent)
1948	1,630	921	56.5	163	10.0	347	21.3	14	0.9	185	11.3
1949	1,127	563	50.0	101	9.0	401	35.6	12	1.1	150	4.3
1950	561	340	60.6	36	6.4	122	21.7	11	2.0	52	9.3
1951	727	508	69.9	107	14.7	54	7.4	4	0.6	54	7.4
1952	967	725	75.0	129	13.3	56	5.8	7	0.7	50	5.2
1953	901	709	78.7	70	7.8	63	7.0	14	1.6	45	4.9
1954	933	689	73.8	67	7.2	104	11.1	14	1.5	59	6.4
1955	928	790	85.1	40	4.3	65	7.0	12	1.3	21	2.3
1956	1,232	779	67.2	121	9.8	233	18.9	14	1.1	13	3.0
1957	1,822	1,204	66.1	274	15.0	268	14.7	18	1.0	58	3.2

Source: Ministerio de Minas e Hidrocarburos, Petróleo y Otros Datos Estadísticos (Caracas, 1965).

$$NPI = -703.076 + 1.371 \quad RV \qquad R^2 = .834$$
$$(.231)$$

where

  NPI = nonpetroleum investment with a one-year lag

and

  RV = retained value of total expenditures.

Nonpetroleum investment almost came up to the retained value amounts during some of these years (compare Table 5.23 and Appendix, Table A.2, column 17). On the basis of this crude test, Venezuela seemed to be devoting to investment purposes an amount almost equivalent to the local payments originating in the petroleum industry. This was an improvement over the previous period.

In summary, the economy's rate of capital formation was most satisfactory during this period, although it was a notch down from the unusually high investment activity of the postwar years.[20] The petroleum industry constituted a declining but significant part of total investment in the period. Investment expenditures in the industry, although expanding at a disappointing rate, still remained quite high as an average during the period, being larger than in any previous period. The oil sector provided a stimulus to the local construction and capital goods industries through these huge investment expenditures.

Finally, investment in the nonpetroleum sectors moved rather consistently with petroleum investment and even more closely with the retained value of total petroleum expenditures. After a one-year lag, changes in the latter were followed by equivalent changes in nonpetroleum gross fixed investment. Thus, there are indications that the behavior of nonpetroleum investment can be explained by the changes in total retained value of oil.

Total Domestic Product and the Expenditures
of the Oil Industry

The value of oil production during this period continued its uninterrupted expansion, although it declined in 1949. To be exact, the expansion from 1948 to 1957 was 141.4 percent, corresponding to a compounded annual average growth rate of 10.3 percent (see Table 5.25). This expansion was smaller than that experienced in the previous period, but nonetheless quite remarkable, especially if the fact that it took place from a higher base value is taken into account.

The participation of petroleum in total GDP (in real terms) hovered between 28.5 percent and 31.3 percent in this period. The share had

TABLE 5.25

Petroleum Gross Domestic Product and the Value
of Oil Production and Retained Value of Total
Expenditures in the Petroleum Industry,
1948-57
(millions of bolívares)

Year	Value of Oil Production	GDP	Retained Value of Total Expenditures in the Petroleum Industry
1948	3,564	2,920	3,167
1949	3,141	2,505	2,385
1950	3,716	2,973	2,451
1951	4,420	3,584	2,809
1952	4,681	3,803	2,990
1953	5,020	3,896	3,329
1954	5,348	4,335	3,542
1955	5,885	4,940	3,542
1956	6,840	5,784	3,806
1957	8,604	7,249	4,840

Source: Ministerio de Minas e Hicrocarburos Petróleo y Otros
Datos Estadísticos (Caracas, 1965), and unpublished statistics; and
data from Appendix, Table A.2, columns 4, 5, 6, 7, 8, 9, 10, 11,
12, and 51.

an erratic movement within this narrow range, experiencing a mild
overall decline from the 1948 level, as can be seen in Table 5.26.[21]
     The strong showing by the petroleum sector resulted from favorable
demand conditions for most of the period. After a mild slump in 1949,
demand picked up, spurred mostly by the Korean hostilities. After
the latter ceased, another moderate lull affected the market, lasting
until 1956, when the situation improved somewhat. During the Suez
Canal crisis that took place in 1957, the demand for Venezuelan oil
and its derivatives skyrocketed, and prices soared. These conditions
prompted increased levels of activity from the oil industry in Venezuela, even though, altogether, the market for oil was not as firm as in
the previous period. As has been seen in the previous section,
investment expenditures were much less affected by all this.
     However, it is through the portion retained in Venezuela that the
increments in the expenditures of the oil industry exert its direct
and most important impact. Therefore, the evolution of retained value
during the period will now be examined.

TABLE 5.26

Share of Petroleum in Gross Domestic Product,
1948-57

Year	Petroleum (millions of bolívares)*	Total (millions of bolívares)*	Share of Petroleum in Total GDP (percent)
1948	3,503	11,225	31.2
1949	3,448	11,726	29.4
1950	3,851	12,593	30.6
1951	4,469	14,270	31.3
1952	4,730	15,202	31.1
1953	4,780	16,257	29.4
1954	5,192	18,222	28.5
1955	5,909	19,645	30.1
1956	6,543	21,281	30.8
1957	7,249	24,295	29.8

*Constant 1957 bolívares.

Source: From Table 5.25; Bernardo Ferrán, lectures on the economic history of Venezuela, given at the Universidad Central de Venezuela, Caracas, 1963; and Banco Central de Venezuela, Memoria (Caracas, several years), and unpublished statistics.

In current bolívares, the retained value of current expenditures more than doubled between 1948 and 1957, but still failed for the first time to grow faster than petroleum GDP. Petroleum GDP increased 148 percent, while retained value of current expenditures only increased 122 percent, both in current bolívares (see Table 5.27). The fact that no new tax increases were imposed on petroleum in this period, coupled with a curtailment in industry employment, determined a lower expansion in the retained value components of value added than in the other components. Except for a mild setback in 1949, the retained value of current expenditures increased every year, although its overall expansion cannot be compared to that of the previous period. As petroleum prices rose throughout the years, the rise in retained value of current expenditures in constant 1957 prices was smaller than in current prices (see Appendix, Table A.2, column 16).

Retained value of current expenditures per barrel of oil produced increased from 1948 to 1957, attaining unequaled highs during this period (see Table 5.27). However, this path was highly erratic over time, and abrupt changes took place quite frequently. Interestingly, the retained value of current expenditures per barrel declined in real terms in the last three years of the period, being much lower in 1957 than in 1948. However, compared with previous ones, the average for this period was nonetheless higher.

The proportion of total value of production that retained value of current expenditures represented decreased sharply at the end of the period. Table 5.28 shows how it hovered at a relatively high level up to 1954 only to fall from 1955 onward. Nevertheless, the average proportion for the period was still higher than that of the previous period.

The retained value of investment expenditures in current bolívares declined from the peak levels of the 1947-49 period, especially if imports of services, which were very low during and before the war, are taken into consideration. If the retained value of both current and investment expenditures are put together in terms of current bolívares, a decline is apparent from the peak 1948 level up to 1952.

TABLE 5.27

Retained Value of Current Expenditures in the
Petroleum Industry, as a Percentage of Total
Current Expenditures in the Industry and per
Barrel of Oil Produced, 1948-57

Year	Retained Value of Current Expenditures (millions of bolívares)	Percentage of Total Current Expenditures	Per Barrel of Oil Produced (bolívares)
1948	2,103	59.0	4.21
1949	1,891	60.2	3.92
1950	2,221	59.8	4.06
1951	2,570	58.1	4.13
1952	2,721	58.1	4.12
1953	3,015	60.1	4.68
1954	3,138	58.7	4.54
1955	3,261	55.4	4.14
1956	3,686	53.9	4.10
1957	4,677	54.4	4.61

Note: The retained value estimates do not include foreign exchange taxes on oil.

Source: Appendix, Table A.2, columns 4, 5, 6, 7, 8, 9, 12, and 21; and Ministerio de Minas e Hidrocarburos, Petróleo y Otros Datos Estadísticos (Caracas, 1965).

It then picks up, surpassing the 1948 level. Nevertheless, this variable's growth (see Table 5.25) is disappointing, compared to the other petroleum indicators already examined in this section. Retained value of total expenditures grew 52.8 percent during the period, equivalent to a compounded annual average of 4.8 percent a year.

In this section, the performance of the oil industry has so far been treated without taking into account the special tax payments for concessions in 1956 and 1957. The performance by the oil industry would certainly look much better if these were added. As pointed out in Chapter 3, these payments are capitalized by the companies and do not affect current expenditures or value added. But, they cannot very well be considered as part of gross domestic investment in the industry and are, therefore, excluded from both the investment and retained value of investment figures for the industry. Nevertheless, these payments are part of the contribution of oil to the Venezuelan economy and have been dealt with accordingly in the section on the industry's fiscal contribution.

If these payments are added to retained value of total expenditures, the results would be quite different. Instead of 3,806 million bolívares and 4,840 million bolívares in 1956 and 1957, respectively, the figures would be 4,780 and 5,982. The expansion throughout the period would become 88.9 percent, for a compounded yearly average of 7.4 percent. Such a performance is still much less impressive than that of the other indicators reviewed above, which is to a great extent due to the lack of expansion in the gross investment of the oil industry throughout the period. [22]

Retained value of total expenditures per barrel shows a decline from the peak 1948 level, even if concession payments are added (see Table 5.28). A comparison with the previous period average shows a gain, though, which would be larger if concessions payments were taken into account. Retained value of total expenditures as a percentage of the value of all petroleum expenditures—value of production plus gross domestic investment—decreased almost continually from 60.9 percent in 1948. In some years, the proportions rose, as in 1950, 1953, and 1954, but these were the exception. Even if concessions payments were added in 1956 and 1957, the share of retained value in total petroleum expenditures would be lower as an average during this period than during the 1943-48 period.

During this period, oil prices increased. Therefore, the increase in retained value of total expenditures expressed in constant 1957 dollars was even lower, as can be seen from Appendix, Table A.2, column 17. The average retained value of total expenditures per barrel during the 1949-57 period, if expressed in constant 1957 prices, drops below the mean for the 1943-48 period. Even if concessions payments are taken into consideration, retained value of total expenditures per barrel, in constant terms, is lower, as an average, and for the year 1957, than the average for the previous period.

TABLE 5.28

Retained Value of Total Expenditures in the Oil Industry
as a Percentage of Total Expenditures and per Barrel of
Oil Produced, 1948-57

Year	Retained Value as a Percentage of Total Expenditures	Per Barrel of Oil Produced (bolívares)
1948	60.9	6.46
1949	55.8	4.95
1950	57.3	4.48
1951	54.5	4.51
1952	52.6	4.51
1953	56.2	5.17
1954	56.3	5.12
1955	51.9	4.50
1956	47.1	4.23
1957	46.4	4.77

Note: Retained value estimates do not include foreign exchange taxes imposed on the oil industry.

Source: Table 5.25; Appendix, Table A.2, columns 3 and 20; and Ministerio de Minas e Hidrocarburos, Petróleo y Otros Datos Estadísticos (Caracas, 1965).

TABLE 5.29

Retained Value in the Oil Industry, as a Percentage
of Total Expenditures and per Barrel of Oil Produced,
Not Including Locally Purchased Foreign Goods, 1948-57

Year	Total Retained Value (millions of bolívares)	Percentage of Total Expenditures	Per Barrel of Oil Produced (bolívares)
1948	3,100	59.6	6.33
1949	2,343	54.9	4.86
1950	2,421	56.6	4.43
1951	2,766	53.7	4.45
1952	2,934	51.6	4.44
1953	3,274	55.3	5.08
1954	3,485	55.2	5.04
1955	3,469	50.9	4.41
1956	3,705	45.9	4.12
1957	4,684	44.9	4.62

Source: From Tables 5.25 and 5.28.

Part of the local procurement undertaken by the oil companies does not end in the purchase of goods produced in Venezuela. Whenever foreign goods are purchased from local importers, the gains to the Venezuelan economy are obviously relatively small. Strictly speaking, only those expenditures destined to pay for local factors, to buy locally produced goods, and to pay taxes to the Venezuelan government should be considered part of retained value. Previous estimates have included these purchases because lack of data made it impossible to take this factor into account in the estimation of retained value. From 1948 the Oficina Técnica de Hidrocarburos began publishing data on local purchases of foreign goods. On the basis of these data, it has been possible to derive a more precise estimate of the retained value of total expenditures, which is presented in Table 5.29.

These estimates of retained value of total expenditures do not depart significantly in their trend from the estimates of retained value presented previously in this section, although their growth since 1948 is smaller. [23]

Although much smaller than in the previous period, the rate of growth in the different indicators of oil activity, such as value of production and retained value, was respectable from 1948 to 1957, especially if concessions payments are taken into account. The only exception was the retained value of investment expenditures, which grew disappointingly. Therefore, the exogenous income-expenditure injections originating in the petroleum industry in this period were substantial, and the total positive contributions of the oil industry to the rest of the Venezuelan economy also appear to have experienced a substantial expansion.

What effects did all this have on the rest of the Venezuelan economy? Were the contributions sufficient to compensate for any unfavorable effects to which the industry might have given rise? And if so, were the net positive effects strong enough to lead to growth in the other sectors?

The Impact of Oil on the Rest of the Economy

The effects of oil in the economy of producing states were not paralleled by population growth. Total labor requirements of the industry actually diminished in absolute terms. A look at the population statistics for the different regional entities or states, compiled in 1950 and 1961, indicate the changes throughout this interval. The average annual rates of growth for the petroleum states expanding their production during the period (Zulia, Anzoátegui, and Barinas) are higher than those for the whole country (see Table 5.30). However, they are smaller than the rate for other areas, notably Caracas. [24] Of course, the petroleum industry also aided the growth in Caracas and in other areas where fast population growth occurred, indirectly

TABLE 5. 30

Average Annual Rates of Growth of Population
for Different States, 1950 and 1961
(percentages)

Region	Rates of Growth
Petroleum states:	
Zulia	4. 95
Anzoátegui	4. 55
Barinas	5. 56
Other states:	
Federal district	5. 74
Aragua	5. 01
Carabobo	4. 51
Miranda	5. 80
Portuguesa	5. 12
Guárico	3. 96
Bolivar	5. 16
Country	3. 99

Source: Ministerio de Fomento, Censo de Población (Caracas, 1950 and 1961).

through purchases and tax contributions. This was especially true of Caracas, where the industry expanded its central administrative headquarters considerably.

As for the Venezuelan economy as a whole, its performance was quite satisfactory. Total GDP doubled in constant prices, doing better than retained value of total expenditures in current terms. It grew 116. 4 percent from 1948 to 1957, which corresponds to an almost 9 percent compounded average rate of increase per year. The higher average investment rate in this period did not bring about a faster rate of growth. This must be interpreted with care, however, as the periods examined are rather short and the difference in rates are quite small.

The average investment rate in this period was 28. 3 percent, higher than the 27. 2 percent average for the previous period. The Venezuelan economy grew at an annual compounded rate of growth of 9 percent from 1948 to 1957 and 13. 5 percent from 1942 to 1948. At first blush, this might appear contrary to Kuznets' findings. However, this evidence must be interpreted with care. The periods examined are rather short, and the difference in rates might not be that large (if any) if the lower 1942 base is taken into account.

In order to better appraise the performance of the other sectors
of the Venezuelan economy, the nonpetroleum GDP should be looked
at. It appears that these sectors grew faster than petroleum during
this period. Nonpetroleum GDP, in constant 1957 bolivares, increased
153. 6 percent, equivalent to a 10. 9 percent annual average compounded rate of growth, from 1948 to 1957 (see Table 5. 31).

The behavior of these different sectors during the period is now
considered. The agricultural sector, including forestry, continued
its disappointing growth in this period. Production increased 29. 3
percent from 1948 to 1957, for a 2. 9 percent annual rate of growth
(see Appendix, Table A. 1). All product groups, except cereals and
the traditional products—coffee and cocoa, had rates of growth higher
than those of the sector as a whole. Sugar, fibers and oils, and
roots and tubers grew fastest, increasing over 100 percent from 1948.
Among roots and tubers, the growth in potato output was extraordinary.
In the cereals group, the production of rice and wheat was especially
disappointing. Then, the doubling in the production of industrial
crops gives evidence of the increasing importance of manufacturing
in the economic life of Venezuela. In toto, the agricultural sector
failed to cover the needs of the Venezuelan population, which expanded at approximately 4 percent per year during this period. [25]

In contrast, the production of manufactures expanded 313. 1
percent from 1948 to 1957 (see Table 5. 32), a 17. 1 percent average
yearly percentage increase. The leather, rubber, and construction
materials industries were the fastest growing. The paper and cardboard industry, the printing industry, the metal industry, and the
vehicle assembly industry also registered high rates of growth,
with the growth in these last two taking place from a particularly
slim base.

The figures that are presented in Table 5. 33 indicate how the
structure of manufacturing was changing. Intermediate and capital
goods industries experienced the fastest growth for the first time,
indicating that the industrial process in Venezuela had achieved a
certain level of sophistication.

The consumption of energy—an indicator of production in the
utilities sector—expanded 39. 4 percent between 1948 and 1950, an
18. 1 percent average rate per year. [26] From 1950 on, there are only
estimates of value added for this sector. Expressed in terms of 1957
bolívares the GDP of this sector grew 244. 9 percent from 1950 to
1957, corresponding to a 19. 3 percent average yearly percentage
increase (see Table 5. 34). This represents a remarkable growth
although from a small base.

Construction activities, the remaining industrial sector, expanded
quite rapidly also. The index of cement consumption, an indicator of
production in this sector, increased 140 percent between 1948 and
1950, which represented an annual average rate of growth of over 50
percent. From 1950 on, GDP estimates for this sector are also avail-

TABLE 5. 31

Nonpetroleum Gross Domestic Product, 1948-57
(millions of constant 1957 bolívares)

Year	Nonpetroleum GDP
1948	5, 462
1949	6, 443
1950	7, 249
1951	8, 185
1952	8, 541
1953	9, 776
1954	11, 205
1955	11, 869
1956	12, 288
1957	13, 854

Source: From Tables 5. 23 and 5. 26.

TABLE 5. 32

Growth of Output in Manufacturing, 1948-57
(index, 1938 = 100)

Year	Index
1948	350
1949	413
1950	538
1951	650
1952	760
1953	880
1954	1, 000
1955	1, 165
1956	1, 273
1957	1, 446

Source: Evelyn M. Baran, The Economic Development of Venezuela
(Ph.D. diss., Radcliffe College, 1959); and Banco Central de Venezuela,
Memoria (Caracas, 1959).

TABLE 5. 33

Manufacturing Production by Industry, and Value Added
for Some Industries, 1948 and 1957

Industry	1948		1957	
	Volume	Index	Volume	Index
Food processing industries:	–	132	–	459
Pasteurized milk[a][b]	15. 7	100	127. 1	810
Milk for butter[a][c]	34. 4	100	50. 0	145
Powdered milk[c]	1. 7	113	4. 5	300
Vegetable oils[c]	10. 1	281	29. 5	819
Peanut oil[c]	0. 5	71	–	–
Sesame oil[c]	1. 3	186	12. 3	1, 757
Coconut oil[c]	1. 3	144	1. 6	178
Cotton oil[c]	0. 2	40	1. 2	240
Canned fish[c]	9. 3	155	13. 7	228
Ground coffee[c][d]	n. a.[o]	–	12. 0	200
Chocolate[a][c]	1. 2	100	2. 2	183
Cookies[c]	6. 3	252	6. 1	244
Pastries[c]	6. 7	216	38. 2	1, 232
Sugar[c]	26. 6	98	192. 8	709
Rice[c]	5. 1	41	27. 1	219
Salt[c]	35. 5	62	85. 7	149
Fruit juices[b][d]	n. a.[o]	–	17. 6	607
Beverage industries:	161. 9	234	408. 9	591
Beer[e]	57. 8	144	153. 9	384
Liquor[e]	5. 6	144	10. 1	259
Rum[e]	4. 6	148	0. 9	29
Gaseous drinks[e]	93. 9	425	244. 0	1, 104
Textile industries:	–	100	–	270
Cotton suits[c]	7. 2	95	–	92
Linen and canvas[c]	3. 7	86	3. 6	84
Cotton cloth[c]	9. 8	104	6. 0	64
Rayon and cotton cloth[c]	n. a.[o]	–	4. 5	–
Cotton knits[f]	0. 3	150	0. 6	300
Cotton bedspreads[g]	0. 07	233	0. 5	1, 667
Cotton blankets[g]	0. 6	150	0. 9	225
Cotton towels[g]	0. 2	50	1. 2	300
Cotton underwear[g]	1. 3	118	1. 5	136
Cotton footwear[g]	1. 6	178	1. 4	156
Rayon cloth[c]	3. 3	194	25. 1	1, 476
Rayon knits[f]	0. 3	750	0. 5	1, 250
Rayon footwear[h]	0. 2	67	0. 05	17
Rayon and cotton footwear[h]	0. 6	86	0. 01	1
Nylon footwear[a][g]	0. 06	100	13. 2	22, 000
Wool suits[c]	0. 09	90	0. 8	778
Wool knits[a][c]	0. 1	100	1. 2	1, 200
Linen cloth[c]	0. 03	30	0. 8	800
Rope[c]	0. 9	129	3. 1	443
Sisal bags[d][g]	n. a.[o]	–	5. 3	1, 060
Leather and hides industry:	–	164	–	905
Leather soles[i]	4. 0	160	5. 0	200
Leather linings[j]	30. 3	168	2, 952. 8	16, 404
Other products[k]	0. 5	167	10. 2	3, 400

	1948		1957	
	Volume	Index	Volume	Index
Paper and cardboard industries[i]	8.7	143	13.6	800
Rubber industries:	72.0	122	1,048.0	1,776
Tires[l]	39.0	115	576.0	1,694
Inner tubes[l]	33.0	132	472.0	1,888
Tobacco industry[g]	1.0	48	3.5	167
Timber industry[k]	58.0	276	206.0	981
Chemical industries:		157		545
Paint[c]	1.4	140	18.1	1,810
Distilled alcohol[e]	3.0	125	5.5	229
Soap[c]	20.0	131	18.2	119
Candles[a c]	2.6	100	5.4	208
Matches[g]	n.a.[o]	–	8.1	–
Industrial gas[a m]	0.7	100	3.0	429
Animal feed[f]	10.3	181	84.9	1,489
Metal industries:	n.a.[o]	–	–	562
Nails[d n]	n.a.[o]	–	7.5	313
Tin cans[d n]	n.a.[o]	–	17.8	848
Vehicle assembly industries:[d]	n.a.[o]	–	–	493
Passenger[l]	n.a.[o]	–	8.9	12,714
Commercial[l]	n.a.[o]	–	5.9	203
Construction materials industries:	215.0	187		2,251
Portland cement[n]	215.0	187	1,747.0	1,519
Lime[d n]	n.a.[o]	–	57.0	116
Cement blocks[d l]	n.a.[o]	–	220.0	105
Cement tubes[d l]	n.a.[o]	–	0.9	–
Mosaics, and so forth[d n]	n.a.[o]	–	616.0	132
Bricks and tiles[d l]	n.a.[o]	–	134.0	151
	Value Added		Value Added	
Furniture[p q]	100		181	
Painting[p q]	100		483	
Machine construction and repair[p q]	100		175	

[a]Index with 1948 = 100.
[b]Thousands of liters.
[c]Thousands of metric tons.
[d]Index with 1950 = 100.
[e]Millions of liters.
[f]Millions of kilograms.
[g]Millions of units
[h]Millions of pairs.
[i]Meters.
[j]Thousands of square feet.
[k]Thousands of cubic meters.
[l]Thousands of units.
[m]Millions of cubic meters.
[n]Millions of metric tons.
[o]Not available.
[p]In constant 1957 bolívares.
[q]Value added.

Source: Juan P. Pérez Castillo, Some Aspects of Venezuela's Economic Development: 1945-1960 (Ph.D. diss., Tulane University, 1963), corrected for certain errors in the computation of the index numbers.

able. As can be seen in Table 5. 34, the construction industry did
not expand as fast as the other components of industrial product from
1950 to 1957, although there are indications that the growth of this
sector was underestimated in the national accounts. Its rate of
increase—in terms of constant 1957 bolívares—was 191. 1 percent
overall during the period, for an average of 9. 7 percent per year.

Extractive activities—oil excluded—expanded over 20 times from
the 1948 base, the highest rate of growth of all (see Table 5. 34).
A very substantial expansion in the mining of iron ore was responsible
for such extraordinary growth. The expansion, which corresponded
to an annual average compounded rate of growth of approximately
42 percent, can be largely explained in terms of the relative unimpor-
tance of mining in the total product of Venezuela at the beginning of
the period. In 1950, the share of GDP, in constant bolívares, corresponding to mining was a little over one-tenth of 1 percent.

Data on tertiary production are available for the first time in
this period. The GDP of this sector, in constant 1957 bolívares, is
presented in Table 5. 34. Total tertiary activities—public services
included—expanded 78. 8 percent from 1950 to 1957, for an 8. 7
percent annual average rate of growth. Commercial activities experienced the fastest expansion within the sector, growing over 100
percent from 1950 to 1957.

Basic to the growth in manufacturing output occurring during this
period was the expansion in aggregate demand resulting from increasing
petroleum activity, high levels of public expenditures, and rising exports. Venezuela's market enlarged to the extent that domestic
production of certain manufactured goods became economically feasible.
At the same time, the government continued its promotion of these
activities by restraining import competition, facilitating loans, and
other similar promotion measures. Lastly, the strong balance-of-
payments position was instrumental in unrestrictedly fulfilling the
requirements of intermediate and capital goods of the sector at
relatively low cost.

The rest of the industrial sector was influenced to an even greater
extent by the expansion of public expenditures. Between 75 percent
and 80 percent of total construction was financed by public institutions
in this period, and the utilities sector was dominated by government
enterprises. [27]

Some of the factors that created a favorable climate for the rising
industrial production were also conducive to higher levels of agricultural production. The meager growth in this sector—in spite of these
incentives—is explained by a lack of appropriate promotion policies.
Even though the need for infrastructure investments was heeded, no
efforts were devoted to the solution of basic institutional problems.
The land tenure system, unavailability of credit and extension services, lack of agricultural research and the implementation of its
findings, and a backward production and marketing organization im-
peded satisfactory progress in agriculture.

TABLE 5.34

Gross Domestic Production in the Utilities,
Construction, and Tertiary Sectors and
Growth of Output in Extractive Activities,
1948-57

Year	Utilities Sector (millions of bolívares)[a]	Construction Industry (millions of bolívares)[a]	Extractive Activities (index)[b]
1948	–	–	248
1949	–	–	293
1950	69	827	293
1951	83	1,032	558
1952	97	1,144	977
1953	119	1,220	1,058
1954	135	1,376	–
1955	159	1,363	–
1956	187	1,605	–
1957	238	1,581	–

Year	Transport and Communications (millions of bolívares)	Tertiary Sector Commerce (millions of bolívares)[a]	Tertiary Sector Services (millions of bolívares)[a]
1948	–	–	–
1949	–	–	–
1950	699	1,726	3,301
1951	706	1,983	3,528
1952	675	2,085	3,760
1953	842	2,291	4,086
1954	876	2,678	4,383
1955	951	2,862	4,636
1956	945	3,156	4,963
1957	940	3,933	5,365

[a]Constant 1957 bolívares.
[b]1936 = 100.

Source: Banco Central de Venezuela, La Economía Venezolana en los Últimos Veinticinco Años (Caracas, 1966), and Memoria (Caracas, 1959); and Evelyn M. Baran, The Economic Development of Venezuela (Ph.D. diss., Radcliffe College, 1959).

The oil industry, particularly through its fiscal sector–balance-of-payments and income-expenditure contributions–was of central importance in bringing about an expansion in the industrial sectors and in the rest of the economy. If the retained value of total expenditures is related to nonpetroleum GDP, with a one-year lag, a respectably high correlation coefficient is found. Simple regression analysis performed on these two variables resulted in the following regression equation:

$$NPP = -3127.553 + 4.043 \quad RV \qquad R^2 = .696$$
$$(1.008)$$

where

NPP = nonpetroleum GDP, with a one-year lag

and

RV = retained value of total expenditures.

Retained value of total expenditures, the summary indicator of all combined contributions of oil, expanded at a satisfactory pace during the period, appearing to have sparked the expansion in the other sectors of the economy. In fact, almost 70 percent of the changes in the latter can be explained by the variation of total retained value. Thus, the petroleum sector appears to have behaved like a leading sector during these years. Given that petroleum activities led the growth of the Venezuelan economy in the 1949-57 period, then any unfavorable effects on the other sectors must have been neutralized by policy decisions or compensated by part of the contributions or favorable effects of the industry.

The industrial statistics available are not fine enough for pin-pointing which were the main industries directly affected by the expansion in petroleum activities. However, it seems reasonable to venture that through the backward linkages of the industry, and of the government expenditures it supports, a strong demand for metal products, energy, construction activities, and services was created. On the other hand, forward-linking industries experienced considerable growth. The output of petroleum products increased seven times during this period. Finally, the use of natural gas for domestic consumption, and of natural gas and heavy oil for the production of electricity, materialized and expanded during these years.

The process of import substitution became a more important force in the economy during this period. It advanced the furthest in industry, aided by multipronged promotion devices. This constituted the first inkling of the possibility of future economic growth with a certain degree of independence from petroleum. Although a somewhat less important but similar expansion had occurred in the previous period, it was spurred by the artificiality of war conditions.

Government policy was less successful in extracting from oil its potential contribution during this period. Therefore, the expansion in retained value resulted, to a great extent, from the automatic growth in the economic activities of the industry, working within a policy framework mostly engineered in the previous period. Furthermore, previous sections indicate that the use of the oil contribution by the economy was somewhat less effective in these years, as a result of a less-enlightened government policy.

The total combined contribution of oil to the other sectors of the economy expanded at a much lower rate during this period, relative to the foregoing one. Yet, the size of the petroleum sector should be taken into consideration when comparing the contributions in each period. Due to the smaller size of the oil industry in the 1943-48 period, the average absolute yearly increase in its total combined contribution was smaller than the corresponding rise in the contributions in the 1948-57 period. In fact, if the overall absolute contributions are compared to the size of nonpetroleum activity at the beginning of the respective periods, which is a more appropriate way of evaluating them, the difference in the increase in the contributions is not so great. During the 1943-48 period, the increase represented 77.3 percent of the value of nonpetroleum GDP in 1942, while for the 1949-57 period, the figure was 71.5 percent. However, the latter period is longer, which raises its corresponding percentage.

Thus, it appears that the actual increase in the total combined contribution of the petroleum sector to the rest of the Venezuelan economy was greater in the earlier period. If the effectiveness in the use of this contribution is considered, the comparison would even be more favorable to the 1943-48 period.

Venezuela grew satisfactorily, even in terms of GDP per inhabitant in constant bolívares. It grew from 2,518 bolívares in 1950 to 3,661 bolívares in 1957, which amounted to a 5.5 percent compounded annual rate. But, more importantly, this period witnessed what apparently were the initial steps in the transformation of Venezuela into an economy less dependent on oil, with the basic conditions and productive structure permitting self-sustained growth.

NOTES

1. The Hydrocarbons Law of 1943 put an end to the haggling over exemptions to imports by petroleum companies. These were to be restricted to the cases in which there was no domestic production of the goods in question. Although the Venezuelan government had objected to a blind application of the exemption provisions in 1938—and from then on it did not grant the exemptions unquestioningly—this was still a controversial and unresolved issue.

2. In order to make this comparison for the government sector as a whole, as the latter has been defined before, it was necessary to assume that the percentage of social and economic expenditures in the federal budget was equally applicable to state and municipal expenditures. No actual data on the composition of the latter are available. Note, however, that they constitute only a very small part of total government expenditures, as is shown in Table 5. 7.

3. Both in 1957 bolívares.

4. In his study, Kuznets compared investment rates and rates of economic growth for particular countries for long periods of time.

5. See Banco Central de Venezuela, Memoria (Caracas, 1949), p. 81.

6. The industry had to provide its workers with certain facilities according to legislation enacted in 1922. This requirement was further strengthened by new legislation in 1928 and, then, by the 1936 labor law and the post-World War II collective agreements.

7. Reference has been made only to those portions of value added in the petroleum industry that are connected with the production of petroleum. Some of the industry's factor and tax payments are capitalized, deriving from the production of capital goods undertaken by the industry for its own use (Appendix, Table A. 2, column 14). If these are added to the estimates presented above, the importance of oil in the economy would be greater.

8. Moreover, as a result of shortages of certain goods during the war and postwar periods and of increased domestic production of industrial goods, the petroleum industry found it increasingly convenient to turn to native sources for its requirements of goods and services.

9. Because the geographic pattern of production and government expenditures converged in Caracas, it turned out that most of the growth taking place outside the petroleum states occurred there.

10. See Economic Commission for Latin America, United Nations, Recent Facts and Trends in the Venezuelan Economy (México, D. F., 1951), p. 54.

11. See Juan P. Pérez Castillo, Some Aspects of Venezuela's Economic Development: 1945-1960 (Ph. D. diss., Tulane University, 1963), Appendix Table G-4.

12. See United Nations, Statistical Yearbook (New York: United Nations, 1954), p. 277.

13. Prices increased much less, close to 50 percent in this period, so the increase in real terms was still formidable.

14. See Banco Central de Venezuela, La Economía Venezolana en los Ultimos Veinticinco Años (Caracas, 1966), Sector Petróleo.

15. As a percentage of total GDP in current bolívares, exports climbed from 32 percent at the end of the previous period to 38 percent in 1957.

16. On this, see Ministerio de Fomento, Anuario Estadístico 1957-1963 (Caracas, 1964).

17. See Banco Interamericano de Desarrollo, Datos Básicos y Parámetros Socio-Económicos de Venezuela, 1950-1965 (Washington, D.C., 1967), Table 2.

18. Only from 1950 on are revenue data presented for the public sector as a whole. Percentage shares from previous years are not directly comparable.

19. It should be remembered that the retained value of total expenditures includes taxes paid to the government by the petroleum industry, an important determinant of public investment, which is part of nonpetroleum investment. It is impossible to separate public from private investment in the Venezuelan national account statistics.

20. Those high rates were actually rather abnormal, as they were mainly caused by the pent-up demand built during the war. Moreover, quite extraordinary investment expenditures took place in the petroleum industry during these years. A continuation of such high investment rates was not to be expected.

21. If the income originated in the oil industry through the production of capital goods for its own use is added, the participation of oil becomes even greater. See Appendix, Table A.2, column 14, for these estimates.

22. This partly resulted from the fact that investment in the industry outstripped the growth of production in the previous period, as capacity expanded, based on the expectation of rising demand, and postponed wartime investment requirements were satisfied. Furthermore, the 1947-49 level of investment was undoubtedly affected by a combination of intensive exploration of new concessions, enormous increase in refining capacity, an expansion of the oleoduct-gas duct-storage-terminal transportation system for the industry.

23. It is impossible to determine if the local purchases of foreign goods are for investment purposes or not. Therefore, this adjustment can only be made for retained value of total expenditures as a whole and not for its current and investment components.

24. The Caracas area continued to be favored in the geographical distribution of government expenditures. So was the state of Bolivar starting at the end of the period.

25. Heavy immigration took place over these years.

26. See Evelyn M. Baran, The Economic Development of Venezuela (Ph.D. diss., Radcliffe College, 1959).

27. See Banco Central de Venezuela, Memoria (Caracas, 1959), pp. 154 ff.

6

THE CONTRIBUTION OF
PETROLEUM AND ITS
EFFECTS ON THE
ECONOMIC DEVELOPMENT
OF VENEZUELA, 1958-73

The next decade and a half in the evolution of the Venezuelan economy, and the influence that oil had on the country's development, will be explored in this chapter. After the climax reached at the end of the previous period, the potential contribution of oil appeared to experience a relative decline. However, in 1973, with an excess demand situation in the world market for oil, which seemingly would keep oil prices at a high level for at least five years more, a reversal of this trend appeared probable.

Again, in order to best examine petroleum's contribution to the economic development of Venezuela and to see how effectively it was used—and thus evaluate the role of oil as a potentially leading sector—two subperiods will be considered. The first begins in 1958, with the revolutionary and democratic regimes that supplanted the military rule of Pérez Jiménez, which brought about a policy of no new oil concessions and tougher tax laws applicable to petroleum. It ends just after Romulo Betancourt had finished his period as the first democratically elected Venezuelan president in 15 years, in 1965. During the second subperiod, the democratic process is consolidated in Venezuela, and an increasingly tougher stance toward the oil industry takes shape. Not only are oil income taxes raised, so that over 80 percent of profits accrue to the state, but new exploration and development of petroleum only takes place through service contracts rather than concessions. By 1973, steps related to the eventual nationalization of the oil concessions, which is supposed to take place in 1983, were taken. However, with the rise of oil prices, there was increasing talk about the possibility of accelerating nationalization, so that it would take place sooner than had been planned.

THE 1958-65 SUBPERIOD

The Foreign Sector Contribution

More detailed balance-of-payments calculations since 1953 have made possible the measurement of the gross balance-of-payments contributions of the oil sector in terms of the current account credits it generates. In current dollars, these credits experienced an overall decline from the peak year of 1957. Its behavior over time was erratic, decreasing from 1957 to 1960 and then increasing to 1965 (see Table 6.1). Oil current account credits also declined in current dollars. Their behavior throughout these years was more erratic than that of total current account credits, with their decline being more pronounced in relative terms. Therefore, the share of oil in the total came down from 90.4 percent in 1957 to 89.1 percent in 1965.

Oil still represented the salient source of export earnings at the end of the period. Thus, its gross balance-of-payments contribution was substantial. On the other hand, the current account credits of the petroleum industry failed to provide an expanding base, which the economy could use to cover increasing needs for payments abroad. As total GDP increased throughout these years, the proportion that exports represented of the total product of Venezuela contracted significantly.

The net balance-of-payments contribution of oil is measured by the foreign currency turned in by the industry as a percentage of all foreign exchange proceeds. This contribution is net in the sense that the oil industry does not use these exchange proceeds at all. They are entirely at the disposal of the rest of the economy. The foreign exchange proceeds derived from oil also contracted during this period, as can be seen in Table 6.2. However, even then, their share in total foreign exchange proceeds increased from 66.4 percent in 1957 to 72.2 percent in 1965.

Only in 1958 and 1959 did the oil industry need to rely on capital inflows for the financing of its operations, particularly its investment program. Since then, the industry has been repatriating its capital. [1]

Doubtless, the Venezuelan economy did not experience an export-oriented development from 1957 on. Although oil bounced back about the middle of the period, this was only a recovery. Inflationary forces were held in check during these years though, and the growth of the economy continued. In order to come up with these results despite stagnating exports, selective exchange controls had to be imposed at the end of 1960, and Venezuela had to dig into its international reserves and negotiate diverse loans. The controls were not harsh, but a divergence between the official and free market foreign exchange selling rates ensued in 1961, culminating on the official devaluation of the bolívar in 1964.

TABLE 6.1

Share of Petroleum in Current Account Credits and in
Total Foreign Exchange Earnings, 1957-65

	Current Account Credits			Foreign Exchange Earnings		
Year	Petroleum (millions of dollars)	Total (millions of dollars)	Share of Petroleum (percent)	Petroleum (millions of dollars)	Total (millions of dollars)	Share of Petroleum (percent)
1957	2,595	2,871	90.4	1,761	2,464	66.4
1958	2,324	2,590	89.7	1,340	1,971	68.0
1959	2,169	2,487	87.2	1,611	2,167	74.3
1960	2,183	2,478	88.1	1,406	2,521	55.8
1961	2,264	2,492	90.9	1,350	1,741	77.5
1962	2,366	2,592	91.3	1,255	1,603	78.3
1963	2,360	2,594	91.0	1,351	1,669	80.9
1964	2,362	2,611	90.5	1,398	1,850	75.6
1965	2,330	2,616	89.1	1,371	1,899	72.2

Source: Banco Central de Venezuela, Memoria (Caracas, several years), and Informe Económico (Caracas, several years).

In the end, all this seems to have provoked a shift in Venezuela's import ratios, and from 1963 on, reserves began piling up again. [2] Finally, both the net barter terms of trade and the import capacity terms of trade of Venezuela deteriorated during this period, with export prices declining sharply and import prices increasing substantially (see Table 6. 2).

The expansion in GDP in real terms amounted to a 6 percent compounded average per year, with unemployment spreading throughout the period. Unemployment could have conceivably been reduced if international reserves would have been used more fully. However, maintaining such a high level of international reserves—close to $600 million at the lowest point—might have been totally justified under the conditions of lack of confidence and uncertainty characterizing this period. Nonetheless, it appears, that this policy was too cautious at the end, when reserve accumulation started again. The level of international reserves is shown in Table 6. 2.

The effective utilization of international means of payment provided by balance-of-payments credits can be measured by the composition of some of the corresponding debits. Concentrating on the composition of imported goods, for the reasons given above, a decreasing trend in the share of investment goods in total imports is found (see Table 6. 3). Both the participation of intermediate and consumer goods in total imports rose, especially the former. Therefore, the evolution of the import pattern of the Venezuelan economy up to 1961 indicates a somewhat ineffective utilization of foreign exchange proceeds, reflecting, to an important degree, a decline in aggregate investment. Nevertheless, the pattern of imports turned for the better from 1962 on. [3]

The importance of oil as a generator of foreign exchange was still large during this period. Nevertheless, oil exports and foreign exchange proceeds failed to expand at a satisfactory pace. If other factors, like the depletion of international reserves, increased foreign lending, and, later, the devaluation of the bolívar, had not compensated for this, the economy would have been more seriously affected. [4] Overall, the utilization of the international reserves of Venezuela improved in comparison with the previous period. In contrast, the allocation of the balance-of-payments credits by Venezuela appears to have deviated from an efficient norm during part of the period, which had not been the case previously.

The Fiscal Contribution of Oil

Although public revenues experienced a sharp setback in 1958, this was almost totally made up in 1959. It is impossible to make a comparison between 1959 and 1960, because of a change in the manner of presentation of the public sector accounts. From 1960 on,

TABLE 6.2

Import Capacity and Net Barter Terms of Trade
and International Reserves, 1957-65

Year	Import Capacity (index)*	Net Barter (index)*	International Reserves (millions of dollars)
1957	136.0	136.0	$1,396
1958	127.8	127.8	1,011
1959	100.0	100.0	709
1960	99.0	94.1	605
1961	99.7	93.7	585
1962	99.9	86.7	583
1963	108.9	93.1	740
1964	114.7	93.1	835
1965	106.1	84.7	853

*1959 = 100.

Source: Banco Central de Venezuela, La Economía Venezolana
en los Ultimos Treinta Años (Caracas, 1971).

TABLE 6.3

Composition of Goods Imports, by Type, 1957-65
(current bolívares)

Year	Investment Goods	Intermediate Goods	Consumer Goods
1957	42.5	39.9	17.6
1958	35.5	42.1	22.3
1959	32.4	40.3	27.3
1960	24.6	45.4	30.0
1961	17.2	51.3	31.5
1962	19.7	53.7	26.6
1963	21.3	56.1	22.6
1964	25.6	54.6	19.8
1965	26.6	55.5	17.9

Source: Computed from Banco Central de Venezuela, Memoria
(Caracas, several years), and Informe Económico (Caracas, several
years).

public revenues are defined as the total revenues of the national government, states, and municipalities, in addition to the revenues received by autonomous administrative institutes in their own right (state enterprises are not included). These revenues increased every year from 1960 on (see Table 6.4), and if 1960 is taken as the base (equal 100), 1965 would represent 148. This is approximately equal to an 8.1 percent rate of growth per year as an average, meaning that during this entire period, public revenues expanded more rapidly than GDP in current bolívares.

Oil revenues increased considerably, after having suffered a decrease in 1958. From then on, their increase was quite rapid (see Table 6.4), which can be attributed to the following: (a) the tax reform of 1958, which introduced the "60-40" sharing of oil benefits in place of the "50-50" formula; (b) the establishment of the "pay-as-you-go" system, which made tax payments due every month of the current year, rather than payable the year after; and (c) the devaluation

TABLE 6.4

Total Public Revenues and Tax Revenues Collected
from Petroleum, Not Including Foreign Exchange
Taxes on Oil, 1957-65

Year	Total[a] (millions of bolívares)	Petroleum[b] (millions of bolívares)	Petroleum Share (percent)
1957	7,283	3,846	52.8
1958	5,870	2,740	46.7
1959	7,023	3,253	46.3
1960	5,548	3,036	54.7
1961	6,366	3,289	51.7
1962	6,539	3,280	50.2
1963	7,340	3,659	49.9
1964	8,036	4,803	59.8
1965	8,202	4,863	59.3

[a]Revenues refer to current revenues (ingresos ordinarios). From 1957 to 1959, the figures cover the whole public sector. From 1960 on, they do not include state enterprises.

[b]Does not include foreign exchange taxes on oil and 1957 concession payments.

Source: Banco Central de Venezuela, Memoria (Caracas, several years), Informe Económico (Caracas, several years), and unpublished statistics; Ministerio de Minas e Hidrocarburos, Petróleo y Otros Datos Estadísticos (Caracas, 1965); and J. J. Bracho Sierra, Cincuenta Años de Ingresos Fiscales (Caracas, 1963).

in the exchange rate of 1964, which augmented petroleum tax receipts in terms of bolívares.

If the foreign exchange tax is also taken into account, a completely different picture of the oil contribution to government revenues is obtained. Considered as a loss of income to the oil sector and as a source of revenue to the government, the proceeds from this tax had increased slowly over time. [5] They jumped to a higher level in 1956 and hovered around it until 1960, as a result of increased investment activity related to the mid-1950 concessions (see Table 6.5). Because the partial devaluation of 1961 did not apply to the petroleum rate, the revenues lost by the petroleum industry as a result of the foreign exchange regulations soared. A dollar sold by the companies to the Central Bank for 3.09 bolívares could be ultimately bought by the purchasers of dollars at 4.50 bolívares or more. However, when, in 1964, the government brought the petroleum rate closer into line with the general official rate, these taxes went down abruptly. [6]

Until now, it has been possible to talk about petroleum taxes with and without the inclusion of the foreign exchange tax. This manner of presentation did not present any problems, as long as the foreign exchange tax followed closely the movement of all the other petroleum taxes. But a computation of petroleum taxes without the inclusion of the exchange tax during this period shows that the contribution of oil to the public sector increased in 1964 and 1965; while, if the exchange tax is included, the opposite conclusion is reached. [7] A similar problem occurs with respect to the 1961 statistics. Although in this case the alternative ways of expressing the contribution of oil coincide in the direction of the change, they differ substantially as to the amount. The increase in oil revenues, not including the foreign exchange tax, is over 200 million bolívares. If the latter is considered, the figure jumps to about 1.9 million bolívares.

Unequivocably, the figures that should be used to indicate the contribution of oil are the ones including the foreign exchange tax. Oil revenues, when defined in this fashion, experienced a decrease in 1958 (see Table 6.5), and from then on, the year to year variations were mixed, with increases in 1959, 1961, and 1963. [8] In 1963, oil revenues were the highest they had ever been, experiencing the above referred cutbacks in 1964 and 1965. Overall, petroleum tax revenues increased 17.2 percent from 1957 to 1965. Over the 1958-65 period, the increase amounted to 63.3 percent. The 1957-65 expansion rate is equal to a compounded annual average of 2.0 percent; in the 1958-65 period, expansion represents approximately a 7.2 percent compounded average rate of growth per year.

The share of oil in public revenues decreased in 1958 and 1959, although it still was much greater than the average share during the 1950-55 period. Total revenues decreased 3.5 percent from 1957 to 1959; oil revenues declined 15 percent during the same time span.

Public revenues before and after 1960 are not comparable. However, from 1960 to 1965, total revenues increased at an average

TABLE 6. 5

Tax Revenue Collected from the Petroleum Industry,
Including Foreign Exchange Taxes on Oil, 1957-65*

Year	Total (millions of bolívares)	Foreign Exchange (millions of bolívares)	Petroleum Share (percent)
1957	4, 249	403	68. 3
1958	3, 050	310	52. 0
1959	3, 609	356	51. 4
1960	3, 342	307	60. 2
1961	5, 247	1, 958	82. 4
1962	5, 101	1, 821	78. 0
1963	5, 625	1, 966	76. 6
1964	4, 901	98	61. 0
1965	4, 980	117	60. 7

*The sizeable 1957 concession revenues are not included.

Source: Computed from Banco Central de Venezuela, La Economía Venezolana en los Ultimos Veinticinco Años (Caracas, 1966), Memoria (Caracas, several years), and Informe Económico (Caracas, several years).

compounded rate of 8. 1 percent yearly. Overall, oil revenues increased a little bit faster (8. 3 percent annually). Therefore, the share of oil in total government receipts increased slightly from 1960 to 1965.

If the 1958-65 period is taken as a whole, it seems that total public revenues fared slightly better than oil revenues. This had not occurred before, which could be taken as a sign of diversification in the Venezuelan economy.

Tables 6. 4 and 6. 5 show that the contribution of oil to public revenues has been quite important, either with or without the foreign exchange tax. The average for the years 1958 and 1959 is 46. 5 percent without the foreign exchange tax and 51. 6 percent with it. For the 1960-65 interval, these percentages are 54. 6 percent and 69. 5 percent, respectively. Expressed as a part of GDP, the contribution of oil through tax funds was 15. 3 percent of GDP with the foreign exchange tax and 12. 4 percent without it during the 1958-65 spell. This is a substantial contribution in terms of the public sector and the economy as a whole.

The Utilization of Oil's Fiscal Contribution

How well were the contributions of oil to government revenues utilized? One thing is evident from the start: there were no accumu-

lations of Treasury reserves during this period. If anything, the
pattern seems to have changed. Balanced budgets are not to be found
until 1963.

Contrary to public revenue data, which present a break in the
middle of the period because of a definitional change, there is con-
tinuity in the public expenditure series. It shows that total expenditures increased at a very fast pace during these years. Between 1957
and 1965, an overall increase of 50. 2 percent was experienced, for
a yearly rise of 5. 2 percent. From 1958 to 1965, the increase came
to 32. 2 percent, which represents a 4. 1 percent rate of growth per
year (see Table 6. 6). When compared with the trajectory of public
revenues, it is seen that public expenditures behaved differently.
They increased substantially up till 1960, when public revenues were
slightly declining. From then on, they rose at a slower pace than
public revenues did.

Thus a good portion of public expenditures had to be debt financed.
While the participation of oil in public finances has been examined
just in relation to tax revenues, the importance of petroleum in all
government revenues is as great or maybe greater. The petroleum
sector had an important share in the financing of the government
deficit, specifically by purchasing a substantial number of Treasury
bills and other credit documents. In fact, the oil sector has contri-

TABLE 6. 6

Total Public Expenditures and the Share of
Public Investment, 1957-65*

Year	Investment Expenditures (millions of bolívares)	Total Expenditures (millions of bolívares)	Share of Invest- ment in Public Expenditures (percent)
1957	3, 693	6, 390	57. 8
1958	3, 190	7, 261	43. 9
1959	2, 692	7, 669	35. 1
1960	3, 881	7, 396	52. 5
1961	3, 925	8, 540	46. 0
1962	3, 376	7, 954	42. 4
1963	3, 129	8, 678	36. 0
1964	3, 118	9, 050	34. 5
1965	2, 842	9, 601	29. 6

*Includes state enterprises.

Source: Banco Central de Venezuela, Memoria (Caracas, several
years), Informe Económico (Caracas, several years), and unpublished
data.

buted more in this respect than any other sector. Clearly, however, petroleum tax revenues did not increase fast enough to obviate the need for deficit financing or to spare the other sectors from higher tax pressures.

As to the basic allocation of public expenditures between capital and current expenditures, reference is made to Table 6.6. Capital expenditures—the best available indication of economic development expenditures—contracted from 1958 to 1965 by 11 percent. There was also a decline from 1957 to 1958. The share of public investment in total investment, which stood at 57.8 percent in 1957, shrank to 29.6 percent in 1965. The process, nevertheless, was not a smooth one, with sharp increases in capital expenditures in 1960 and 1961, after decreases in 1958 and 1959. From 1962 on, capital expenditures declined again. The same pattern is exhibited by capital expenditures expressed as a share of total expenditures.

The average share of capital expenditures was somewhat smaller during this period when compared with the previous one. From 1950 to 1957, the average share of capital expenditures in the public sector was 45.4 percent, while from 1958 to 1965 it was 39.5 percent. Nevertheless, if 1956 and 1957 are excluded, the comparison is not so much in favor of the former.

On the other hand, during this period, the allocation of investment funds seems to have improved considerably. Waste was greatly eliminated. The apportionment of investment funds among different sectors was more closely in agreement with sound investment criteria, and the breakdown between investments in directly productive activities and social overhead capital seems to have improved also.

Finally, how do capital expenditures in the public sector compare with oil revenues during this period? At the beginning, public investments, including those in state enterprises, were usually larger than oil revenues, with foreign exchange taxes not included. From 1963 on, however, the pattern was inverted, with capital expenditures usually being much smaller than petroleum taxes. If proceeds from the foreign exchange tax are included, then the revenues derived from the oil sector were higher than public investments in every year. However, for the whole period, it is evident that the increments in oil revenues were not devoted to increased public investment, whether oil taxes are included or not. Yet, up to 1960 (see Table 6.7), oil revenues and government investment are closely tied.

The government used oil revenues for current expenditures to a greater extent during this period than in the past, which certainly jibes with the lower rate of capital accumulation found. The "sow the oil" policy, which asserted that oil funds were to be devoted to economic development expenditures, appears not to have been followed.

Summary

To review, oil revenues failed to expand at an appropriate pace during this period, and, as a result, the other sectors of the economy

TABLE 6. 7

Changes in Oil Revenues and Changes in
Public Investment, 1957-65*
(millions of bolívares)

Year	Yearly Change in Oil Revenues	Yearly Change in Public Investment
1957	–	–
1958	-1, 106	-502
1959	513	-498
1960	-217	1, 189
1961	253	44
1962	-9	-549
1963	379	-247
1964	1, 144	-11
1965	60	-276
Period change	1, 017	-850

*Not including foreign exchanges taxes on oil; includes state enterprises.

Source: Tables 6. 4 and 6. 6.

had to bear an increasing tax pressure. Nevertheless, two different stages must be distinguished: (a) up to 1960, in which petroleum taxes experienced a declining trend from 1957 levels; and (b) from 1961 on, in which an opposite trend sets in, with the peak attained in 1963 but with sharp decreases in 1964 and 1965.

On the other hand, it is difficult to determine if the contribution of oil was used more effectively than in the previous period. Oil funds devoted to capital formation were disappointingly low, and the share of capital expenditures in the total activities of the public sector decreased. But these things were compensated for by a fuller use of revenues–since the government did not indulge in the accumulation of treasury reserves–and a more efficacious allocation of investment funds.

Overall, the impact of the oil sector on the rest of the economy through the government was disappointing during this period, if compared with the previous one, because of a less-important petroleum revenue contribution, which was not utilized more effectively. This was especially true in the first part of the period, with all of the increases in oil-derived tax revenues from the 1957 base taking place only after 1961.

The Contribution of Petroleum Investment

The behavior of the gross fixed domestic investment of Venezuela was also disappointing during this period. Investment decreased in absolute terms, expressed in constant 1957 bolívares, from 1957 to 1961. It rebounded from then on, but never attained the 1957 level.

As a percent of GDP in 1957 prices, investment declined up to 1963, then enlarged its participation in 1964 and 1965. In Table 6.8, it can be seen that the Venezuelan economy reduced its investment rate from 26.5 percent in 1957 to less than 13.1 percent in 1963. By 1965, the investment rate had shown a slight recuperation, up to 14.4 percent. [9]

Petroleum investment experienced a similar declining trend, which started in 1959 instead of 1958. In 1963, there was a reversal in the trend, but even then, the gross fixed domestic investment in the industry in 1965 was just a shade over one-third of petroleum investment in 1957 (see Table 6.8). This decline was much greater than that experienced by total investment.

The composition of petroleum investment changed radically during this period. Investment in refining and transport experienced a sharply declining trend. On the other hand, investment in the production of crude oil, even though decreasing in absolute terms, increased its share from 66.1 percent of the total in 1957 to 87.0 percent in 1965. The share devoted to marketing also expanded greatly up to 1964— even experiencing an absolute increase up to that year—but contracted in 1965, to wind up with a moderate increase (see Table 6.9).

Investment in the petroleum industry was a diminishing portion of total investment from 1958 on, although it recuperated slightly at the end of the period. In Table 6.8, the time path of this percentage is shown. Investment, in turn, represented a smaller share of GDP. In fact, from 1958 to 1965, the investment rate was only slightly higher than in the 1936-42 period, while in the interim years, it had been significantly above that rate. As to the share of petroleum investment, it was even lower during these years than in the 1936-42 period. The average of petroleum investment in constant terms was lower during the 1958-65 period than in the 1948-57 period.

Nonpetroleum gross fixed investment, in constant 1957 prices, experienced a decline up to 1961 and then reversed its trend (see Table 6.10). By the end of the period, it had risen 6.7 percent from the 1957 level, for a 0.8 percent yearly compounded average growth. Although this is not a satisfactory rate, it is much better than the performance of petroleum investment.

The disappointing performance of total investment during the early part of the period resulted from the following forces:

1. After the Suez Canal crisis, which increased Venezuelan oil prices substantially, the world market for crude oil and products was

TABLE 6.8

Total and Petroleum Gross Fixed Domestic Investment and the
Investment Rate, 1957-65

Year	Total Investment (millions of bolívares)*	Petroleum Investment (millions of bolívares)*	Petroleum's Share in Total (percent)	Investment Rate (percent)
1957	6,429	1,822	28.3	26.5
1958	6,180	1,828	29.6	25.7
1959	6,054	1,263	20.9	23.5
1960	4,725	723	15.3	17.5
1961	4,019	488	12.1	14.1
1962	4,196	422	10.1	14.1
1963	4,307	440	10.2	13.1
1964	5,178	622	12.0	14.2
1965	5,558	641	11.5	14.4

*Constant 1957 bolívares

Source: Table 6.11; Banco Central de Venezuela, Memoria (Caracas, several years), Informe Económi-co (Caracas, several years), and unpublished statistics; and Ministerio de Minas e Hidrocarburos, Petróleo y Otros Datos Estadísticos (Caracas, 1965).

TABLE 6.9

Composition of Petroleum Gross Fixed
Domestic Investment, 1957-65

Year	Production (millions of bolívares)	Share Corresponding to Production (percent)	Transport (millions of bolívares)	Share Corresponding to Transport (percent)	Refining (millions of bolívares)
1957	1,204	66.1	274	15.0	268
1958	1,150	64.3	384	21.5	173
1959	888	70.4	158	12.5	123
1960	551	75.5	95	13.0	37
1961	426	82.6	24	4.7	30
1962	362	76.4	53	11.2	25
1963	404	79.5	52	10.2	20
1964	581	77.2	49	6.5	75
1965	718	87.0	41	5.0	29

Year	Share Corresponding to Refining (percent)	Marketing (millions of bolívares)	Share Corresponding to Marketing (percent)	Other (millions of bolívares)	Share Corresponding to Other (percent)
1957	14.7	18	1.0	58	3.2
1958	9.7	17	1.0	64	3.5
1959	9.7	20	1.6	73	5.8
1960	5.1	21	2.9	26	3.5
1961	5.8	14	2.7	22	4.2
1962	5.3	15	3.2	19	3.9
1963	3.9	10	2.0	25	4.4
1964	10.0	27	3.6	21	2.8
1965	3.5	12	1.5	25	3.0

Source: Ministerio de Minas e Hidrocarburos, Petróleo y Otros
Datos Estadísticos (Caracas, several years).

141

characterized by excess supply. By then, Venezuelan oil was at a disadvantage because of relatively high costs, and its export volume was rising very slowly. [10] Such a situation, coupled with no new concessions, political uncertainty, and lack of confidence in the Venezuelan economy, led the oil companies to follow restrictive policies with regards to investment.

2. The other sectors of the economy were affected by the gloomy outlook for petroleum and by the lull in its activity. But because government policy partly neutralized such contraction, effective demand never actually weakened very much. In fact, the capital goods sector, still very small in Venezuela, was severely hit, with only moderate curtailments taking place in the consumer goods sectors. Therefore, in the end, nonpetroleum investment expenditures did not diminish as much as could have been expected, with a 25 percent reduction from 1957 to 1961, the trough year in the recession. Thus, the contraction was relatively mild, when compared with the 75 percent reduction experienced by oil investment over the same years.

The relationship of petroleum investment and nonpetroleum investment weakened throughout these years, as the economy became much

TABLE 6.10

Nonpetroleum Gross Fixed Domestic Investment
and Retained Value of Total Expenditures in the
Petroleum Industry, 1957-65*

Year	Nonpetroleum Investment (millions of constant 1957 bolívares)	Total Retained Value (millions of current bolívares)
1957	4,607	5,087
1958	4,532	5,691
1959	4,791	5,474
1960	4,002	5,388
1961	3,531	6,885
1962	3,774	6,880
1963	3,867	7,140
1964	4,556	7,457
1965	4,917	7,610

*Total retained value includes foreign exchange taxes on oil.

Source: Tables 6.8, and Appendix, Table A.2, columns 4, 12, and 21.

more independent of oil. Short-term countercyclical policies had much
to do with this, with investment in oil and in the rest of the economy
moving in opposite direction in certain years. The relationship of
nonpetroleum gross fixed investment (lagged one year) with the retained value of total oil expenditures is somewhat closer, but the
correlation between them is still quite low.

During this period, nonpetroleum investment was a substantial
share of the total retained value of oil, although a much lower one
than in previous periods. On the other hand, the average productivity
of public investment appears to have increased. There was a cut in
waste, and more thought appears to have been given to investment
decisions. As the Venezuelan economy improved its institutions, it
became more mobile, flexible, and informed, with the profit-conscious
class of entrepreneurs becoming more numerous and sophisticated.
As a result, a better allocation of investment resources probably
occurred in the private sector also.

In short, both petroleum and nonpetroleum investment moved
disappointingly from 1958 to 1965. This was especially so in the
early part of the period. The behavior of petroleum investment was
particularly distressing, with its level dropping as much as 75 percent
in the trough year. The signs of some independence from oil, which
came to the fore in the last period, were stronger during these years.
Nonpetroleum investment experienced an overall expansion during the
period, in the face of a contraction in petroleum investment.[11] A
very weak connection was found between the former and the retained
value of total oil expenditures.

Total Domestic Product and the Expenditures
of the Oil Industry

Increments in the total income and expenditures originating in an
exogenous sector constitute injections into the economic flows of a
country. An income-expenditure effect is derived from these injections, as they run their course through the producing and consuming
sectors of an economy. Have such repercussions arisen from the
petroleum industry in this period?

In a previous section, the behavior of petroleum investment
expenditures was examined. Similar attention should now be given
to the variables related to value of production. The latter declined
from the 1957 level up to 1960 and then started moving up again. A
big jump in 1964 resulted from the extension of the devaluation to
the oil sector (and, thus, covers the whole Venezuelan economy).
A similar trend was followed by the GDP of petroleum in current bolívares (see Table 6.11).

In constant terms, petroleum's GDP grew at a 3.4 percent compounded annual average per year in this period. As a percentage of

TABLE 6.11

Value of Oil Production and the Share of Petroleum
in Total Gross Domestic Product, 1957-65

Year	Value of Oil Production (millions of bolívares)	Petroleum GDP (millions of bolívares)	Petroleum GDP (millions of constant 1957 bolívares)	Total GDP (millions of constant 1957 bolívares)	Share of Petroleum (percent)
1957	8,604	7,249	7,249	24,295	29.8
1958	7,644	6,301	6,710	24,078	27.9
1959	7,343	5,977	7,307	25,799	28.3
1960	7,302	5,911	7,697	27,038	28.5
1961	7,475	6,274	8,003	28,488	28.1
1962	7,958	6,759	8,491	29,841	28.5
1963	7,910	6,748	8,574	32.947	26.0
1964	10,948	9,328	9,100	36,345	25.0
1965	11,216	9,680	9,444	38,612	24.5

Source: Banco Central de Venezuela, La Economía Venezolana en los Ultimos Veinticinco Años (Caracas, 1966), Memoria (Caracas, several years), Informe Económico (Caracas, several years), and unpublished statistics; Ministerio de Minas e Hidrocarburos, Petróleo y Otros Datos Estadísticos (Caracas, 1965).

total GDP in constant 1957 prices, the petroleum sector hovered between 28. 0 percent and 30. 0 percent. This means that petroleum had
become a less-important part of total GDP. The average share in the
previous period was 30. 1 percent, as compared to 27. 4 percent from
1958 to 1965. In 1965, the share was 24. 5 percent, as against 29. 8
percent in 1957 (see Table 6. 11). [12]

The total expenditures of an exogenous sector constitute the
leverage on which its income-expenditure effects are based. But
actually, only a part of such total expenditures has an immediate and
significant influence over the other sectors of the economy. This is
the retained value portion of total expenditures, as defined in preceding chapters. The concept of retained value is also an approximate
summary indicator of the total combined contribution of a sector to an
economy. Therefore, the movements of the retained value of oil
expenditures over the period, as well as its impact on the rest of the
economy, must also be examined.

In this period, the manner in which the retained value of total
expenditures is calculated must be altered, so as to incorporate the
contribution of oil to government revenues through the exchange rate
tax. In the past, the trend in such tax revenues was substantially
the same as that for all petroleum tax revenues. This, plus the
awkwardness of the levy—which makes its classification difficult—
and the fact that these taxes had to be estimated in an imprecise
manner, prompted us to exclude such taxes from the previous retained
value figures.

However, the exchange rates for the economy and for the petroleum
sector altered drastically during this period, with the differential in
these two rates abruptly becoming very wide in certain years. In turn,
this caused exceptional variations in the petroleum foreign exchange
tax receipts. As a result, if the foreign exchange tax receipts are
included, the whole picture of the industry's retained value of expenditures is changed, and a more accurate representation of the actual
changes in retained value is obtained. [13]

It is not possible to determine accurately which portion of the
foreign exchange tax contribution of oil is attributable to current
expenditures and which to capital expenditures during these years.
Thus, only total retained value figures are used in this section, with
no separate calculation presented of the retained values of current
and capital expenditures of the oil industry.

Retained value of total expenditures, defined in this fashion,
increased in 1958 and then declined up to 1960. It subsequently
increased up to 1965, mainly as a result of the increased exchange
rate tax in 1961, 1962, and 1963, and also because of increased
income and royalty taxes in 1964 and 1965. Overall, it increased
50 percent, which is equivalent to a compounded annual average
increment of 5. 2 percent from 1957 to 1965 (see Table 6. 12). The

TABLE 6.12

Retained Value of Total Expenditures in the Oil
Industry, as a Percentage of Total Expenditures
in the Oil Industry and per Barrel of Oil Produced,
1957-65*

Year	Retained Value of Total Expenditures (millions of bolívares)	Percentage of Total Expenditures	Per Barrel of Oil (bolívares)
1957	5,087	48.7	5.02
1958	5,691	60.3	5.98
1959	5,474	63.6	5.41
1960	5,388	64.9	5.18
1961	6,885	86.1	6.46
1962	6,880	81.6	5.89
1963	7,140	84.7	6.02
1964	7,457	63.5	6.00
1965	7,610	63.3	6.00

*Includes foreign exchange taxes on oil and excludes concession
payments in 1957.

Source: Tables 6.8, 6.10, and 6.11, Appendix, Table A.2, column
20; and Ministerio de Minas e Hidrocarburos, Petróleo y Otros Datos
Estadísticos (Caracas, 1965).

increase would be less in constant 1957 bolívares, as the implicit
deflator for petroleum GDP increased in 1964 and 1965 (see Appendix,
Table A.2, column 17).

However, if the extraordinary payments for oil concessions taking
place in 1956 and 1957 are included in the retained value figures for
those years, then the 1957-65 increment drops to 22.2 percent overall,
which corresponds to a 2.5 percent annual average compounded rate
of growth. The increase in real terms is, again, something less than
that.

The retained value of total petroleum expenditures per barrel of
oil produced, including exchange taxes, also increased during the
period in both current and constant prices. Not only was an overall
increase registered, but the average for this period was greater than
the average for the previous one—all this in the face of decreasing
oil prices.

Retained value of total expenditures represented a higher average
share of the value of production plus investment expenditures in the

petroleum industry during the 1958-65 period than in the preceding one. This is so even considering the concession payments in 1957. The percentage share was much higher in 1965 than in 1957.

During this period, the government was able to increase retained value from the 1957 levels in the face of declining investment. This was made possible through higher income tax rates for petroleum, a raise in the petroleum foreign exchange tax rate, increased tax revenues resulting from the 1964 devaluation, and more effective tax enforcement. Another contributing factor of lesser importance was increasing local procurement by the oil companies.

However, in absolute terms, the total combined growth-promoting contributions of the oil industry to the economy expanded at a slow and unsatisfactory pace during this period. Such a performance stands in contrast with those in the previous periods. It is possible, but by no means certain, that excessive tax pressures affected the investment decisions—and, perhaps, the export potential—of the oil industry in these years.

Notwithstanding the weak contribution of petroleum, Venezuela's GDP grew 59 percent in real terms from 1957 to 1965. This is equivalent to a compounded average rate of increase of 6.0 percent a year (see Table 6.11).[14] This is quite an impressive gain in the light of unsatisfactory growth in the oil industry, the reduction in total investment, and the uncertain conditions referred to in the investment section. The growth appears even more remarkable if we take into account that 1957 was a boom year for oil and a record year for the Venezuelan economy. Yet, on the whole, the rate of economic growth was lower than in the previous period, in consonance with the lower investment rate from 1958 to 1965. This certainly agrees with the findings of Simon Kuznets, which have been discussed above.

Moreover, the increment in nonpetroleum GDP was even greater, as can be seen from Table 6.13. From 1957 to 1965, this aggregate increased 96.3 percent, representing an annual average compounded rate of growth of 8.8 percent.[15] Government policy was quite effective in neutralizing the adverse effects taking place in the first part of the period. Although the petroleum sector expanded more slowly than the economy as a whole, it rebounded in the second part of the period, to ease the burden of the government sector. However, it seems that both the government sector and the import-substituting industries were the most important leading sectors in the economy during this period, with petroleum providing added support in the second half. The nonpetroleum part of the Venezuelan economy continued the trend initiated at the end of the war, gaining considerably in strength and independence. In fact, the take-off of the Venezuelan economy probably began in the 1958-65 period.

The agricultural sector, forestry included, grew satisfactorily from 1957 to 1965, in contrast with previous periods. As can be seen in Appendix Table A.1, it expanded at a compounded annual

TABLE 6.13

Nonpetroleum Gross Domestic Product, 1957-65
(millions of constant 1957 bolívares)

Year	Nonpetroleum GDP
1957	13,854
1958	14,167
1959	16,143
1960	17,458
1961	18,939
1962	19,491
1963	22,426
1964	25,166
1965	27,193

Source: Tables 6.8 and 6.11.

average growth rate of 6.1 percent. Cereals, fibers and oil, sugar, animal products, and forestry products had the highest rates of growth. The production of fibers and oils and cereals about doubled in this span, and animal products nearly accomplished it. Among cereals, the production of rice expanded close to 10 times, although from a low base. Sesame and cotton were the main cause of the expansion in fibers and oils. Dairy products, eggs, and poultry were the most rapidly expanding categories among animal products.

The governments that succeeded the military regime of Marcos Pérez Jiménez implanted basic institutional reforms in the rural areas and devoted a larger share of public resources to agricultural investment and agricultural credit. Measures such as land redistribution, more extensive production and investment credits, sound and far-reaching extension services, and well-thought out overhead facilities were responsible for the performance of this sector.

Manufacturing activities had big gains in this period. The index of manufacturing production grew 104 percent, including petroleum refining, for a 9.3 percent compounded average yearly increase. As petroleum refining—which represented over 10 percent of manufacturing production throughout this period—had a slower growth, if it is excluded the rate of growth of manufacturing would be even greater. [16]

In Tables 6.14 and 6.15, manufacturing output is presented in a disaggregated fashion. Up to 1963, the paper and cardboard industry and the tobacco industry (see Table 6.14) had the fastest expansion. Table 6.15 is expressed in terms of the product originated in each industry in constant 1957 bolívares, with the year 1953 as the base. Table 6.15, in contrast with the previous table, presents a more comprehensive coverage of the manufacturing sector (petroleum refining excluded).

TABLE 6.14

Manufacturing Production by Industry and Commodity, 1957 and 1963
(index, 1945 = 100)

Industry	1957 Volume	1957 Index	1963 Volume	1963 Index
Food processing industries:	–	459	–	635
Pasteurized milk[a]	127.1	810	178.9	1,139
Milk for butter[b]	50.0	145	45.0	90
Powdered milk[b]	4.5	300	20.9	1,393
Vegetable oils[b]	29.5	819	35.4	983
Peanut oil[b]	–	–	–	–
Sesame oil[b]	12.3	1,757	22.7	3,243
Coconut oil[b]	1.6	178	0.5	56
Cotton oil[b]	1.2	240	3.5	700
Canned fish[b]	13.7	228	17.4	290
Ground coffee[b][c]	12.0	200	17.6	293
Chocolate[b]	2.2	183	2.0	175
Cookies[b]	6.1	244	9.3	372
Pastries[b]	38.2	1,232	46.9	1,513
Sugar[b]	192.8	709	275.6	1,013
Rice[b]	27.1	219	26.7	215
Salt[b]	85.7	149	76.4	133
Fruit juices[a][c]	17.6	607	30.7	1,059
Beverage industries:	408.9	591	665.7	962
Beer[d]	153.9	384	248.8	620
Liquor[d]	10.1	259	11.3	290
Rum[d]	0.9	29	0.2	6
Gaseous drinks[d]	244.0	1,104	405.4	1,834
Textile and clothing industries:	–	270	–	480
Cotton suits[b]	7.0	92	12.7	167
Linen and canvas[b]	3.6	84	5.9	137
Cotton cloth[b]	6.0	64	38.4	409
Rayon and cotton cloth[b]	4.5	100	7.5	167
Cotton knits[d][e]	0.6	300	0.8	400
Cotton bedspreads[f]	0.5	1,667	0.3	1,000
Cotton blankets[f]	0.9	225	1.5	375
Cotton towels[f]	1.2	300	2.3	575
Cotton underwear[f]	1.5	136	n.a.[p]	–
Cotton footwear[f]	1.4	156	1.7	189
Rayon cloth[b]	25.1	1,476	34.0	2,000
Rayon knits[e]	0.5	1,250	0.4	1,000
Rayon footwear[g]	0.05	17	n.a.[p]	–
Rayon and cotton footwear[g]	0.01	1	n.a.[p]	–
Nylon footwear[f]	13.2	22,000	18.3	30,500
Wool suits[b]	0.8	800	0.8	800
Wool knits[b]	1.2	1,200	1.7	1,700
Linen cloth[b]	0.8	800	n.a.[p]	–
Rope[b]	3.1	443	2.7	386
Sisal bags[c][f]	5.3	1,060	5.8	1,160
Leather industries:	–	905	–	1,071
Leather soles[h]	5.0	200	4.9	196
Leather linings[i]	2,952.8	16,404	3,485.4	363
Other products[j]	10.2	3,400	21.6	7,200
Paper and cardboard industries[k]	13.6	800	40.0	2,353

(continued)

Table 6.14 continued.

Industry	1957 Volume	1957 Index	1963 Volume	1963 Index
Rubber industries:	1,048.0	1,776	1,567.0	2,656
Tires[l]	576.0	1,694	978.0	2,876
Inner tubes[l]	472.0	1,888	589.0	2,356
Tobacco industry[f]	3.5	167	8.3	395
Timber industry[j]	206.0	981	171.0	814
Chemical industries:	−	545	−	1,565
Paint[b]	18.1	1,810	19.4	1,940
Distilled alcohol[m]	5.5	229	9.6	400
Soap[b]	182.0	119	25.5	167
Candles[b]	5.4	208	6.0	231
Matches[c][f]	8.1	100	12.8	158
Industrial gas[n]	3.0	429	3.5	500
Animal feed[e]	84.9	1,489	305.0	5,351
Metal industries:	−	562	−	853
Nails[c][o]	7.5	313	4.0	167
Tin cans[c][o]	17.8	848	34.4	1,638
Transport equipment, assembly, and repair industries:	−	493	−	740
Passenger[l]	8.9	12,714	16.5	23,571
Commercial[l]	5.9	203	5.7	197
Construction materials industries:	−	2,241	1,570.0	1,927
Portland cement[o]	1,747.0	1,519	48.0	1,365
Lime[c][o]	57.0	116	28.0	98
Cement blocks[c][l]	22.0	105	1.0	133
Cement tubes[d][l]	0.9	100	401.0	111
Mosaic, and so forth[c][o]	616.0	132	107.0	86
Bricks and tiles[c][l]	134.0	151	−	120

[a]Thousands of liters.
[b]Thousands of metric tons.
[c]Index, 1950 = 100.
[d]Index, 1957 = 100.
[e]Millions of kilograms.
[f]Millions of units.
[g]Millions of pairs.
[h]Meters.
[i]Thousands of square feet.
[j]Thousands of cubic meters.
[k]Thousands of tons.
[l]Thousands of units.
[m]Millions of liters.
[n]Millions of cubic meters.
[o]Millions of metric tons.
[p]Not available.

Source: Juan P. Pérez Castillo, Some Aspects of Venezuela's Economic Development: 1945-1960 (Ph. D. diss., Tulane University, 1963), corrected for certain inaccuracies in the computation of the index numbers.

TABLE 6.15

Indices of Product Originated in the Manufacturing Sector, by Industry, 1957-65

(Index, 1953 = 100)

Industry	1957	1958	1959	1960	1961	1962	1963	1964	1965
Food processing	161.2	160.8	184.5	202.5	224.0	244.1	257.1	295.1	322.0
Beverage	133.0	166.3	190.6	204.3	200.0	203.3	207.3	216.1	229.9
Tobacco	125.5	137.3	153.6	239.0	260.3	279.2	296.5	312.0	346.1
Textile	200.7	215.7	257.2	257.9	294.3	339.1	375.3	436.8	440.2
Clothing	207.5	205.1	219.6	190.5	199.5	185.4	178.3	233.1	199.1
Paper and cardboard	320.3	347.6	537.1	627.2	736.5	770.3	927.9	1,186.0	1,269.2
Printing	180.3	217.3	221.6	217.0	203.6	216.9	280.4	237.3	262.1
Leather	187.3	203.6	246.9	312.6	301.0	266.9	246.1	314.1	262.0
Chemical	193.5	204.2	238.2	220.4	248.6	277.3	299.1	371.2	409.9
Timber	185.0	178.4	246.5	139.3	142.3	144.3	159.3	192.1	206.7
Furniture	206.4	183.7	201.5	169.4	179.8	208.3	223.0	242.8	329.0
Rubber	224.0	260.0	289.1	299.2	312.8	362.0	374.0	420.3	475.7
Construction materials	174.5	159.4	186.9	152.6	152.3	152.1	156.2	189.7	220.0
Construction, assembly, and repair of machinery	149.4	167.0	176.3	178.9	190.1	268.7	298.1	399.4	554.1
Construction, assembly, and repair of vehicles	151.0	161.0	172.2	157.8	169.2	168.2	205.2	281.0	353.0
Metal	371.3	487.3	579.8	620.2	656.6	764.8	721.9	893.1	923.5
Basic metals	401.6	308.5	486.3	379.3	509.5	1,703.2	2,975.1	3,531.3	4,389.0
Jewelry	152.2	216.6	217.6	303.0	256.9	181.7	216.6	306.9	313.8

Note: Product originated in terms of constant 1957 bolívares.

Source: Banco Central de Venezuela, La Economía Venezolana en los Ultimos Treinta Años (Caracas, 1971), and Informe Económico (Caracas, 1969).

Several industries grew faster than the manufacturing sector as
a whole from 1957 to 1965. They mostly were capital goods industries;
rubber, vehicle construction, assembly and repair; machinery construction, assembly and repair; and metals. These represented about 12
percent to 13 percent of total manufacturing over these years. Some
intermediate industries, namely the chemical and paper and cardboard
industries, expanded faster than total manufacturing too, also from
a slim base. Of the consumer goods industries, only tobacco and
textiles expanded significantly faster than the overall manufacturing
sector. Among these, the fastest growing from 1957 to 1965 were the
machine construction and repair industry, the paper and cardboard
industry, and the basic metals group.

The performance of the rest of the industrial sector was mixed
in character, as Tables 6.16 and 6.17 show. The utilities sector
expanded close to 210 percent from 1957 to 1965. This represents
an annual average compounded rate of growth of approximately 15.2
percent. On the other hand, construction activities contracted
slightly over these years. As in the previous period, the performance
of these sectors is measured in terms of GDP in constant 1957 bolívares.

The key to the growth in the manufacturing sector was the import
substitution drive, which attained prominence as the most dynamic
force in Venezuelan economic growth during this period. The process
of import substitution began to affect intermediate goods, and even
some capital goods lines, but basically fed on consumer goods industries. Other important factors in the expansion of manufactures
were the fostering policies of the government, especially credit
facilities and tax and tariff rebates.

The tremendous expansion in the utilities sector resulted to a
great extent from the growth of industry and agriculture and the urbanization process they helped generate. However, the fulfillment of
previously unsatisfied needs for these services (utilities) was also
an important factor. [17] The contraction in the construction sector
is explained in terms of the reduction in investment expenditures
that took place in this period. This affected the capital goods
industries through its major component: the construction industry.

Extractive activities, petroleum excluded, rose slightly, as
Table 6.18 shows. This can again be explained in terms of the
factors affecting the iron industry, which represents close to 90 percent of the product originated in this sector. As iron faced an unfavorable situation in the international markets from 1960 to 1963, the
product originated in mining contracted, pari passu with the reduction
in the production of iron. Together with iron, it rebounded strongly
in 1964 and 1965, surpassing the 1957 level.

Tertiary activities greatly expanded from 1957 to 1965. Their
expansion was even faster than that of industry. As shown in Table
6.19, it amounted to about 90 percent overall, for an annual average
rate of growth of 8.3 percent. Services experienced the strongest

TABLE 6.16

Gross Domestic Product in the Utilities Sector,
1957-65
(millions of 1957 bolívares)

Year	GDP
1957	238
1958	281
1959	336
1960	371
1961	422
1962	501
1963	590
1964	663
1965	738

Source: Banco Central de Venezuela, La Economía Venezolana en los Últimos Veinticinco Años (Caracas, 1966), and Informe Económico (Caracas, 1965).

TABLE 6.17

Gross Domestic Product in Construction
Activities, 1957-65
(millions of 1957 bolívares)

Year	GDP
1957	1,581
1958	1,618
1959	1,707
1960	1,647
1961	1,471
1962	1,420
1963	1,340
1964	1,496
1965	1,545

Source: Banco Central de Venezuela, La Economía Venezolana en los Últimos Veinticinco Años (Caracas, 1966), and Informe Económico (Caracas, 1967).

TABLE 6.18

Gross Domestic Product in Mining,
Petroleum Excluded, 1957-65
(millions of constant 1957 bolívares)

Year	GDP
1957	383
1958	379
1959	420
1960	463
1961	358
1962	333
1963	282
1964	390
1965	425

Source: Banco Central de Venezuela, La Economía Venezolana en
los Ultimos Treinta Años (Caracas, 1971), and Informe Económico
(Caracas, 1969).

expansion, with an overall increase of 136 percent. Commerce and
transport and communications activities expanded at a much slower
pace—about 35 percent—from 1957 to 1965 (see Table 6.19).

Although the oil industry did not lead the economic growth of
Venezuela in this period, the importance of its contributions to the
industrial strength of the country cannot be overlooked. The backward
linkages of the industry were partly responsible for the growth in the
metal (especially basic metals) and machinery industries, while the
forward linkages were basic in the expansion of fertilizers, the petro-
chemical industry, and several uses of natural gas.

The decline in external petroleum prices constituted the big
difference in the contribution of oil to the rest of the Venezuelan
economy during this period. Since 1936, the general trend has been
one of rising prices. This meant externally determined increases in
petroleum and total GDP. The opposite was true in this period. The
total contribution of petroleum over these years was constrained by
a declining value for each barrel of oil produced.

Although encouraging progress was experienced in the nonpetroleum
part of the economy, overall, the Venezuelan economy did not gain
that much in per capita terms. The very high rate of growth of population in Venezuela partly explains this. Total GDP per inhabitant
enlarged from 3,661 to 4,427, in constant 1957 bolívares, for a 20.9
percent increase overall. This represents a compounded annual
average of 2.4 percent.

However, a most important phenomenon was occurring. As the economy of Venezuela grew, a new pattern of production and trade emerged. This change had started back in the late war years and had ripened sufficiently to pass its first test respectably. Such factors were considerably aided during the 1957-65 period by a substantial reduction in excess capacity. [18] However, it became evident that the Venezuelan economy had become sufficiently diversified to be adequately prepared for short-cycle slumps in the oil sector.

The secondary and tertiary sectors increased their importance considerably during this period. Agriculture, with its share still decreasing over time, grew relatively faster over these years, in consonance with the country's rapid population growth. Exports of manufacturing goods greatly expanded, and the prospects for continued expansion seemed encouraging.

THE 1966-73 SUBPERIOD

The Foreign Sector Contribution

Oil's contribution through the external sector was more accentuated during the last period to be examined, that is, the years 1966-73.

TABLE 6.19

Gross Domestic Product in the Tertiary Sector,
by Category, 1957-65
(millions of constant 1957 bolívares)

Year	Transport and Communications	Commerce	Services	Total
1957	940	3,933	5,365	10,238
1958	1,002	3,803	5,825	10,630
1959	1,090	4,003	6,296	11,389
1960	1,011	3,976	6,989	11,976
1961	996	3,811	8,381	13,188
1962	996	4,051	9,595	14,642
1963	1,045	4,315	10,946	16,306
1964	1,181	4,932	11,987	18,100
1965	1,267	5,455	12,665	19,387

Source: Banco Central de Venezuela, La Economía Venezolana en los Últimos Treinta Años (Caracas, 1971), and Informe Económico (Caracas, 1969).

However, the improvement occurred toward the end of the period, with a large expansion in petroleum exports and a favorable and considerable rise in Venezuela's foreign trade being experienced in 1973. As the outlook for Venezuelan oil became more attractive, a future could be foreseen in which petroleum's contribution to the economy through the external sector could be compared in its relative importance to the prosperous times of the 1950s.

The current account credits of Venezuela's balance of payments appear in Table 6.19, with petroleum's share also indicated. The same table shows the amount of foreign exchange received by Venezuela due to these and other balance-of-payments credits. Just a quick glance is sufficient to conclude that the year 1973 constitutes a jump in the time series.

Oil foreign exchange earnings, for example, increased roughly 60 percent during the years 1965 to 1972; nevertheless, this figure doubles if one considers the year 1973 as the final one in the period. This means a very quick increase in the cumulative yearly growth rate, which reaches 10.5 percent if 1973 is taken as the end of the period. (The yearly growth rate increases to 12.1 percent if we consider 1966 as the base year). It should be pointed out that oil's current account credits did not increase as fast. Even though it was not possible to obtain the corresponding estimate for 1973 in the Central Bank's statistics, an estimate could be made, based on the data provided by the Ministry of Mines and Hydrocarbons. By relating exports at realized or sale prices with those at reference or fiscal prices, obtained from the Ministry of Mines, oil's credits are estimated at realized or sale prices as $4,416 million. Therefore, the increase in these credits was 89.5 percent as a whole, equivalent to an annual compounded growth rate of 8.5 percent, with respect to 1965, and of 97.2 percent, in relation to 1966, corresponding to a yearly compounded rate of 10.2 percent.

The fact that the increment in petroleum's foreign exchange earnings was superior to the increase in its current account credits denotes the pressure that the Venezuelan government has been exerting to enlarge the obligations that the petroleum companies must settle in bolívares in Venezuela. This is also reflected in total foreign exchange earnings, which grow faster than total credits, even though this is also due to the behavior of the capital account transactions in Venezuela's balance of payments.

In general, we may conclude that the expansion in Venezuela's current account credits, and, in particular, petroleum's contribution through the external sector, were satisfactory during the period 1966-73. However, it should again be underlined that this was so mainly because of the jump that occurred in 1973. On the other hand, the contribution in terms of exchange earnings is even more positive. Partly because of these favorable conditions, Venezuela's GDP was able to expand, and the percentage that balance-of-payments current

TABLE 6.20

Petroleum's Share in Current Account Credits and Foreign Exchange Earnings, 1965–73

Year	Petroleum (millions of dollars)	Total (millions of dollars)	Petroleum's Share (percent)	Petroleum (millions of dollars)	Total (millions of dollars)	Petroleum's Share (percent)
1965	2,330	2,616	89.1	1,371	1,899	72.2
1966	2,239	2,539	88.2	1,369	2,050	66.8
1967	2,361	2,695	87.6	1,536	2,259	68.0
1968	2,398	2,738	87.6	1,587	2,304	68.9
1969	2,360	2,761	85.5	1,595	2,382	67.0
1970	2,436	2,894	84.2	1,686	2,640	63.9
1971	2,935	3,396	86.4	2,165	3,421	63.3
1972	2,910	3,432	84.8	2,190	4,081	53.7
1973	—	—	—	3,045	5,587	54.5

*The 1973 data have not yet been made available by the Central Bank.

Note: All figures at realized or sale prices.

Source: Banco Central de Venezuela, Informe Económico (Caracas, 1973).

account credits represented of GDP (at current prices) declined from 30. 9 percent to 27. 8 percent.

Before considering the utilization of oil's contribution through the external sector, it is necessary to emphasize two relatively important points related with the considerations made above. First, it is evident that oil's share in Venezuela's external sector decreased slightly during the period 1966-73 (see Table 6. 20). Second, as Table 6. 21 shows, it was the rise in the price of oil that fundamentally determined the satisfactoriness of its contribution during the period.

The series appearing in Table 6. 21 shows that the net terms of trade index rises quickly beginning in 1971, surpassing, in 1973, the 1959 base. If this index is computed based on reference or fiscal prices, the same trend is found with a sharper increase, however (see Table 6. 22).

It has been seen that gross (in terms of current account credits) and net (in terms of foreign exchange earnings) contributions were satisfactory in the period examined. How were these contributions utilized? In the first place, it is seen that Venezuela's international reserves increased continually throughout these years, reaching levels comparable to those in developed countries toward the end of the period. The reserves, in dollars, as can be seen in Table 6. 21, tripled

TABLE 6. 21

Net Barter Terms of Trade, Import Capacity, and
International Reserves, 1965-73

Year	Net Terms of Trade (index)*	Import Capacity (index)*	International Reserves (millions of dollars)
1965	84. 7	106. 1	853
1966	81. 4	99. 9	772
1967	82. 5	106. 2	874
1968	83. 1	106. 8	928
1969	77. 9	102. 4	939
1970	73. 5	99. 0	1, 023
1971	86. 7	111. 0	1, 479
1972	85. 0	101. 3	1, 747
1973	100. 9	126. 3	2, 389

*1959 = 100.

Source: Banco Central de Venezuela, La Economía Venezolana en los Ultimos Treinta Años (Caracas, 1971).

TABLE 6.22

Import Capacity and Net Barter Terms of Trade
at Reference Prices, 1968-73
(index, 1968 = 100)

Year	Import Capacity	Net Barter
1968	100.0	100.0
1969	102.8	100.4
1970	95.5	95.4
1971	113.3	110.1
1972	119.7	111.7
1973	147.7	142.5

Source: Banco Central de Venezuela, Informe Económico (Caracas, 1973).

during this period, after experiencing a shortfall in 1966. The annual compounded rates of increase were 17.5 percent for the period in question and 13.7 percent if 1965 is taken as the base year. Therefore, excessive reserves were again accumulated, while the economy grew at a rate (4.8 percent a year, compounded) which, although satisfactory, seemed insufficient, given the underemployment of the Venezuelan labor force. Yet, it is possible that Venezuela's absorptive capacity of investment was limited by certain bottlenecks during these years. On the other hand, the high level of reserves, and, thus, the strong import capacity of the Venezuelan economy, continued to allow the maintenance of very low inflation rates. Nevertheless, toward the end of the period, the scarcity of a series of basic foodstuffs, the generalization of price hikes throughout the world, and Venezuela's tariff reforms led to rates of price increases that had not been felt for many years in Venezuela.

How were the foreign exchange earnings put to use, that is, those that did not end up enlarging Venezuela's international reserves? An important contribution of oil's exchange earnings was to allow the processes of capital accumulation, production, and spending to take place unimpeded by any important constraint. This has prevented the appearance of bottlenecks in terms of availability of goods and services and seems to have been one of the main reasons for Venezuela's growth.

However, the effective use of these external resources requires that the importation of goods and services maintain a certain path throughout time. This is determined by the importance that capital formation holds in the process of economic development and by the stages generally traced by a country's industrial growth. An effective use is indicated by a relative increase in capital goods imports and a decrease of consumption goods imports. The evolution of the import components, according to type of goods, appears in Table 6.23, and it is seen that, during this period, imports of capital goods increased to about 30 percent of total imports, while the imports of consumption goods decreased to less than 15 percent. This implies that the net resources contributed by the petroleum sector for import financing were well employed during the period 1966-73.

Altogether, oil's contribution through the external sector was still considerable during this period. In relative terms, oil was the most important factor in the enormous increase in the Venezuelan economy's current account credits (especially occurring in its exports of goods and services). It also had a very high participation in its total foreign exchange earnings. Thus, its relative contribution was similar to that made in the previous period (1957-65). However, its contribution was much more satisfactory during the most recent period, when the absolute growth in current account credits and foreign exchange earnings is considered. On the other hand, the use of the contribution was much more effective during the years 1966-73. The pattern of imports and its evolution throughout the period fitted the development and industrial growth norm mentioned above, and the price increases in the period were reasonably contained considering the circumstances. The only negative aspect in the utilization of petroleum's contribution was the accumulation of international reserves

TABLE 6.23

Composition of Imported Goods,
According to Type, 1965-73
(current bolívares)

Year	Investment Goods	Intermediate Goods	Consumption Goods
1965	26.6	55.5	17.9
1966	27.5	55.5	17.0
1967	25.8	56.9	17.4
1968	27.5	55.2	17.2
1969	30.0	53.4	16.6
1970	27.0	57.4	15.6
1971	29.1	56.0	14.9
1972	30.5	53.6	15.9
1973*	30.6	54.5	14.9

*First semester only.

Source: Banco Central de Venezuela, unpublished data.

to a degree that could be considered excessive. Given the problems facing the Venezuelan society, to have vast capital reserves yielding very low returns is difficult to justify. It should be recognized that this is a very debatable point; it should also be made clear that, in 1973, the Venezuelan authorities became quite preoccupied about the allocation of international reserves. In fact, this happened exactly when foreign reserve flows grew to such an extent that it became evident that some sterilization was required, given the danger of upsetting the country's internal monetary flows.

The Fiscal Contribution of Oil

The government's overall fiscal revenues, excluding those of government firms, increased twofold during the period being examined. Again, the jump experienced by petroleum revenues in 1973 was the principal cause of this extraordinary increase. Whether 1965 or 1966 is taken as base, the result is very similar when the increase is expressed in terms of annual compounded growth rates. These turn out to be between 10 percent and 11 percent as an average.

The petroleum sector contributed to this expansion by more than doubling the revenues it paid the Venezuelan government. However, it should be pointed out that, in 1969 and 1970, the relative share of petroleum's fiscal revenues decreased to less than 60 percent of the total (roughly 55 percent). The following years it experienced a recovery culminating in 1973, when petroleum-derived revenues represented 64 percent of total fiscal revenues. The average yearly compounded growth rate of revenues from petroleum fluctuated between 11 percent and 12 percent, respectively, whether the last year of the preceding period or the first year of this period is taken as base. *

These fiscal revenue growth rates, which are a bit larger than those of GDP at current prices, are due, in great part, to the fiscal pressures applied to the petroleum sector during the period. The government forced the petroleum companies to apportion 80 percent of their profits to the state and 20 percent to themselves, basically through use of the income tax. At the same time, they were made to pay, using reference or fiscal prices and not-realized or sale prices as base, although the latter are the ones the companies declared they had received. Finally, oil revenues also increased toward the end of the period, mostly as a result of the rapid rise in oil prices, even though the volume of oil sold also expanded significantly.

---

*The growth rates of both oil and total fiscal revenues are smaller if 1965 is used as a base year and larger if 1966 is utilized. The basic data for these calculations appear in Table 6.24.

TABLE 6.24

Total Government and Oil-Derived Revenues,
Not Including Petroleum's Foreign Exchange
Taxes, 1965-73*

Year	Total (millions of bolívares)	Petroleum (millions of bolívares)	Petroleum's Share (percent)
1965	8,202	4,863	59.3
1966	8,430	5,143	61.0
1967	9,600	5,866	61.1
1968	9,865	6,075	61.6
1969	9,804	5,597	57.1
1970	10,854	5,885	54.2
1971	13,172	7,860	59.7
1972	13,979	8,138	58.2
1973	17,867	11,440	64.0

*Ordinary revenues only; it includes neither public enterprise revenues nor concession or service contract payments.

Source: Banco Central de Venezuela, Informe Económico (Caracas, various years), and unpublished data; Ministerio de Minas e Hidrocarburos, Petróleo y Otros Datos Estadísticos (Caracas, 1972), and unpublished data.

TABLE 6.25

Taxes Collected from the Petroleum Industry,
Including Petroleum's Foreign Exchange Taxes
and Petroleum's Share in Total Fiscal Revenues,
1965-73

Year	Foreign Exchange (millions of bolívares)	Total (millions of bolívares)	Petroleum's Share (percent)
1965	117	4,980	60.7
1966	117	5,260	62.4
1967	131	5,997	62.5
1968	135	6,210	62.9
1969	136	5,733	58.5
1970	143	6,028	55.5
1971	184	8,044	61.1
1972	186	8,324	59.5
1973	259	11,699	65.5

Source: Derived from data appearing in Banco Central de Venezuela, La Economía Venezolana en los Ultimos Treinta Años (Caracas, 1971), and Informe Económico (Caracas, several years); and Table 6.24.

If the revenues resulting from the exchange rate differential
applied to the oil sector are added, the contribution of oil would
still be greater. The tax revenues derived from foreign exchange
petroleum transactions rose at the same rate as the rest of its fiscal
contribution, reaching the sum of 259 million bolivares in 1973.
Table 6.25 shows the magnitude of the exchange rate differential
contribution, which, when added to the rest of oil's fiscal contribution, increased its share in total government revenues to more than
65 percent in 1973.*

It is evident that oil's contribution to public finances is extreme-
ly important in Venezuela. Moreover, during this period, its importance
grew, contradicting the trend toward diversification, which became
clear in the preceding period. Petroleum's participation in fiscal
revenues during the 1966-73 period, represented 59.6 percent of the
total, as an average. If the foreign exchange tax is included, this
expands to 61.0 percent. In terms of GDP at current prices, oil's
contribution amounted to 18.2 percent and 18.8 percent respectively.
All of this is a clear indication of the importance of petroleum's fiscal
contribution and that it had become more relevant in this period.

The Utilization of Petroleum's Fiscal Contribution

One characteristic of these last years, as in the preceding period,
was to have deficits in the government budgets. Only in 1973 was
there a surplus. This could easily be attributed to the fact that fiscal
revenues in this year were greater than expected. The two years
registering the greatest deficits were 1970 and 1972. This points to
the fact that oil revenues were used in their entirety during the period
and were even complemented by an increase in the public debt. Contrasting with the 1950s, when the Venezuelan Treasury accumulated
reserves, the government did not sterilize petroleum's fiscal revenues
and continued to increase the public debt and the influence of the
public sector in the nation's economy.

Comparing Table 6.26 with Table 6.24, it is clearly seen that
the deficits have not been very large. It is also evident that the
share of capital expenditures in total expenditures, after having
increased during the years 1967, 1968, and 1969 to more than 36
percent as an average, decreased to roughly 30 percent toward the
end of the period. Now, if the entire period is averaged out, the
share of public investment would be 33 percent. Thus, one-third of
public expenditures was channelled to capital formation.

_____

*It should be kept in mind that reference is being made to ordinary
fiscal revenues only. Therefore, payments resulting from service
contracts signed with petroleum companies, are not included. However, these payments were much less than those resulting from the
concessions awarded in 1957.

TABLE 6.26

Total Expenditures and Capital Expenditures of
Government, Excluding Public Enterprises,
1965-73

Year	Capital Expenditures (millions of bolívares)	Total Expenditures (millions of bolívares)	Investment's Share in Total Expenditures (percent)
1965	1,964	8,251	23.8
1966	3,072	8,809	34.9
1967	3,576	9,668	37.0
1968	3,774	10,615	35.6
1969	4,234	11,516	36.8
1970	3,814	12,137	31.4
1971	4,591	13,971	32.9
1972	4,687	15,102	31.0
1973	5,351	17,386	30.8

Source: Banco Central de Venezuela, Informe Económico (Caracas, several years).

TABLE 6.27

Changes in Petroleum's Fiscal Revenues and in
Government Investment, 1965-73*
(millions of bolívares)

Year	Annual Change in Petroleum Revenues	Annual Change in Government Investment
1965	–	–
1966	280	1,108
1967	723	504
1968	209	198
1969	-478	460
1970	288	-420
1971	1,975	777
1972	278	96
1973	3,302	664
Total change	6,577	3,387

*Including neither taxes on petroleum's foreign exchange nor the investment of public firms.

Source: Tables 6.24 and 6.26.

164

As can be deduced from the above statements, public expenditures expanded considerably in this period. Just like public revenues, these expenditures doubled, growing at an average compounded growth rate of 10.2 percent per annum. Government capital spending did not increase as fast, but it did grow at 8.2 percent, as an average, from 1966 to 1973 (see Table 6.26). If the growth in public expenditures is compared to that experienced in the preceding period, it must be concluded that government activities were quite dynamic during the more recent period, and, looked at from this angle, it seems that oil's contribution was used much more efficiently. Also, the trajectory of government expenditures during these years was similar to that of government revenues, with no undue accumulation of treasury reserves. As for government capital expenditures, their evolution has not been as favorable, when contrasted with that in the period 1957-65. During the previous period, 40 percent of government spending was allocated to what was called, in a broad sense, "development expenditures." As has been seen, during the years 1966 to 1973, only one-third of government expenditures was devoted to development expenditures. In this sense, oil's contribution was not employed as effectively.[19]

However, it should be pointed out that the 1957-65 series and the most recent one are not strictly comparable. The last one excludes government enterprises, while the first one includes them. It has been impossible to homogenize the series, because the Central Bank does not have data on the capital and total spending of public firms for most of the recent years. Given that the expenditures of public firms were small relative to total government expenditures, and since their nature should not be that different from the rest of public spending, the rate of growth of total expenditures and its share of capital spending should not differ significantly, whether public firms are included or not. Moreover, given that the differences in the rates of development expenditures (capital spending) between both periods are noteworthy, it is difficult to imagine that the conclusions reached could be altered by the inclusion or not of public firms.

As to the effectiveness in the use of the funds devoted to public investment, even though not comparable to the waste that characterized the 1950s, its allocation seems to have been less rational and efficient than in the preceding period. The continuous increase in petroleum revenues seemed to bring about a relaxation in the management of the fiscal funds, which contrasted with the care shown in the preceding period. This was particularly the case in the allocation of investments to agriculture, which was again hurt by sharing insufficiently in public finances. However, a very successful effort was undertaken in the industrial field. Because of the latter, an acceptable balance was maintained between investments in infrastructure and direct investments in productive activities.

Another indication of the effectiveness in the utilization of the funds generated by petroleum can be seen when comparing the change in oil-derived revenues with those of government investment during these years. Table 6.27 shows that annual changes in these variables have almost always been positive, which again contrasts with the preceding period. It is easy to see that the yearly increases have been much greater in the fiscal revenues generated by petroleum. Looking at the period as a whole, it is even clearer that the increase in petroleum's fiscal contribution was not utilized for investment or developmental purposes, as it should have been to be consonant with the broad interpretation of the "sow the oil" motto.

Approximately one-half of the increments in oil's fiscal revenues seem to have been devoted to public investment, even though it should be pointed out that the gaps between oil revenues and public investments began to appear in 1970, when oil revenues started to expand rapidly. It should be recognized, however, that government investment has been defined as excluding state enterprises, and, as such, it appears in Table 6.27; on the other hand, petroleum's foreign exchange tax revenues have not been included among the oil revenues. Considering all these factors, it should be concluded that, continuing the preceding period's trend, petroleum's fiscal contribution was not well utilized to promote Venezuela's economic development during this period. [20]

Summary

Petroleum's fiscal contribution was very important during this period, even more so than in the anteceding one. Oil's fiscal revenues grew rapidly due to a favorable world market situation, government pressure to increase petroleum taxes and the prices charged for Venezuelan oil. Through this rapid expansion, the petroleum sector gave the necessary support for an expansion in the rest of the economy, given its high share in total fiscal revenues and the fast pace at which these revenues grew, helped to a great extent by those contributed by oil.

Nevertheless, the utilization of the fiscal contribution, in many ways left a lot to be desired. Although the petroleum funds were used almost in their entirety, since there was no accumulation of Treasury reserves, the share of capital outlays decreased and the yearly increases in petroleum funds were not channelled into investment during the period. On the other hand, the allocation and application of the government investment funds seems not to have been well planned during these years.

Therefore, even though oil's fiscal contributions increased during the period, in great part due to policies of the Venezuelan government, the authorities did not use this contribution as effectively as in the preceding period.

The Contribution of Petroleum Investment

Venezuela's gross fixed investment increased rapidly during the 1966-73 period, especially from 1968 on. In 1973, investment at 1957 prices almost doubled if compared to 1965, the last year of the previous period. This represents a complete turnabout, as real investment, although underestimated, appeared to decrease in the preceding period. This can be explained in terms of a more effective rate of capital utilization during 1958-65, a smaller savings rate, and a restraint of investment in the petroleum sector. The first two aspects appear not to have operated during the years 1966 to 1973, seeming to imply that a point was reached when it was necessary to expand productive capacity, given the decrease in slack from the late 1950 levels.

Table 6.28 shows that the investment rate, that is, gross fixed investment divided by GDP, both at 1957 prices, increased during the period being considered. In 1973, the investment rate appeared just to be on the verge of returning to the greater than 20 percent levels that had characterized the Venezuelan growth process, which was based on a fast rate of capital accumulation from the end of World War II up to the early 1960s.

Petroleum investment revived in the years 1968 to 1971, driven by the new service contracts between the government and the oil companies, by investments on petroleum desulfurization, by new explorations, and by the push to increase known reserves. Nevertheless, it decreased abruptly during the last two years of the period, declining to figures that were lower than 10 percent of total Venezuelan investment, which had not occurred for over 30 years. The petroleum sector's investment, as a percentage of total investment, followed the course set by the former, surpassing the 20 percent level during the middle of the period and declining toward the end. After all, even though investment in the petroleum sector grew since the beginning of the period, its annual compounded rate of growth was 2.8 percent, while that of total investment was roughly around 9.0 percent.

As for the composition of petroleum investment, significant changes occurred. Investment in petroleum production per se greatly declined, contrary to what had occurred in the previous period. With respect to investment in transport capacity, its percentage in terms of total petroleum investment increased substantially, contradicting the previous period trend. Investment in refining facilities increased somewhat, again contradicting the tendency of the preceding period, in which it had considerably decreased proportionally. [21] All these investment data appear in Table 6.29.

The lack of dynamism of investment in the petroleum sector during the 1966-73 period is noteworthy. Petroleum's investment average share of total investment had never been so low in previous periods,

TABLE 6.28

Total and Petroleum Gross Fixed Investment and
the Investment Rate, 1965-73*

Year	Total Investment (millions of bolívares)	Petroleum Investment (millions of bolívares)	Petroleum's Share in Total Investment (percent)	Investment Rate (percent)
1965	5,558	641	11.5	14.4
1966	5,920	637	10.8	15.1
1967	6,118	639	10.4	14.9
1968	7,164	1,141	15.9	16.6
1969	7,496	1,505	20.1	16.6
1970	7,635	1,207	15.8	15.4
1971	8,532	1,118	13.1	17.0
1972	9,499	815	8.6	18.4
1973	11,068	800	7.2	20.3

*Constant bolívares of 1957.

Source: Table 6.31; Banco Central de Venezuela, Informe Económico (Caracas, 1969 and 1972); Ministerio de Minas e Hidrocarburos, Petróleo y Otros Datos Estadísticos (Caracas, 1972); and unpublished data from both the Banco Central and the Ministerio de Minas e Hidrocarburos.

not even during the years 1936-42, when oil was just becoming a prime mover in the Venezuelan economy. It is evident that oil's contribution, from the point of view of investment expenditures, even though significant, cannot be considered important during the recent period. In fact, this confirms a tendency set in the preceding period, which shall probably continue indefinitely, since Venezuelan oil production will, at most, be maintained at the present absolute levels over the next years.

The weakness of investment in the petroleum sector in this period makes the dynamism of investment in the nonpetroleum sectors stand out even more. In real terms (at constant 1957 prices), gross fixed investment in the nonpetroleum part of the economy grew at a higher rate than total gross fixed investment, as can be seen by comparing Tables 6.28 and 6.30. The average annual compounded nonpetroleum investment growth rate was 9.6 percent.

The recuperation of the economy's investment outlays occurring during this period should be noted. As to the relationship that had existed between investment in the petroleum sector and that in the

TABLE 6.29

Composition of Gross Fixed Investment in the Petroleum Sector, 1965-73

Year	Production (millions of bolívares)	Production's Share (percent)	Transportation (millions of bolívares)	Transportation's Share (percent)	Refining (millions of bolívares)
1965	718	87.0	41	5.0	29
1966	502	78.7	65	10.2	38
1967	514	79.4	39	6.0	52
1968	870	73.6	58	4.9	185
1969	855	54.3	178	11.3	387
1970	943	72.9	107	8.3	216
1971	945	73.4	134	10.4	170
1972	758	75.8	67	6.7	131
1973	829	74.0	201	17.9	47

Year	Refining's Share (percent)	Marketing (millions of bolívares)	Marketing's Share (percent)	Other (millions of bolívares)	Other's Share (percent)
1965	3.5	12	1.5	25	3.0
1966	6.0	13	2.0	20	3.1
1967	8.0	21	3.2	21	3.2
1968	15.7	8	0.7	61	5.2
1969	24.6	17	1.1	137	8.7
1970	16.7	20	1.5	8	0.6
1971	13.2	11	0.9	27	2.1
1972	13.1	7	0.7	37	3.7
1973	4.2	5	0.4	39	3.5

Source: Ministerio de Minas e Hidrocarburos, Petróleo y Otros Datos Estadísticos (Caracas, 1972), and unpublished data.

TABLE 6. 30

Nonpetroleum Gross Fixed Domestic Investment
and Retained Value of Total Expenditures in the
Petroleum Industry, 1965-73*
(in millions of constant 1957 and
current bolívares)

Year	Nonpetroleum Investment (constant)	Total Retained Value (current)
1965	4, 917	7, 610
1966	5, 283	7, 099
1967	5, 479	6, 636
1968	6, 023	7, 940
1969	5, 991	7, 678
1970	6, 428	8, 149
1971	7, 414	10, 511
1972	8, 684	9, 801
1973	10, 268	15, 108

*The total retained value includes petroleum foreign exchange taxes.

Source: Table 6. 28; and Appendix, Table A. 2, columns 3-12 and 19-21.

rest of the economy, which had become weaker during the previous period, it totally disappeared during these last years. This constitutes another proof of the increasing coming of age of the Venezuelan economy.

Investment in the petroleum sector was revived somewhat at the beginning of the period by service contract concessions and by some investments at the refining stage (mainly in oil desulfuration); toward the end, petroleum was affected by the policy of conservation of oil resources and by the excess capacity existing in the industry. Contrastingly, investment in the rest of the economy expanded, as excess capacity in many sectors and aggregate demand grew as a result of the expansion of the public sector and of petroleum sector export values, the latter toward the end of the period.

As for the relationship between total gross fixed investment and the retained value of total petroleum expenditures it seems to have been rather close during these years. The last variable is an expression of short-run activity in the oil sector, being expressed in current terms and, thus, reflecting changes in oil prices. Furthermore, it also reflects the increasing pressure applied by the Venezuelan government in order to increase the proportion of the industry's total expenditures retained by Venezuela. Thus, the evolution of total retained value of petroleum does not have to coincide with that of real investment in the petroleum sector, which responds to longer-run forecasts, reacts more sluggishly to current events, and is deflated to reflect real values. This explains why nonpetroleum investment accompanied the evolution of one (total retained value) and not the other (petroleum investment).

During this period, investment in the nonpetroleum part of the economy still represented a substantial part of oil's total value, even though a somewhat smaller one than in the previous period and, therefore, even smaller than in preceding sub-periods. Even though it is still a controverted point, it would seem that the productivity of Venezuelan investments, especially in the case of public investment, seemed at best to have been equivalent to that of the previous period. As a whole, the petroleum's sector direct and immediate contribution, through the retained value of its total expenditures, was not employed as well as in the previous period, in terms of an increase in quantity or quality of the country's productive capacity through capital formation.

In summary, the contribution of petroleum investment to the Venezuelan economy during this period was the smallest of all time periods that have been examined. Furthermore, the use of this contribution apparently was not more fruitful than in earlier periods. Even though the relationship between investments in the petroleum and nonpetroleum sectors was weak, the latter increased substantially during the years 1966-70. It is important to underline that nonpetroleum investment followed closely the trajectory of the total retained value of petroleum's expenditures, indicating that, although the impact of oil on total investment through its investment expenditures had not been significant, its total impact was.

Total Gross Domestic Product and the Expenditures of the Oil Industry

In order to study the impact of the current expenditures of the oil sector on the rest of the economy, the value of oil production will be examined more closely. In current terms, the value of oil production increased very slightly up to 1971, when it experienced a considerable increment. An even heartier increase in 1973. Actually, the latter part of the period represents a violent turnabout from the trend that Venezuelan oil had been observing ever since the mid-1960s. This was due to an increase in the demand for oil in the world markets, which was faster than foreseen, and to the increasing influence of the main oil-producing nations, banded together in the Organization of Petroleum Exporting Countries (OPEC), in fixing oil prices. As for oil's GDP, in current bolívares, after declining in 1966, it experienced a continuous growth, with higher increments toward the end of the period. The compounded yearly rate of growth in the value of oil production was 7.2 percent, equivalent to an overall increase of 74.8 percent (see Table 6.31) during the period.

As for oil's GDP in current terms, it grew at an average compounded rate of 8.9 percent per annum during the period examined, faster than the value of production (see Table 6.31). Adjusting these figures for price inflation, and expressing them in 1957 bolivares, one finds that the GDP of the petroleum sector declined roughly 34 percent during the period as a whole, which represents a compounded yearly rate of decline of 0.4 percent as an average. Throughout the period, the share of petroleum's GDP in total GDP, in real terms, decreased substantially. This meant a continuation of the trend that was apparent in the previous period—a decrease in the relative importance of oil in the economy. By 1973, the share of oil in total GDP had been reduced to 15.9 percent. During the interval examined, the share of oil in total GDP decreased to less than 20 percent for the first time, beginning in 1971. The average share for the period as a whole was 20.7 percent, comparable only to that found in the initial period, covering the years 1936-42. [22]

After decreasing in 1966, oil's total retained value grew almost continuously during the following years, with slight reductions in 1969 and 1972. These increases were basically caused by the rise in oil prices, through their effect in the value of oil production, by stronger tax pressures, and by the government tending to augment the share of the total expenditures of the industry retained in Venezuela. From 1965 to 1973, the total retained value of oil expenditures grew 98.5 percent, representing a yearly compounded growth rate of 8.9 percent. Using 1966 as the base year, the overall expansion of the total retained value during the period would have been 112.8 percent, equivalent to a yearly compounded rate of increase of 11.4 percent. At 1957 prices, this increment would be much less, as can be seen in column 17 of the Appendix, Table A.2.

Petroleum's total retained value per barrel of oil produced, including petroleum foreign exchange taxes, doubled during the period, expanding at the same yearly rate of total retained value. If total retained value per barrel of oil is expressed in 1957 prices, there still is an increase, but of much smaller importance.

As for retained value's share in total expenditures (value of production plus investment in the oil sector), it remained at about 65 percent until the final part of the period, when it rose to about 70 percent. Even though the share was increasing over the period, going from 63.3 percent in 1965 to 72.9 percent in 1973, the overall average was slightly lower than that of the preceding period. Actually, this was due to very high participation shares in the years 1961, 1962, and 1963, which were principally determined by the wide differential that existed between the foreign exchange rates applicable to oil and

TABLE 6.31

Value of Oil Production and Share of Oil in Total Gross Domestic Product, 1965-73
(in millions of bolívares and percentages)

Year	Value of Production (in current bolívares)	Oil's GDP (in current bolívares)	Oil's GDP (in constant 1957 bolívares)	Total GDP (in constant 1957 bolívares)	Share of Petroleum
1965	11,216	9,680	9,444	38,612	24.5
1966	10,415	9,269	8,990	39,287	22.9
1967	10,923	9,970	9,625	41,104	23.5
1968	11,197	10,186	9,794	43,223	22.7
1969	10,824	10,460	10,058	45,077	22.3
1970	11,449	11,244	10,874	49,437	22.0
1971	13,859	12,775	9,842	50,120	19.6
1972	13,234	13,085	8,404	51,615	16.3
1973	19,607	19,176	8,646	54,502	15.9

Source: Banco Central de Venezuela, La Economía Venezolana en los Ultimos Treinta Años (Caracas, 1971); Informe Económico (Caracas, several years), and unpublished statistics; Ministerio de Minas e Hidrocarburos, Petróleo y Otros Datos Estadísticos (Caracas, 1972), and unpublished statistics.

to the rest of the economy, which resulted in very sizeable foreign exchange taxes on oil.

Contrary to the previous period, oil's total combined contribution to the economy grew very fast during the recent years. However, this high growth rate cannot be considered comparable to that experienced in the earlier periods, since it was not smooth, occurring mainly from 1971 on. Impelled in part by the growth in petroleum's contributions, expressed through the retained value of total petroleum expenditures, the GDP of Venezuela increased by 41.2 percent in real terms from 1965 to 1975. This is equivalent to a 3.5 percent yearly compounded growth rate, which is not very satisfactory (see Table 6.31).

It is important to make clear that these rates of change are calculated from our GDP estimates at 1957 prices. This series, which differed very little from those estimates presented by Venezuela's Central Bank in earlier periods, represents toward the end of the period examined, an attempt to link two different series. This had to be done, because for the last years of the period, the Central Bank has only published estimates of real GDP in terms of 1968 prices. The linkage was made on the basis of Central Bank estimates at both 1957 prices and 1968 prices for the years 1968 and 1969. It should be pointed out that, if instead of linking them, the two series are

TABLE 6.32

Total Retained Value, as a Percentage of Total
Expenditures in the Petroleum Industry and per
Barrel of Oil Produced, 1965-73

Year	Share of Total Expenditures (percent)	Per Barrel of Oil (bolívares)
1965	63.3	6.00
1966	64.2	5.77
1967	66.0	5.91
1968	64.1	6.02
1969	61.9	5.85
1970	63.9	6.02
1971	69.4	8.12
1972	68.9	8.32
1973	72.9	12.29

Note: Total retained value includes oil foreign exchanges taxes.

Source: Previous Tables 6.30 and 6.31; and Ministerio de Minas e Hidrocarburos, Petróleo y Otros Datos Estadísticos (Caracas, 1972), and unpublished data.

kept separate, GDP growth estimates for the period would not be
affected by much. [23] Moreover, considering that growth estimates
toward the end of the period are calculated in constant 1968 bolívares,
which have a smaller purchasing power than those of 1957, it is not
surprising to find that growth is somewhat smaller in terms of the
latter.

On the other hand, it is not difficult to explain the apparently
small repercussion of the petroleum sector over the economy as a
whole. It has been already noted that the effects of petroleum operate
with a lag on Venezuela's overall economic activity and that petroleum
expansion really took place in the last couple of years of the period
considered. Moreover, when the expansion is expressed in real terms,
then the effects of the terms of trade in total income are not noticeable.
Given that the terms-of-trade effect was unquestionably favorable,
especially in the last year of the period under examination, the conversion of petroleum income into real terms tends to underestimate the
impact of petroleum on the economy.

Total growth between 1966 and 1973 amounts to 38. 7 percent,
corresponding to a yearly compounded growth rate of 4. 8 percent.
It should be pointed out that the estimated growth was smaller in the
period considered, even though it had a higher investment rate than
in the previous one. It appears that in the present period, it was
necessary to undertake a faster increase in the process of capital
accumulation, after having reduced excess capacity in the 1958-65
period. Once again, this appears to show the dangers of relating
the investment rate with the rate of growth of gross product during
relatively short periods, since contradictions may appear with the
direct relationship, found by Kuznets when longer historical periods
are examined.

Examining now the behavior of the GDP of the nonpetroleum part
of the economy (see Table 6. 33), it is found that its total increase
was 57. 1 percent from 1966 to 1973. An increase of 65 percent is
found, if the last year of the preceding period (1965) is taken as the
base. Although these figures are greater than those corresponding
to the growth of total GDP, they represent annual compounded average
changes of 6. 5 percent and 6. 7 percent, respectively, which are
significantly smaller than those experienced by the nonpetroleum
GDP in the previous period. [24]

The expansion of the petroleum sector's contributions to the
Venezuelan economy was only important toward the end of the period
and, in real terms, oil's GDP decreased. Therefore, it is not surprising that petroleum's impact during this period was much weaker
than in the preceding one. The indication that, even toward the
end of the period, the carry-over of the oil sector's impulse to the
rest of the economy seems to have been weak appears to be partly
explained by the apparent loss of dynamism of the industrial import
substitution process and to the slackening of the agricultural sector's
growth rate.

TABLE 6. 33

Nonpetroleum Gross Domestic Product, 1965-73
(millions of constant 1957 bolívares)

Year	Nonpetroleum GDP
1965	27, 193
1966	28, 598
1967	29, 891
1968	31, 316
1969	33, 164
1970	37, 157
1971	38, 325
1972	42, 300
1973	44, 862

Source: Tables 6. 28, 6. 30, 6. 31, Appendix, Table A. 2, column 19.

The Venezuelan economy, which had taken-off in the previous subperiod, showed that it was not yet sufficiently independent of oil so that its nonpetroleum sector would not become affected by the adverse conditions encountered by Venezuelan oil up to the end of the 1966-73 period. The signs that the process of import substitution was reaching a point of maturity and that the agricultural sector's growth process was being hindered by adverse policies and conditions appear to have been important factors also.

Although the agricultural production series, which had helped to interpret the sector's economic evolution, was recently discontinued, the estimates of GDP at 1957 prices in agriculture point out that the sectoral growth was less than 4. 0 percent yearly, compounded, as an average, during these years (see Table 6. 34). The unavailability of volume indices, as well as the change in the base of the GDP series, renders different the detailing of those products that grew faster during this interval. The substantial decrease in the agricultural growth rate, when compared with the previous period, seems to have been due, to a great extent, to the fact that the priority given to agriculture was not so high in this period. The enthusiasm for agrarian reform policies, which greatly stimulated agrarian production, began declining as the years passed, and, at the end of the period, the lack of dynamism in this sector constituted a general preoccupation in Venezuela.

Manufacturing production indices and the detailed estimates of physical volumes presented in the first part of this chapter were also discontinued during the present term. However, value added at 1957

prices by industrial category, were estimated until 1972, and the
manufacturing industry's GDP for the entire period was also available.
By concentrating on the latter, and linking those series in 1957 prices
with those in 1968 prices, both published by the Central Bank, the
overall performance of the manufacturing sector can be evaluated.
The cumulative growth in real GDP of manufacturing was above 6 percent per year as an average in this period. [25] These series include
oil refining in the manufacturing sector. Evidently, the growth in
manufacturing was much slower during this period, when compared
with previous periods, and particularly with the pace of growth during
the years 1958-65.

Data on the value added, by type of manufacturing industry, are
shown in Table 6.35. Those industries experiencing fastest growth
were of the capital goods type: metallurgy and construction, assembly,
and repair of machinery. The lumber and printing industries, producing
in great part intermediate and capital goods, also grew very fast.
These industries expanded at a faster pace than the manufacturing
sector as a whole. It should be noted that no consumer goods-type
industry grew faster than manufacturing as a whole, confirming the
previously noted tendency of concentrated expansion in the capital
and intermediate goods industries, although at more moderate absolute
rates than in the preceding period.

As for the rest of the secondary activities, the production of water
and electrical services more than doubled, as can be seen on Table 6.34.

TABLE 6.34

Gross Domestic Product in Agriculture, and
Electricity and Water, 1965-73
(millions of 1957 bolívares)

Year	Agricultural GDP	Electricity and Water GDP
1965	2,546	738
1966	2,653	808
1967	2,798	894
1968	2,938	1,041
1969	3,030	1,147
1970	3,246	1,287
1971	3,219	1,422
1972	3,282	1,517
1973	3,471	1,682

Source: Derived from Banco Central de Venezuela, La Economía
Venezolana en los Ultimos Treinta Años (Caracas, 1971), and Informe
Económico (Caracas, 1969 and 1972).

TABLE 6.35

Indices of Value Added in the Manufacturing Sector, by Industry, 1965-72[a]

Industry	1965	1966	1967	1968	1969	1970	1971	1972	Percentage Change	
					Index[b]				1972/1965	1972/1966
Food processing	322.0	312.9	335.2	336.6	345.0	363.6	396.0	428.9	33.2	37.1
Beverage	229.9	238.7	257.9	263.7	291.4	308.9	326.8	357.2	55.4	49.6
Tobacco	346.1	349.4	376.2	400.5	411.3	432.3	460.0	526.7	52.2	50.1
Textile	440.2	441.4	459.1	487.3	515.6	531.6	572.5	644.1	46.3	45.9
Clothing	199.1	206.6	213.0	214.5	231.4	245.3	271.8	289.5	45.4	40.1
Paper and cardboard	1,269.2	1,283.3	1,336.6	1,485.0	1,498.4	1,597.3	1,677.3	1,851.6	45.9	44.3
Printing	262.1	282.3	331.3	372.0	403.4	430.4	466.6	506.3	93.1	79.3
Leather	262.0	295.6	279.1	263.0	257.5	276.3	289.0	305.8	16.7	3.5
Chemical	409.9	412.8	452.4	489.5	526.2	555.7	597.9	642.7	56.8	55.7
Timber	206.7	194.4	203.2	239.5	236.1	270.6	294.4	338.0	63.5	73.9
Furniture	329.0	356.5	377.1	389.5	426.1	449.1	473.8	498.9	51.6	39.9
Rubber	475.7	504.5	472.5	543.0	557.1	590.5	638.3	688.7	44.8	36.5
Construction materials	220.0	217.0	236.2	244.4	228.8	237.0	270.9	312.1	41.9	43.8
Construction, assembly, and repair of machinery	554.1	605.9	692.9	769.8	890.7	925.4	948.5	1,149.6	107.5	89.7
Construction, assembly, and repair of vehicles	353.0	371.0	356.6	375.7	416.3	371.8	397.8	446.7	26.5	20.4
Metal	923.5	905.6	980.6	1,030.6	1,265.6	1,471.9	1,675.0	1,933.0	109.3	113.4
Basic metals	4,389.0	4,096.0	4,878.1	5,823.0	5,165.0	5,934.6	6,124.5	6,332.7	144.3	154.6
Jewelry	313.8	307.4	321.6	337.7	349.9	372.6	391.2	435.8	38.9	41.8

aCalculated in terms of constant 1957 bolívares.
b1953 = 100.

Source: Banco Central de Venezuela, La Economía Venezolana en los Últimos Treinta Años (Caracas, 1971); Informe Económico (Caracas, 1971); and unpublished data.

This expansion was of the order of 10.8 percent, when expressed in compounded annual average rates. However, these services represented a very small part of total GDP. The construction sector's growth was a shade lower than that of electricity and water, since they almost doubled, attaining a compounded annual average growth rate of 9.4 percent during this time period. However, it must be recognized that construction has a greater weight on total GDP (see Table 6.36) being these estimates of value added, the ones which are being used to evaluate the behavior of the different components of Venezuela's economy.

As pointed out before, the process of import substitution of manufactures, concentrated on intermediate and capital goods, was the main agent in the development of this sector. However, everything seems to indicate that the existence of a limited market and other production difficulties, together with the lack of an effort oriented to support the more efficient manufacturing lines, especially those with an export potential, were the key factors determining a smaller vitality in this sector.

The rapid growth of the utilities sector (electricity and water) was based not so much on the expansion of manufacturing and agriculture, but on the dynamism of the construction sector. In this respect, what occurred in this period differs again from the experience in the previous one, when manufacturing and agriculture grew more rapidly. It should also be considered that, even though the pace of

TABLE 6.36

Gross Domestic Product in the Construction
Sector, 1965-73
(millions of 1957 bolívares)

Year	GDP
1965	1,545
1966	1,648
1967	1,682
1968	2,040
1969	1,975
1970	1,959
1971	2,289
1972	2,867
1973	3,176

Source: Banco Central de Venezuela, La Economía Venezolana en los Últimos Treinta Años (Caracas, 1971), and Informe Económico (Caracas, 1969 and 1972).

TABLE 6. 37

Gross Domestic Product of the Mining Sector,
Excluding Petroleum, 1965-73
(millions of 1957 bolívares)

Year	GDP
1965	425
1966	427
1967	411
1968	366
1969	454
1970	484
1971	454
1972	412
1973	512

Source: Derived from Banco Central de Venezuela, La Economía
Venezolana en los Ultimos Treinta Años (Caracas, 1971), and Informe
Económico (Caracas, 1969 and 1972).

the expansion in electricity and water slowed down during this period,
they still maintained a high growth rate, which can be partially attributed to the fact that those services were not yet sufficient to fill the
needs of the entire Venezuelan society. At the same time, the expansion in the construction sector was mostly determined by the recovery
of gross fixed investment that took place in the 1966-73 period, as
well as the high level of government expenditures taking place during
those years.

The growth of the mining sector during these years, after petroleum is excluded, was slow as it was in the preceding period. Mining
activities expanded 20 percent overall, tantamount to a compounded
annual rate of approximately 2. 5 percent. This sector's GDP at
1957 prices, moved somewhat erratically, with a considerable jump
in 1973. If it had not been for this large increase, the sector's
value added would have decreased during the years examined.

Finally, the rate of growth of tertiary activities also declined
during these years. There generally exists a close relationship
between the rate of growth of manufacturing and that of the tertiary
sector, and this has been found to be applicable to Venezuela also.
In this period, the expansion of tertiary activities in real terms was
also smaller than the one in manufacturing. However, it was still
larger than the expansion in primary activities, including oil. As
may be seen in Table 6. 38, tertiary activities increased more than
50 percent overall, which represents a compounded annual growth

rate of approximately 5. 3 percent as an average. Of all tertiary activities, transportation and communication, having grown by 70 percent,
experienced the largest expansion in the period. Commercial and
service activities grew at a smaller but still respectable rate of about
49 percent during these years. Given that commerce and services
constitute most of the tertiary sector, the growth in transportation and
communication did not have a significant effect on the magnitude of
the expansion in tertiary production.

It was only toward the end of the period that oil began again to
contribute substantially to the growth of the rest of the Venezuelan
economy, through the increase in the retained value of its total
expenditures. Although there has generally been a lag between the
growth in petroleum's contributions and the growth of the economy's
nonpetroleum sectors, the response to the substantial expansion of
the oil sector from 1971 on appears to have been exceptionally delayed.
This may have been due to the irregularity in the growth of total retained value of oil expenditures, which jumped ahead in 1971, contracted
in 1972, and advanced even more in 1973. But it could have also
been that the mechanism of transmission of the oil sector's expansion
to the rest of the economy might not have been operating so effectively during the 1970s given the structural change experienced by
the economy of Venezuela. On the other hand, the effectiveness in
the use of petroleum's contributions (especially the fiscal one) left

TABLE 6. 38

Gross Domestic Product of the Tertiary Sector,
by Category, 1965-73
(millions of 1957 bolívares)

Year	Transportation and Communications	Commerce	Services	Total
1965	1, 267	5, 455	12, 665	19, 387
1966	1, 306	5, 695	13, 202	20, 203
1967	1, 310	5, 907	13, 550	20, 832
1968	1, 460	6, 344	14, 119	21, 293
1969	1, 466	6, 501	15, 075	23, 042
1970	1, 739	7, 139	15, 924	24, 802
1971	1, 870	7, 431	16, 642	25, 943
1972	2, 047	7, 809	17, 845	27, 701
1973	2, 154	8, 199	18, 838	29, 191

Source: Derived from Banco Central de Venezuela, La Economía
Venezolana en los Ultimos Treinta Años (Caracas, 1971), and Informe
Económico (Caracas, 1969 and 1972).

a lot to be desired during this period, and this may also help explain the slower and weaker reaction.

By some combination of these reasons, the impact of petroleum in 1971 and the following years does not seem to have brought about a corresponding increase in the real product of the nonpetroleum part of the economy. Yet, it did bring about a considerable increase in the Venezuelan investment rate. [26] Also, the favorable terms-of-trade effects, resulting from the rapid rise in petroleum prices, substantially raised the total income of the Venezuelan society, in current terms, through its international exchange.

All of this underlines the need to carefully analyze the effects that the expansion of retained value of total petroleum expenditures had on the nonpetroleum GDP during this period. This will probably shed further light on the operation of the mechanism of transmission of an oil expansion to the rest of the economy, under the conditions given by the change in Venezuela's economic structure. It is also possible that what appears to be a time lag in the reaction of the nonpetroleum sectors to a considerable increase in the petroleum contributions is actually a sample of the increasing independence of the rest of the economy since the end of the 1950s.

The per capita growth of the Venezuelan economy in real terms was rather small during these years, because of its high population growth rate. Per capita GDP grew from 4,427 bolívares to 4,810 bolívares (constant 1957 bolívares), representing an overall increase of 8.6 percent from 1965 to 1973. When expressed as an average yearly compounded rate, this figure amounts to roughly 1.0 percent. However, the nonpetroleum sector expanded at a rate that, if not comparable to that of the previous period, at least could be considered satisfactory. At the same time, these sectors continued to bolster their independence from oil, which began to constitute a smaller part of Venezuela's GDP in real or constant terms.

What seems to demand greater attention is the finding of ways to improve, through economic policy measures, the transmission of the positive benefits that the petroleum sector could be able to generate in the future, given that the means of ensuring that its adverse conditions are not carried over to the rest of the economy, seem to have been developed during the 1960s. Equally important is the thinking through of new strategies for expanding the nonpetroleum sectors, since the process of import substitution of manufactured products appears to have lost its dynamism in Venezuela. [27]

NOTES

1. Ministerio de Minas e Hidrocarburos, Petróleo y Otros Datos Estadísticos (Caracas, 1965), p. 131.

2.   Reserves were still relatively high when the exchange controls were established in 1960, but they had halved between 1957 and 1960.

3.   Note that in this period these calculations were made in terms of current bolívares.

4.   However, it must be recognized that Venezuela had been able to put these reserves aside as a result of a strong showing by the petroleum industry in previous periods.

5.   The foreign exchange tax proceeds calculated in this fashion differ from the foreign exchange profits reported by the government because of the following: (a) during a given year, the amount of foreign currency turned in by the petroleum companies is not necessarily equal to the amount sold by the Central Bank, and on which profits are made; and (b) the government reports the combined net profits in the Central Bank's operations, and usually there have been losses as a result of subsidies to other sectors, as well as profits derived from other industries, and also the expenses incurred in the operation of the program are deducted. Moreover, the figures presented in this study are an approximation obtained by multiplying the foreign exchange sold by the oil companies to the Central Bank during a year by the difference between the petroleum buying rate and the official rate (called "controlled official rate" since 1960) up to 1960, and the petroleum buying rate and the controlled free buying rate from 1961 to 1964. From 1964 on, the difference again reverted to the pre-1961 system. This is an approximation, because the actual profits derived from oil result from complicated operations, with different types of buying and selling rates by the Central Bank and the commercial banks and changes in these rates over time. Moreover, not all petroleum-supplied foreign exchange has been bought by the Central Bank at the established rates. Whenever the supply of foreign exchange from petroleum companies exceeds the demand for foreign exchange by the Venezuelan economy, a lower buying rate can apply, corresponding to the gold import point. On certain occasions, this rule has been put into effect.

6.   In January 1964, the petroleum rate was devalued to 4.40 bolívares per dollar.

7.   If the exchange tax is not included, oil revenues amount to 4,803 million bolívares in 1964 and 4,863 million bolívares in 1965, a rise from the tax level of 3,659 million bolívares in 1963. With the exchange tax included, the 1963 figure is 5,625 million bolívares, with 4,901 million bolívares and 4,980 million bolívares, respectively, in 1964 and 1965.

8.   Keep in mind that, in 1956 and 1957, the oil industry made concession payments of 974 million bolívares and 1,142 million bolívares, respectively, to the Venezuelan government.

9.   As shall be seen later, the GDP series has been revised by the Central Bank, while the investment figures were not. As the GDP

estimates were corrected upwards, there is reason to believe that gross fixed investment has been underestimated in turn. This would particularly affect the investment rate, which is the relation between those two variables.

10. From 1957 to 1965, production rose at a compounded annual average rate of 2.9 percent, as can be seen in Appendix, Table A.2, column 20.

11. This does not mean that the Venezuelan economy could continue to achieve long-run growth in per capita terms without at least some moderate expansion in the oil sector at this moment. However, the rest of the economy was beginning to move on its own to a greater extent. A continuation of this trend would eventually lead to a situation in which the rest of the economy would not be much affected by the oil sector in the determination of its level of activity, except in the short run.

12. All of these estimates would have been larger if they had included the income originated in the production of capital goods for the petroleum industry's own use (shown in Appendix, Table A.2, column 14).

13. These receipts are defined as the loss of income to the petroleum sector of a less-favorable conversion of foreign currency into bolívares.

14. This figure may be exaggerated, as the national account figures were revised in 1970 by the Central Bank. The revisions of the GDP were generally upward, but were only covered back to 1960. Thus, it might be inferred that the 1957-59 figures shown in Table 6.11 are underestimated.

15. The growth rate in nonpetroleum GDP is probably overestimated, because the revisions undertaken by the Central Bank in the GDP figures largely affected the nonpetroleum sectors.

16. It was not possible to present accurate estimates of the overall increase in manufacturing production without petroleum refining for the whole period. See Banco Central de Venezuela, La Economía Venezolana en los Ultimos Treinta Años (Caracas, 1971), Sector Secundario.

17. Note that the base from which this growth took place is comparatively small. Thus, the relative rate of increase is exaggerated.

18. Witness the slow growth of investment vis-à-vis the total GDP.

19. Curiously, investment outlays expanded year after year (see Table 6.26), with the exception of 1970. However, its share of total expenditures declined significantly during the interval, although erratically, since it practically increased until 1969, declining from then on.

20. Toward the end of the period, government investment, excluding state enterprises, accounted for less than one-half of oil's total revenues.

21. It is interesting to note that, toward the end of the period, investment in petroleum refining had increased, until it represented 25 percent of overall investment in the petroleum sector.

22. As in preceding periods, the product originated by the petroleum sector in the production of capital goods for its own use has not been included. These estimates appear in the Appendix, Table A. 2, column 14.

23. See GDP estimates at constant prices in Banco Central de Venezuela, Informe Económico (Caracas, 1969, 1972, and 1973).

24. This conclusion would still hold, even after taking into account the possible overestimation of the growth in nonpetroleum GDP during the 1958-65 interval.

25. See the manufacturing industry's GDP in Banco Central de Venezuela, Informe Económico (Caracas, 1969, 1972, and 1973).

26. It is possible that the increase in investment might have been tied to the slow reaction of the rest of the economy. The economy appears to have been affected by restrictions in capacity and even bottlenecks in certain sectors, which required a special effort in the investment sector.

27. Economic policies to ensure the sustained and fast growth of the agricultural sector should be considered here. This will allow Venezuela to continue and conclude a take-off period in the 1970s and to foresee the possibility of self-sustaining growth from the 1980s on.

Almost every peripheral country in the not-too-distant past had a pattern of trade based on the export of primary products and the importation of industrial goods. The major source of growth in these countries was the export sector, or one or a few lines in it. Such sector lines usually constituted a sizeable portion of the product originated in these countries.

If these activities expand satisfactorily over a long period of time (two to three decades), would their influence upon the other sectors be sufficiently strong so as to bring about a parallel expansion of the economy? As has been seen in Chapter 2, there are affirmative and negative views on this question, while others believe there is no general rule.

Such periods of expansion in primary export activities in peripheral countries occurred in the past. Hence, history might contribute to settling this debate. Even though the expositors of these views also hold contradictory beliefs as to the historical outcomes, no effort has been made to resolve the debate in an empirical fashion.

It is our belief that in peripheral countries with the characteristics described above, primary export sectors or lines can transmit their growth to the whole economy. This usually takes place automatically, but, in many cases, it requires an efficacious manipulation of the potentially leading sector's impact upon the rest of the economy.

The Venezuelan case from 1936 to the present is a test case for these views. Petroleum activities in Venezuela represented 7 percent or 8 percent of national income and over 20 percent of GDP at the beginning of the period. In terms of retained value of total expenditures, petroleum activities grew at a 12.3 percent compounded average yearly increase from 1936 to 1973. Even in terms of GDP in constant 1957 bolívares, the growth amounted to more than a 6.5 percent clip yearly. It is clear that petroleum fits the definition of "potentially leading sector" during these years.

In 1936, the Venezuelan economy exported almost exclusively primary products and produced very little of its industrial goods at home. Primary activities dominated the economy, and a great portion of the industrial establishments were small scale and of the craft and artisan type.[1] Petroleum was the main source of growth in Venezuela throughout the historical time span examined, as was shown in preceding chapters.

Exports accounted for 23.7 percent of total GDP in 1936, even though world trade had not recuperated from the jolt of the Depression. By 1940, the participation of exports in total GDP had gone up to 31.1 percent. Thus, just before the war, Venezuela was in every sense an open economy—tied to the advanced nations through the international markets. It traditionally had depended on the international economy for an important portion of its necessities and requirements and as a basic source of its economic progress.

In its expansion, the Venezuelan oil industry contributed to the growth of the other sectors. Its main contributions came through: (a) its financing of the public sector and the provision of services of an essentially public character by the industry, while absorbing a minimal portion of the government's budget (see Table 7.1); (b) the foreign exchange earnings supplied; (c) the increase in the economic wealth and the productive capacity of the nation taking place through petroleum investment, and the strengthening of the Venezuelan capital goods industry that it brought about; and (d) the income and current expenditures originated in the oil industry, and the multiplier-accelerator repercussions they created throughout the economy, leading to an increase in aggregate demand and a larger volume of savings.

With respect to the two latter contributions, special importance must be attached to the retained portions of petroleum's investment and current expenditures, which have a more direct and immediate impact on the rest of the economy. In fact, although there are many other contributions, the retained value of total expenditures is an approximate reflection of the combined total.

The petroleum industry provided a large share of the total foreign exchange earnings of the economy. While at the beginning, net capital inflows constituted an important part of these earnings, this has not been the case since the late 1950s. Petroleum exports have risen tremendously over time, at an average compounded increase of 6.5 percent per year. This contribution, and the effects related to it—such as import availability and inflation-combating capabilities—have been called the balance-of-payments contribution of oil.

Oil has contributed a large share of government revenues, as well. Taxes derived directly from the oil sector rose at an annual average compounded rate of 15.1 percent, with their share in total tax revenues having increased since 1936. As in the balance-of-payments contribution, other effects related to oil taxes are part and

TABLE 7. 1

Share of the Expenditures of the Central Government
Corresponding to Mines and Hydrocarbons, 1940- 73
(percentages)

Year	Share
1940	2. 4
1945	4. 0
1950	6. 7
1955	3. 1
1960	1. 6
1965	1. 6
1970	2. 0
1973	2. 8

Note: For the years 1940, 1945, and 1950, the shares refer to
the Development Ministry. The Department of Mines and Hydrocarbons
was part of this ministry then. From 1955 on, the shares refer to the
Ministry of Mines and Hydrocarbons.

Source: Banco Central de Venezuela, La Economía Venezolana en
los Últimos Treinta Años (Caracas, 1971).

parcel of its public sector contribution, such as the low tax pressure
on other sectors and the possibility of extending public services
while averting deficit financing.

The investment contribution of petroleum has not been as impressive. In real terms, oil investment only grew at a compounded annual
average rate of growth of 4. 1 percent. Yet, if 1958 is taken as the
terminal year, then the growth is much higher, amounting to an 11. 1
percent annual average compounded rate. Despite the fact that the
share of oil in total investment declined throughout time, the investment contribution of petroleum has been important, especially in
helping the development of the construction and metal industries.

The exogenous income— expenditure injections of oil into the
flow matrix of the Venezuelan economy—has been of considerable
importance. As petroleum is export oriented, a change in its prices
does not directly or necessarily affect internal prices in Venezuela.
Thus, the income-expenditure injections, expressed in current terms,
are the relevant ones. Total current petroleum expenditures rose at
an annual average compounded rate of more than 11 percent. The
GDP of the petroleum industry, in current terms, grew at a similar
pace. Clearly, the overall expenditure contribution, which embraces
other related effects, experienced a formidable increase from 1936 to
1965.

No other contributions have been examined in detail. But the tremendous increase in the retained value of total expenditures suggests that their growth has been comparably fast. Total retained value increased at a 12.3 percent annual average compounded rate of growth. This means that, in 1973, the retained value of total expenditures in the oil industry was 74 times larger than in 1936.

Over the years, total retained value has increased more than the total expenditures of the oil industry. Thus, the percentage share of total retained value in the latter rose. The behavior of the share of retained value in the total expenditures of the oil industry has been mostly determined by the policies of the Venezuelan government. The main variables juggled have been the native wage bill of the industry, its local purchases, and the taxes it pays the Venezuelan government. [2] In some occasions, the share changed as a result of industry decisions, however.

The government was quite successful in enlarging the retained value portion up to 1948. From 1948 to 1957, the pressure was off. When it resumed in 1958, it was concurrent with a confidence crisis in the oil industry with respect to the economic and political future of Venezuela and with misgivings about the status of the companies and the organization of the Venezuelan oil industry in the years ahead. As a result, investment dropped off considerably, and exports stagnated.

For the manipulation of the portion of total expenditures retained in Venezuela, tax policy is mainly used. In previous chapters, the question of the effects of high tax pressure on oil sales has been briefly considered. Up to 1957, an increasing tax pressure on the oil industry did not affect petroleum exports. But then, increasing tax pressure from 1958 to 1965 brought about a reduction in exports (see Table 7.2). Even if decreasing oil prices are taken into account, the growth in oil exports from 1957 on is much slower, as the figures in Table 7.3 show, notwithstanding that total world exports of oil continued to expand at a brisk pace from 1958 to 1965. Thus, the high tax pressure in that period appeared to have had a negative effect on oil exports.

This illustrates the fact that there are limits to the juggling of the retained value portion of total expenditures, and that, at a certain point, an increase of, say, 1 percent in the tax rate on oil might actually bring about a decrease in total retained value or a smaller rise than if no change in taxes would have taken place. Thus, the maximization of the absolute size of retained value of total expenditures over the long run, which has to be the central objective of petroleum policy in Venezuela, might require the sacrifice of immediate gains under certain circumstances.

However, the situation changed considerably in the late 1960s and 1970s. A conservationist policy with respect to petroleum was prevalent. Venezuela felt that the expansion in the production of oil was not appropriate, given the increasing exhaustion of the reserves

TABLE 7.2

Tax Pressure on the Oil Industry and Oil Exports,
1936-73

Year	Tax Pressure* (percent)	Exports (millions of dollars)
1936	10.47	133
1937	8.40	167
1938	21.13	187
1939	18.46	170
1940	17.53	262
1941	15.83	324
1942	19.11	206
1943	22.00	254
1944	25.48	342
1945	31.73	332
1946	29.19	485
1947	29.34	664
1948	30.05	1,069
1949	28.05	966
1950	28.85	1,124
1951	29.68	1,297
1952	29.54	1,384
1953	27.99	1,428
1954	29.43	1,564
1955	30.50	1,791
1956	31.46	2,086
1957	32.58	2,570
1958	38.62	2,299
1959	37.38	2,128
1960	36.58	2,149
1961	38.34	2,213
1962	41.07	2,343
1963	41.97	2,336
1964	45.73	2,341
1965	45.46	2,305
1966	46.17	2,221
1967	49.42	2,333
1968	49.12	2,425
1969	55.17	2,449
1970	54.14	2,496
1971	54.43	3,127
1972	62.75	3,509
1973	66.56	5,294

*Defined as taxes accrued over value of production.

Source: From Appendix, Table A.2, column 21; Banco Central de Venezuela, La Economía Venezolana en los Ultimos Treinta Años (Caracas, 1971); Ministerio de Fomento, Anuario Estadístico (Caracas, several years); and Ministerio de Minas e Hidrocarburos, unpublished statistics

of this nonrecuperable resource. This was especially the case because such resources were being produced by foreign companies. At this juncture, the continued pressures to increase the retained value portion out of the total oil expenditures made sense, given the goals of the government. Of course, a policy objective that is implied as a corollary is the discouragement of investment in, and exports of, oil, except if they are the result of substantially higher oil prices. The former may involve a sacrifice in the absolute figures of retained value of oil expenditures.

It is clear that the contribution of the oil industry to the other sectors of the Venezuelan economy has been considerable. To a

TABLE 7.3

Volume of Oil Exports, 1950-73
(thousands of cubic meters)

Year	Exports
1950	82,619
1951	93,566
1952	99,491
1953	96,423
1954	104,118
1955	117,433
1956	134,539
1957	149,498
1958	141,432
1959	149,586
1960	156,238
1961	160,420
1962	175,165
1963	178,362
1964	186,935
1965	188,748
1966	184,635
1967	195,061
1968	196,009
1969	197,929
1970	201,343
1971	191,723
1972	180,095
1973	185,616

Source: Ministerio de Minas e Hidrocarburos, Petróleo y Otros Datos Estadísticos (Caracas, 1972), and unpublished statistics.

great extent, the policy decisions of the Venezuelan government brought this about. The government was also instrumental in reaping the potential benefits of petroleum's contributions. However, frequently, these contributions were inefficiently utilized.

In general, it should be noted that government policies determining the contribution of oil and directing their use left ample room for improvement. Seemingly, the government did not have clearly defined policy objectives in relation to the petroleum industry and its influence on the economy, or, if it had, it did not consistently follow them.

THE PERFORMANCE OF THE VENEZUELAN
ECONOMY SINCE GÓMEZ'S DOWNFALL

The economy of Venezuela experienced a considerable expansion from 1936 on. Total GDP, in 1957 prices, grew at a 6. 5 percent average annual compounded rate of growth. Nonpetroleum GDP expanded at a 7. 0 percent annual average rate. This is one of the fastest growth rates during a close-to-four-decade time span in contemporary economic history. Notwithstanding a very high rate of growth of population, per capita GDP, in constant 1957 bolívares, increased at an approximate compounded average of 3. 25 percent yearly.

In the meantime, the Venezuelan economy experienced a strong industrialization process. If oil and mining are excluded, secondary activities were the most dynamic sector in the economy during this interval. The process gained strength from 1942 on and based itself in an expansion of the market and in the substitution of industrial imports. As a result, by 1973, Venezuela had become a semiindustrialized society. The agricultural sector grew disappointingly during most of these periods, however, while the tertiary sector expanded more or less in consonance with the overall growth of the economy.

Enormous progress took place in the Venezuelan infrastructure from 1936 to 1973. The basic conditions for a take-off were completed by the late 1950s. In the 1960s, a new era dawned in Venezuela, with the economy becoming increasingly resilient and taking off into self-sustained growth. Assuming no long-run stagnation or slow growth in the value of oil exports in the future, the achievement of self-generating growth appears to be within the reach of Venezuela in another 10 years or so.

Even though it slackened considerably during the 1960s, investment in real terms increased at an 8. 4 percent average compounded annual rate from 1936 to 1973 in Venezuela. Even though the rate of capital accumulation picked up in the early 1970s, its rate of expansion was significantly greater up to 1957. The growth in investment was higher in the nonpetroleum part of the economy. From 1936 to 1973, nonpetroleum gross fixed domestic investment, in 1957 bolívares, experienced an annual average compounded rate of growth of 9. 4 percent.

From 1936 to 1955, total GDP, in 1957 bolívares, expanded at a 9.2 percent rate of growth per year as an average. During this period, the average investment rate, in constant bolívares, was 23.8 percent yearly. From 1955 to 1973, the rate of growth decreased to a yearly average of 5.75 percent. At the same time, the rate of capital formation also decreased to an annual average of 18.6 percent. Although the differences are small, these facts show that increases in capital formation were tied to higher rates of growth over the long-run, which is in agreement with Kuznet's findings. It should be noted that this test is more fitting to Kuznets' proposition than those reported in previous chapters, as they cover a longer time span. Kuznets usually used two or three decades in his empirical studies, using 15-year periods only as an exception.

THE DISTRIBUTION OF THE GAINS FROM GROWTH

The absolute increase in retained value of total expenditures of the oil industry from 1936 to 1973 comes to about 5.9 times the total GDP of Venezuela in 1936, if both are expressed in current bolívares. The growth of the Venezuelan economy, resulting to an important degree from the massive influence of oil, was considerable. Yet, the rise in product and income per capita could be impressive and still not affect most of the people, because of an unequal income distribution.

The process of economic development in Venezuela has been marred by such income distribution problems. Not only do they relate to the personal distribution of income, but also to the regional one.

Only very recently has some attention been devoted to the study of the personal distribution of income in Venezuela. Empirical proof of the skewness of the personal income distribution was first presented by the Commission to Study the Fiscal System of Venezuela, directed by Carl Shoup. [3] Since then, various studies have appeared, based on a national survey of income and expenditures undertaken by Cordiplan in 1962, * and another nationwide data collection effort on housing, which included information on income, which was carried out by the National Savings and Loan Bank and the National Housing Commission. [4] They tend to confirm what the Shoup Commission found in 1957.

The effects of a highly concentrated distribution of personal income on economic development have been subject to controversy. According to some economists, an unequal income distribution facilitates a high savings rate, which is essential for growth. Others believe that a less-skewed income distribution is tied to the expansion of the middle class, and thus to a more numerous entrepreneurial class, while bringing about larger internal markets.

---

*Cordiplan is the national planning agency of Venezuela.

Various studies have been conducted on the effects of greater or less equality in the distribution of income on growth. [5] The general conclusion has been that rather important changes in the former have relatively weak effects on growth. In the case of Venezuela, it appears that the inequality in its personal income distribution did not hamper the development process noticeably. The high savings rate usually sustained by Venezuela during these decades can be partly explained in terms of the distribution of income. Even though the domestic market would have been larger if greater equality had prevailed, the substantial immigration that took place after World War II and the elaborate business promotion system of the government assured a strong business activity and a healthy demand for capital in Venezuela.

A worrisome fact, however, is that the personal distribution of income in Venezuela appears to be getting worse. This is the con- clusion reported in a recent article that attempted to compare the various estimates of the pattern of personal income distribution across time, starting with the Shoup study. [6] Furthermore, if the functional distribution of income, represented by the factor shares, is considered, the distribution of income, after becoming generally more equal up to 1963, has begun to move in the opposite direction (see Table 7.4).

As to the regional distribution of income, previous chapters have shown that, up to 1950, growth was highly concentrated in Caracas and in the areas where petroleum operations were taking place. From then on, other territories began to increase their participation in the economic growth of the country (for example, the state of Bolivar in the Guayana region and the Maracay, Valencia, and Barquisimeto areas), but Caracas and its environs still gained the most. It was only from the 1960s on that centers of economic activity not related to the exploration of oil began to show a dynamism comparable to that of Caracas.

Regional disparities in growth rates usually occur while a nation grows. Although such disparities are, to some extent, essential to economic development, a great deal of regional inequality can be eliminated without affecting the rate of development of the country. In fact, by so doing, the rate of economic growth might be improved sometimes. In this sense, the performance of the Venezuelan economy left much to be desired.

In conclusion, the outstanding performance of the Venezuelan economy in terms of economic growth was accompanied by an unjust distribution of income. However, the pace of economic growth and development does not appear to have been significantly affected by such income distribution problems.

Even though the labor share in the national income of Venezuela has had an irregular movement throughout time, it has grown consider- ably, if 1936 is taken as the initial period. Furthermore, various indices of wages, prices, and real wages confirm the gains in real standards of living of the labor force from the mid-1930s on. [7]

TABLE 7.4

Share of Labor in National Income,
1936, 1949, and 1950-73

Year	Share of Labor (percents)
1936	46
1949	61
1950	60
1951	58
1952	55
1953	58
1954	57
1955	56
1956	55
1957	52
1958	54
1959	60
1960	61
1961	62
1962	60
1963	61
1964	56
1965	56
1966	57
1967	58
1968	58
1969	58
1970	57
1971	57
1972	56
1973	57

Source: Evelyn M. Baran, The Economic Development of Venezuela (Ph. D. diss., Radcliffe College, 1959); and Banco Central de Venezuela, Memoria (Caracas, 1959), and Informe Económico (Caracas, various years).

Yet, there are indications that some labor groups only reaped minimal gains over these years. These are easily recognized by a comparison of the employment and product-originated shares of the various groups. Improvements in productivity and real income have been especially small for agricultural workers and quite limited for a large chunk of the workers in the service sector. Furthermore, these 35 years of development seem to have left by the wayside increasing numbers of un- and underemployed workers. All these conditions define limitations to, and reductions of, the welfare gains derived by many Venezuelans from the growth process described previously.

In 1936, Venezuela, a peripheral country, with its pattern of trade based on primary type exports, imported most of the industrial goods it required. It specialized in the production of oil for the world markets, with this product providing its main source of growth. The rest of the Venezuelan economy successfully grafted its expansion onto that of petroleum. Although there were unfavorable effects stemming from the petroleum industry during the time interval examined, they were neutralized by public policies and overcome by the contributions of the industry, allowing the Venezuelan economy to expand briskly.

In this context, it should be mentioned that Venezuela grew in spite of the play of some of the adverse factors mentioned by the development economists, whose views were examined in Chapter 2. Some of these were the following: (a) unfavorable movement of the terms of trade during certain periods; (b) a very high rate of population growth, which was partly the result of the openness of the economy; (c) the organization of petroleum operations in units that had enclave-like characteristics (leakages, a monopsony-monopoly position, and so forth; (d) immigration of foreign labor into the oil industry and the rest of the economy; (e) factor proportions that stressed the utilization of capital rather than labor in the advanced sector; (f) fierce competition of imports with native goods; and (g) the absence of the basic preconditions for a take-off. Other factors which, according to these economists, impede the carry-over of a primary type export expansion, never did materialize in the Venezuelan case. For instance, the quite famous demonstration effect did not have a significantly deleterious effect on the rate of savings, and perverse factor movements were not important either.

The Venezuelan economy from 1936 to 1973 fits our hypothesis quite well. The petroleum industry acted as a leading sector during most of this time span, bringing about the development of the economy. Government policy had a central role in neutralizing some of the ill effects of the industry, extracting a sizeable contribution from petroleum and determining its effective use. Moreover, the Venezuelan experience underlines the importance of the catalytic role of government policy in bringing about a carry-over of the export expansion into the rest of the economy. In many cases, the automaticity assumed by the classical and neoclassical economists and their followers, by some staple and regional economists, and by some economic historians does not work in peripheral countries.

The case of petroleum in Venezuela seems to contradict the viewpoints which deny that primary production for exports can bring forth economic growth in the rest of the economy or which make this conditional to the presence of certain social and economic factors. Certainly, these preconditions or factors were not present in Venezuela during most of the overall time period covered by this study.

It shows that a potentially leading primary type export sector is not incapable of bringing about the economic development of a peripheral country with a pattern of trade based on primary product exports. Although a cursory examination of the evidence in many countries for different historical time periods suggests that this experience can be generalized, yet a greater number of case studies are required before definite conclusions can be reached on this issue. Not only would a wider range of countries be needed, but a greater coverage from the standpoint of products.

The effectiveness of primary product exports as leading sectors in the economic development of peripheral countries is an issue with important and timely policy implications. In many peripheral countries, policy decisions have emphasized import substitution as the all-important source of economic growth. Primary product exports are slighted as sources of growth. The case against primary exports has been built in such strong terms (in contrast with the support of import substitution) that other types of exports also have been discriminated against by extension.

Although there are other reasons determining this aversion toward primary type exports, to an important degree it stems from the belief that these products cannot efficiently transmit their expansion to the other sectors of the economy and that no successful development process could be ignited if they are relied upon. The empirical evidence examined suggests that this belief is ill-founded. Granted that testing of these ideas remains incomplete, a reexamination of the economic policies of many peripheral countries is suggested by the conclusions of this study.

Let us emphasize that, even if the results were more general they would not imply that primary exports should revert to a central role in the economies of peripheral countries.

> The determination of how, and up to what point, it be
> economically expedient to reduce the import coefficient,
> and the adoption of basic decisions with respect to the
> reallocation of resources so that exports may be expanded
> and diversified, with due consideration of the various
> alternatives for optimum use of resources, constitutes
> the cornerstone of a development policy. [8]

Our results would recommend the formulation of such policies only after a careful evaluation of all alternatives, including those in which primary exports play an important role. They suggest that, in scanning for an optimum growth path, the ineffectiveness of primary exports as leading sectors should not be taken for granted. For some nations "the basic international trade problem . . . is not so much how to control its trade, but rather to achieve a more extensive carry-over from its export trade to its domestic economy."[9]

Lately, developing countries are reconsidering their development strategies, as a result of the radical and, perhaps, sustainable improvement in the world markets of many primary products, the balance-of-payments pressures coupled with unsatisfactory growth rates suffered by some of them, difficulties in furthering the import substitution drive, and on the realization that part of the obstacles to the export of manufactures might result from policies biased against primary exports and favoring import-substituting industrialization. The conclusions of this study could be helpful in this process of policy reexamination.

NOTES

1. See Banco Central de Venezuela, El Ingreso Nacional de Venezuela (Caracas, 1949).

2. The government manipulated other variables, such as the price of oil by-products in the local market; the level of skills of the Venezuelan workers in the industry; the use of company roads, schools, and hospitals by the general public; and processing and further use of crude oil and its by-products.

3. See Carl Shoup, The Fiscal System of Venezuela (Baltimore: Johns Hopkins Press, 1959).

4. Consult CORDIPLAN, Primera Encuesta Nacional de Ingresos y Gastos Familiares en Venezuela (Caracas, 1962). Also Comisión Nacional de la Vivienda and Banco Nacional de Ahorro y Préstamo, Estudio del Mercado Real de Vivienda (Caracas, 1970).

5. See, for example, William Cline, Potential Effects of Income Redistribution on Economic Growth: Latin American Cases (New York: Praeger, 1972).

6. Hector Valecillos, "Consideraciones en torno a la Distribución del Ingreso en Venezuela y Examen de sus Posibles Cambios Recientes," in Cuadernos de la Sociedad Venezolana de la Planificación, nos. 108-10. Also consult this essay for tabular information on the patterns of income distribution in Venezuela. It should be noted that during the Pérez Jiménez years, the distribution of income also seems to have suffered a setback, as Table 7.4 suggests.

7. Wage information is quite scarce in Venezuela, and, generally, unreliable. However, with data presented in the Memorias of the Banco Central de Venezuela, the following real wage index was constructed covering from the mid-1940s to the mid-1950s:

Year	Index
1946 (first semester)	100. 0
1948 (first semester)	133. 2
1950 (first semester)	140. 2
1952 (first semester)	152. 6
1954 (first semester	180. 1
1955 (second semester)	186. 0

Unfortunately, the Central Bank discontinued the calculation of the series on which this index is based. From then on, the information is less satisfactory, but consult Dirección General de Estadísticas y Censos, Anuario Estadístico (Caracas, various years), and Encuesta Nacional de Hogares por Muestreo (Caracas, various years).

8. United Nations, The Economic Development of Latin America in the Post-War Period (New York, 1964), p. 9.

9. Gerald Meier, International Trade and Development (New York: Harper and Row, 1963), p. 185.

TABLE A.1

Agricultural Production, by Product, 1945, 1949, 1950, 1957, 1958, and 1965
(thousands of metric tons and index, 1945 = 100)

Product	1945	Index	1949	1950	1957	Index	1958	1965	Index
Total	1,857.7	(100.0)	—	1,733.8	2,622.7	(139.8)	2,555.0	4,227.3	(225.4)
Farm food crops:	1,332.2	(100.0)	—	1,197.6	1,709.3	(128.3)	1,602.2	2,619.3	(196.6)
Cereals:	530.4	(182.7)	383.8	353.5	364.8	(125.7)	379.6	722.2	(248.8)
Corn	483.3	(190.4)	323.3	310.3	340.1	(134.0)	357.6	521.0	(205.3)
Shelled rice	41.7	(140.9)	35.9	38.6	21.8	(73.6)	19.1	199.9	(675.3)
Wheat	5.4	(78.3)	4.6	4.6	2.1	(30.4)	2.9	1.3	(18.8)
Legumes:	53.7	(124.6)	64.3	62.1	82.6	(191.6)	80.8	49.2	(114.2)
Beans	30.0	(135.7)	28.4	32.0	44.3	(200.5)	42.5	26.1	(118.1)
Pigeon peas	7.7	(154.0)	6.5	5.1	11.3	(226.0)	8.2	5.4	(108.0)
Kidney beans	8.0	—	15.7	17.0	24.2	(302.5)	27.3	16.2	(202.6)
Peas	8.0	—	13.7	8.0	2.8	(35.0)	2.8	1.5	(18.8)
Roots and tubers:	166.2	(101.3)	257.8	264.1	430.0	(262.2)	417.5	630.1	(384.2)
Cassava	95.9	(100.0)	148.6	137.6	190.3	(198.4)	189.1	301.4	(314.3)
Yautia	19.4	(100.0)	29.6	33.9	40.9	(210.8)	46.0	96.6	(497.9)
Yams	17.6	(100.0)	26.7	25.8	60.7	(344.9)	64.6	71.5	(406.3)
Sweet potatoes	8.0	(100.0)	12.0	18.7	15.8	(197.5)	21.2	22.2	(277.5)
Celery	3.6	(100.0)	5.6	10.3	7.1	(197.2)	10.9	33.3	(925.0)
Mapuey	5.7	(100.0)	8.7	8.4	9.3	(163.2)	15.9	9.2	(161.4)
Potatoes	16.0	(114.3)	26.6	29.4	105.9	(156.4)	69.8	135.9	(970.7)
Fruits and vegetables:	581.9	—	—	515.5	853.9	(165.6)	738.7	1,217.8	(236.2)
Bananas	310.0	—	n.a.[b]	246.6	417.3	(169.2)	359.0	418.1	(169.5)
Plantains	155.9	—	155.9	149.4	269.3	(180.3)	218.8	547.1	(366.2)
Other fruits	60.3	—	61.5	63.6	71.8	(112.9)	7.07	98.9	(155.5)
Vegetables	55.7	—	57.0	55.9	95.5	(170.8)	90.2	153.7	(275.0)

Industrial crops:	142.1	(110.0)	156.5	157.8	321.3	(226.1)	282.6	524.8	(369.3)
Fibers and oils:	20.3	(161.1)	22.6	22.3	59.0	(468.3)	58.6	129.1	(1,024.6)
Sesame	6.2	(310.0)	8.2	5.3	21.0	(1,050.0)	19.8	54.1	(2,705.0)
Peanuts	0.3	-	0.2	0.9	2.3	(766.7)	0.8	1.8	(600.0)
Copra	5.2	(100.0)	4.9	5.4	13.6	(261.5)	8.5	15.3	(294.2)
Raw cotton	7.1	(68.9)	7.7	8.4	15.2	(147.6)	22.8	44.6	(433.0)
Sisal fiber	1.5	(100.0)	1.6	2.3	6.9	(460.0)	6.7	13.3	(886.7)
Others:	121.8	(100.0)	133.9	135.5	262.9	(215.8)	224.0	395.7	(324.9)
Sugar	26.6	(97.8)	41.0	50.4	192.8	(708.8)	156.3	240.4	(1,251.5)
Unrefined sugar	88.5	(177.0)	83.6	77.9	63.6	(127.2)	62.7	46.3	(92.6)
Tobacco	6.7	(100.0)	9.3	7.2	5.9	(88.1)	5.0	9.0	(134.3)
Coffee	53.4	(91.9)	50.7	34.0	50.3	(86.6)	61.8	54.4	(93.6)
Cacao	23.8	(157.6)	15.0	16.9	15.2	(100.7)	14.8	21.9	(145.0)
Animal products:	324.2	(116.7)	324.6	327.5	526.6	(189.6)	593.6	1,006.9	(326.5)
Meat	73.4	(104.7)	81.4	87.5	113.5	(161.9)	134.7	194.1	(276.9)
Poultry	2.0	(100.0)	1.8	1.5	9.1	(455.0)	11.4	42.3	(2,115.0)
Fish	79.8	(145.9)	65.2	61.6	83.6	(152.8)	77.1	119.3	(218.1)
Eggs	3.1	(206.7)	3.2	3.3	4.7	(313.3)	5.1	25.1	(1,673.3)
Dairy products	168.9	(113.0)	173.0	173.6	315.7	(211.2)	365.3	626.1	(418.8)
Milk	78.9	(127.3)	73.0	69.1	215.2	(347.1)	252.3	417.5	(673.4)
Cheese	90.0	(102.9)	100.0	104.5	100.5	(114.9)	113.0	208.6	(238.4)
Forestry[a]	152.4	(154.3)	200.3	193.5	273.1	(276.4)	268.7	438.1	(433.3)

[a]Cubic meters.
[b]Not available.

Source: Derived from Juan P. Pérez Castillo, Some Aspects of Venezuela's Economic Development, 1945-1960 (Ph.D. diss., Tulane University, 1963), and expanded to 1965 using the same sources.

TABLE A. 2

Basic Data, 1936-73
(in millions of bolívares unless otherwise indicated)

Years	(1) Implicit Deflator of Total GDP* (index, 1937 = 100)	(2) Total Gross Fixed Domestic Investment	(3) Petroleum Gross Fixed Domestic Investment
1936	49.0	272	88
1937	54.0	403	136
1938	52.0	549	235
1939	52.0	683	213
1940	52.0	671	135
1941	57.0	505	113
1942	67.0	483	104
1943	73.0	493	161
1944	76.0	806	266
1945	78.0	1,339	439
1946	81.0	1,805	683
1947	91.0	3,165	1,127
1948	102.0	4,390	1,630
1949	95.0	4,235	1,127
1950	92.9	2,731	561
1951	91.5	3,251	727
1952	91.7	4,031	967
1953	91.4	4,293	901
1954	92.3	4,786	933
1955	92.6	4,583	928
1956	95.5	5,087	1,232
1957	100.0	6,429	1,822
1958	101.7	6,044	1,788
1959	95.5	6,048	1,262
1960	94.7	4,768	730
1961	94.8	4,253	516
1962	95.0	4,716	474
1963	96.9	5,081	511
1964	97.8	6,397	753
1965	98.2	7,508	804
1966	100.1	7,431	638
1967	101.3	7,930	647
1968	103.6	9,382	1,182
1969	104.6	9,606	1,574
1970	107.2	9,939	1,294
1971	115.1	11,553	1,287
1972	112.7	13,723	1,000
1973	140.1	16,928	1,121

*Up to 1949, the wholesale price index.

Years	(4) Depreciation and Amortization Charges of the Oil Industry	(5) Profits after Taxes in the Oil Industry	(6) Interest Pay- ments by the Oil Industry
1936	68	182	–
1937	74	223	–
1938	92	169	–
1939	92	182	–
1940	100	145	–
1941	111	279	–
1942	88	119	–
1943	151	98	–
1944	158	259	–
1945	151	274	–
1946	179	446	–
1947	190	742	–
1948	246	1,075	4
1949	325	711	6
1950	420	951	9
1951	495	1,209	7
1952	530	1,264	5
1953	558	1,274	5
1954	613	1,417	5
1955	680	1,715	5
1956	732	2,121	4
1957	812	2,753	3
1958	836	1,610	3
1959	939	1,350	3
1960	948	1,289	4
1961	929	1,473	4
1962	911	1,703	2
1963	876	1,681	4
1964	871	2,458	8
1965	899	2,656	23
1966	856	2,529	24
1967	873	2,649	3
1968	892	2,741	3
1969	913	2,697	2
1970	1,044	2,896	4
1971	1,160	2,874	22
1972	1,104	2,714	24
1973	1,075	3,947	25

(continued)

Years	(7) Current Goods Imported by the Petroleum Industry	(8) Current Services Imported by the Petroleum Industry	(9) Transfers Abroad by Foreign Workers in the Petroleum Industry
1936	5	–	4
1937	9	–	8
1938	7	–	9
1939	9	–	11
1940	8	–	12
1941	6	–	9
1942	5	–	12
1943	5	–	10
1944	1	–	7
1945	0	–	9
1946	20	4	10
1947	37	4	17
1948	104	5	27
1949	95	56	57
1950	28	37	50
1951	34	45	60
1952	44	58	64
1953	34	71	63
1954	35	73	67
1955	41	112	71
1956	44	178	75
1957	75	195	89
1958	50	188	97
1959	45	143	96
1960	37	62	92
1961	32	93	75
1962	51	80	60
1963	35	63	57
1964	39	164	70
1965	46	116	114
1966	–	–	106
1967	–	–	88
1968	–	–	88
1969	–	–	141
1970	–	–	88
1971	–	–	79
1972	–	–	65
1973	–	–	59

Years	(10) Wages and Salaries in the Oil Industry	(11) Capital Goods Imported by the Petroleum Industry	(12) Capital Services Imported by the Petroleum Industry
1936	51	26	–
1937	67	54	–
1938	54	66	–
1939	72	58	–
1940	97	45	–
1941	93	39	–
1942	109	35	–
1943	93	25	–
1944	109	96	–
1945	151	193	–
1946	237	216	8
1947	395	440	9
1948	524	556	10
1949	582	521	12
1950	521	228	103
1951	561	398	90
1952	621	591	107
1953	654	446	141
1954	726	382	147
1955	745	423	224
1956	775	755	357
1957	878	1,268	445
1958	900	729	377
1959	940	477	287
1960	999	271	134
1961	1,002	163	186
1962	875	287	160
1963	867	282	125
1964	968	286	329
1965	1,003	303	233
1966	1,072	–	–
1967	1,090	–	–
1968	1,014	–	–
1969	959	–	–
1970	1,084	–	–
1971	1,100	–	–
1972	1,153	–	–
1973	1,296	–	–

(continued)

Years	(13) Implicit Deflator of Petroleum Gross Domestic Product (index, 1957 = 100)	(14) Petroleum National Income in Capital Goods Production	(15) Retained Value of Investment Expenditures in the Oil Industry
1936	31.7	–	62
1937	32.0	–	82
1938	30.9	66	169
1939	29.3	57	155
1940	31.9	32	90
1941	35.8	31	74
1942	37.1	31	69
1943	36.9	39	136
1944	40.2	47	170
1945	39.4	63	246
1946	46.5	86	459
1947	65.2	106	678
1948	83.4	152	1,064
1949	72.7	108	494
1950	77.2	91	230
1951	80.2	118	239
1952	80.4	124	269
1953	81.5	119	314
1954	83.5	108	404
1955	83.6	111	281
1956	88.4	128	120
1957	100.0	145	163
1958	93.9	130	682
1959	81.8	92	498
1960	76.8	81	325
1961	78.4	61	167
1962	79.6	55	27
1963	78.7	68	104
1964	102.5	75	138
1965	104.5	68	268
1966	103.1	–	–
1967	103.3	–	–
1968	104.0	–	–
1969	104.0	–	–
1970	103.4	–	–
1971	129.8	–	–
1972	155.7	–	–
1973	221.8	–	–

Year	(16) Retained Value of Current Expenditures in the Petroleum Industry (millions of constant bolívares)	(17) Retained Value of Total Petroleum Expenditures (millions of constant bolívares)	(18) Retained Value of Investment Expenditures (millions of constant bolívares)
1936	448	568	127
1937	506	637	152
1938	466	677	325
1939	549	757	298
1940	564	710	173
1941	598	703	130
1942	477	568	103
1943	821	1,007	186
1944	1,087	1,311	224
1945	1,563	1,878	315
1946	1,766	2,333	577
1947	2,146	2,891	755
1948	2,522	3,565	1,053
1949	2,601	3,121	638
1950	2,877	3,149	394
1951	3,204	3,467	362
1952	3,384	3,676	408
1953	3,699	4,050	508
1954	3,758	4,249	670
1955	3,901	4,230	591
1956	4,113	4,245	524
1957	4,677	4,840	554
1958	5,282	5,979	1,083
1959	5,950	6,448	786
1960	6,341	6,782	455
1961	6,207	6,365	334
1962	6,464	6,488	166
1963	6,600	6,690	197
1964	7,194	7,308	386
1965	7,230	7,444	399
1966	–	6,886	–
1967	–	7,392	–
1968	–	7,635	–
1969	–	7,383	–
1970	–	7,881	–
1971	–	8,098	–
1972	–	6,295	–
1973	–	6,812	–

(continued)

Year	(19) Value of Oil Production (millions of constant bolívares)	(20) Quantity of Oil Produced (millions of barrels)	(21) Taxes Included in Petroleum's Value Added
1936	1, 318	155	42
1937	1, 581	186	40
1938	1, 598	188	90
1939	1, 742	205	84
1940	1, 564	184	78
1941	1, 930	227	98
1942	1, 258	148	77
1943	1, 522	179	132
1944	2, 184	257	212
1945	2, 746	323	336
1946	3, 298	388	430
1947	3, 697	435	701
1948	4, 165	490	1, 071
1949	4, 097	482	881
1950	4, 650	547	1, 072
1951	5, 287	622	1, 312
1952	5, 610	660	1, 383
1953	5, 474	644	1, 405
1954	5, 882	692	1, 574
1955	6, 690	787	1, 795
1956	7, 641	899	2, 152
1957	8, 604	1, 014	2, 803
1958	8, 083	951	2, 952
1959	8, 593	1, 011	2, 745
1960	8, 857	1, 042	2, 671
1961	9, 061	1, 066	2, 866
1962	9, 928	1, 168	3, 268
1963	10, 081	1, 186	3, 320
1964	10, 557	1, 242	5, 023
1965	10, 778	1, 268	5, 099
1966	10, 102	1, 230	4, 788
1967	10, 574	1, 293	5, 355
1968	10, 766	1, 319	5, 536
1969	10, 408	1, 312	5, 889
1970	11, 073	1, 353	6, 217
1971	10, 677	1, 295	7, 619
1972	8, 500	1, 178	8, 090
1973	8, 840	1, 229	12, 833

Year	(22) Local Purchases by the Petroleum Industry
1936	–
1937	–
1938	–
1939	–
1940	–
1941	–
1942	–
1943	–
1944	–
1945	–
1946	–
1947	–
1948	144
1949	98
1950	72
1951	99
1952	134
1953	143
1954	154
1955	180
1956	226
1957	322
1958	322
1959	298
1960	251
1961	241
1962	255
1963	329
1964	461
1965	571
1966	427
1967	442
1968	573
1969	711
1970	804
1971	826
1972	602
1973	720

(continued)

211

Source: All the data referring to the year 1973 were in unpublished form at the time of writing and were supplied on a confidential basis by various organizations.

Column 1. From 1950 on, it is derived from the current and constant price total GDP series. These appear in Banco Central de Venezuela, Memoria (Caracas, several years), and Informe Económico (Caracas, several years), and in unpublished tables made available by the same source.

Column 2. Derived from unpublished statistics of the Banco Central de Venezuela up to 1949. The figures were originally expressed in constant 1957 bolívares. They were converted into current bolívares by using the general wholesale price index. From 1950 on, they are taken from Banco Central de Venezuela, Memoria (Caracas, several issues), and Informe Económico (Caracas, several issues). For this period, the correction factor was an unpublished wholesale index of investment goods prices used by the Banco Central de Venezuela. Total investment was corrected to take account of the differences between the Banco Central estimates of petroleum gross fixed domestic investment and our estimates.

Column 3. As has been said above, these figures include some capital charges that cannot be considered investment, like concession costs, capitalized taxes, and so forth (however, the 1956-57 concession payments are not included). It was impossible to iron out this problem with the data at hand. From 1936 to 1942, the figures were derived directly from the "big three" oil-producing groups in Venezuela (Standard of New Jersey, Shell, and Gulf). An adjustment was made to obtain industry-wide estimates. From 1943 to 1947, the data are taken from Ministerio de Fomento, Anuario Petrolero (Caracas, 1949). The rest of the figures came from Ministerio de Minas e Hidrocarburos, Petróleo y Otros Datos Estadísticos (Caracas, several issues).

Column 4. From 1936 to 1942, figures were derived from our survey of the three main company groups in the oil industry, adjusted to cover the whole industry. From 1943 to 1946, they were taken from Joseph Pogue, Oil in Venezuela (New York, 1949). From 1947 on, they come from Ministerio de Minas e Hidrocarburos, Petróleo y Otros Datos Estadísticos (Caracas, several issues). These charges represent overestimates of the normal depreciation allowances used in national accounting.

Column 5. For the years 1936 to 1942, the figures are derived from our survey of the three main oil company groups, adjusted to represent the whole industry. From 1943 to 1946, they are taken from Ministerio de Fomento, Anuario Petrolero (Caracas, 1949 and 1950), and from then on, from Ministerio de Minas e Hidrocarburos, Petróleo y Otros Datos Estadísticos (Caracas, several issues). Oil profits are expressed in relation to value of output rather than to value of sales.

Column 6. From unpublished and confidential data made available by Oficina de Economia Petrolera, Ministerio de Minas e Hidrocarburos. Not available before 1947.

Column 7. For the years 1936 to 1940, they are taken from Ministerio de Fomento, Estadística Mercantil y Marítima (Caracas, several issues). These data were adjusted into c.i.f. (cost, insurance, freight) data by calculating freight and insurance on the basis of 12 percent of f.o.b. (free on board) value. This percentage appears to be a sensible one for oil company imports and was also used by the Ministry of Mines and Hydrocarbons in some of its estimates. For the 1941 to 1952 period, they are taken from Ministerio de Minas e Hidrocarburos, Memoria (Caracas, 1961). For the 1953 to 1970 period, the data are taken from Banco Central de Venezuela, La Economía Venezolana en los Ultimos Treinta Años (Caracas, 1971), and Informe Económico (Caracas, 1971, 1972, and 1973), converted from dollars to bolívares by using the exchange rate applicable to petroleum. Freight and insurance costs were added from unpublished data supplied by the Banco Central so as to have all the series in c.i.f. terms. Current imports were taken as a residual after estimating the portion corresponding to capital goods imports. The latter were estimated on the basis of the economic classification of imports by type of goods and type of importer appearing in Banco Central de Venezuela, Memoria (Caracas, 1949-65), adjusted for erroneous inclusion of some capital goods under the raw materials subclassification. Up to 1949, the shares of current and capital goods imports were based on Ministerio de Fomento, Estadística Mercantil y Marítima (Caracas: Ministerio de Minas e Hidrocarburos, several issues). The percentage of capital goods imports in total imports by the petroleum companies was estimated in relation to the classification of imports into dutiable, free of duty, and exonerated (this last category is the one exempted from duty as part of the concession privileges). Such estimation was undertaken on the basis of information given by industrial and government sources.

Column 8. The value of the total services imported by the petroleum industry is derived from unpublished data supplied by the Banco Central de Venezuela. The value of current services is estimated as one-third of the total on the basis of information supplied by the petroleum industry and government sources.

Column 9. For the years 1936 to 1945, the figures presented were obtained under the assumption that the relationship that prevailed between wages and salaries, and transfers abroad, in later years, also held during the early years. From 1946 to 1952, they were estimated from unpublished data compiled by the Banco Central de Venezuela on wages and salaries and other transactions paid in dollars by the petroleum industry. No discrimination existed between wages and salaries and other transactions. It was assumed that, from 1946 to 1952, the relationship between wages and salaries and transfers abroad followed the 1953 to 1965 pattern.

Column 10. From 1936 to 1946, Ministerio de Fomento, Anuario Petrolero, 1949-1950 (Caracas, 1950). From then on, Ministerio de Minas e Hidrocarburos, unpublished statistics. These wages and salaries do not include those charged to capital account. From 1936 to 1946, the portion of total wages and salaries charged to capital account were estimated.

Column 11. See notes for column 7, which explain how these figures were estimated.

Column 12. See notes for column 8, which explain the way in which current services imported were estimated. Imports of capital services are a residual.

Column 13. Derived from estimates of petroleum GDP, in current and constant prices, taken from Banco Central de Venezuela, Memoria (Caracas, several years) and Informe Económico (Caracas, several years), and from unpublished data provided by the same source. Before 1950, current petroleum GDP is converted into a constant price series by using a weighted index of petroleum prices computed from Ministerio de Minas e Hidrocarburos statistics.

Column 14. Estimated by information derived from the Ministerio de Fomento, Memoria (Caracas, several years), and Anuario Petrolero, 1949-1950 (Caracas, 1950), for the first few years. From the middle of the 1940s on, the data were derived from the Ministerio de Minas e Hidrocarburos, Petróleo y Otros Datos Estadísticos (several years), and unpublished data from the same source.

Column 15. Defined as investment expenditures in the petroleum industry minus imports of capital goods and services. From columns 3, 11, and 12.

Column 16. From the corresponding chapter tables showing retained value of current expenditures, converted into constant bolívares by using the implicit deflator of petroleum GDP.

Column 17. From the corresponding chapter tables presenting retained value of total expenditures, converted into constant bolívares by using the implicit deflator of petroleum GDP.

Column 18. Same as column 15, deflated by the wholesale price index from 1936 to 1949 and, from then on, by an investment goods price index obtained in unpublished form from the Banco Central de Venezuela.

Column 19. From figures presented in tables in Chapters 4, 5, and 6, deflated by the implicit deflator of petroleum GDP.

Column 20. From Ministerio de Minas e Hidrocarburos, Petróleo y Otros Datos Estadísticos (Caracas, 1965).

Column 21. From 1936 to 1938, based on petroleum tax receipts presented in Manuel R. Egana, Tres Décadas de Producción Petrolera (Caracas, 1947), adjusted to exclude estimated capital taxes. From 1938 to 1942, taken from Ministerio de Minas e Hidrocarburos, Petróleo y Otros Datos Estadísticos (Caracas, 1965). Data on indirect taxes were derived from J. J. Bracho Sierra, Cincuenta Años de Ingresos

Fiscales (Caracas, 1963). Adjustments were also performed to exclude capitalized taxes. For the years 1943 to 1946, from Ministerio de Fomento, Memoria (Caracas, several years) and Bracho Sierra, op. cit. From then on, based on Ministerio de Minas e Hidrocarburos, Memoria (Caracas, 1965), and Banco Central de Venezuela, Informe Económico (Caracas, several years), and unpublished statistics from the same source. From 1943 on, only taxes charged to current production are included.

Column 22. Taken from Ministerio de Minas e Hidrocarburos, Informe de Conservación (Caracas, several years).

ABOUT THE AUTHOR

JORGE SALAZAR-CARRILLO is Technical Coordinator in ECIEL (Program of Joint Studies on Latin American Economic Integration) and Special Advisor to its Coordinator General. He has been connected with the Brookings Institution for many years, having been a Senior Fellow and now being a member of the Brookings' Associated Staff.

In addition to contributing several articles and essays to journals and books, and participating in the editorial boards of the Review of Income and Wealth and the Handbook of Latin American Studies, he is the author of a forthcoming ECIEL book, Wage Differentials in LAFTA Countries. Dr. Salazar-Carrillo has been consultant of various firms and international agencies, and is on leave from Georgetown University, where he is a Professorial Lecturer in the Department of Economics, the Latin American Studies and the Interamerican Labor Economics Programs.

Dr. Salazar-Carrillo studied law at the Universidad de la Havana and economics at the University of Vilanova at Havana, Cuba. He studied business administration at the University of Miami, where he obtained his B.B.A. Dr. Salazar-Carrillo left his country to study at the University of California (Berkeley), where he obtained an M.A. and a Ph.D. in Economics, as well as a Certificate in Economic Development Programming.

ARAB OIL: Impact on Arab Nations and Global
Implications
> edited by Naiem A. Sherbiny and Mark A.
> Tessler

CHINA'S PETROLEUM INDUSTRY: Output Growth
and Export Potential
> Chu-yuan Cheng

DEVELOPMENT OF THE IRANIAN OIL INDUSTRY:
International and Domestic Aspects
> Fereidun Fesharaki

ECONOMIC GROWTH AND EMPLOYMENT
PROBLEMS IN VENEZUELA: An Analysis of
an Oil-Based Economy
> Mostafa F. Hassan

EXPROPRIATION OF U.S. PROPERTY IN SOUTH
AMERICA: Nationalization of Oil and Copper
Companies in Peru, Bolivia, and Chile
> George M. Ingram

THE MULTINATIONAL CORPORATION AS A FORCE
IN LATIN AMERICAN POLITICS: A Case Study of
the International Petroleum Company in Peru
> Adalberto J. Pinelo

THE UNITED STATES AND INTERNATIONAL OIL:
A Report for the Federal Energy Administration
on U.S. Firms and Government Policy
> Robert B. Krueger*

*Also available in paperback as a PSS Student Edition.